H. J. Eysenck was born in Berlin in 1916. He left Germany in 1934 to study French and English History and Literature at the Universities of Dijon and Exeter. Having studied Psychology at the University of London, obtaining a PhD in 1940, he was appointed Research Psychologist at the Mill Hill Emergency Hospital in 1942. The research he carried out there formed the basis of *Dimensions of Personality*. At the end of the war H. J. Eysenck was appointed Psychologist to the Maudsley Hospital, where his research formed the basis of *The Scientific Study of Personality*. In 1950 he was appointed Reader and Director to the Psychological Department at the Institute of Psychiatry, University of London, and in 1955, Professor of Psychology. It was during these years that he wrote *The Structure of Human Personality* and *Psychology of Politics*.

Professor Eysenck has held Visiting Professorships at the University of Philadelphia (1949) and at the University of California (1954). He has authored to date 17 books, been the editor of six more, and has contributed numerous articles and papers to learned journals.

Crime

H. J. Eysenck

and Personality

Paladin

Granada Publishing Ltd, 3 Upper James Street, London W1

First published in Great Britain by
Routledge & Kegan Paul Ltd 1964
Published by *Paladin* 1970
Copyright © H. J. Eysenck 1964
Made and printed in Great Britain by
Hazell Watson & Viney Ltd, Aylesbury, Bucks
Set in Monotype Fournier

This book is sold subject to the condition that it shall not, by way of trade *or otherwise*, be lent, re-sold, hired out or otherwise *circulated* without the publisher's prior consent in any form of binding or cover other than that in which it is published *and without a similar condition including this condition being imposed on the subsequent purchaser*.

This book is published at a net price and is supplied subject to the Publishers Association Standard Conditions of Sale registered under the Restrictive Trade Practices Act, 1956.

To Sybil

Contents

Introduction   11

1. Is Human Conduct Predictable?   17

2. The Nature of Personality   37

3. The Mark of Cain   58

4. The Biological Roots of Personality   76

5. Is Conscience a Conditioned Reflex?   106

6. Crime and Conditioning   130

7. Punishment or Cure?   150

8. The Task of Society   171

9. Some Questions Answered   193

Epilogue   202

References   205

Index   209

In nature there are neither
rewards nor punishments—
there are only consequences.

R. G. INGERSOLL

Introduction

There can be little controversy about the severity of the problem of crime and delinquency in our society. Even in purely material terms, the total cost of crime to the community was estimated by the Wickersham Commission in 1931 to have been about 1,000 million dollars in the United States, and this sum is likely to have more than doubled by now. The personal cost, in loss of life, personal unhappiness, injury, or suffering inflicted on prisoners and dependents alike, is impossible to estimate.

Man has, almost from the beginning of civilized life, formulated theories to explain the occurrence of criminal activity, and to understand the wrongdoer. Explanations were first couched in religious and philosophical terms; but in recent years social science has entered the field, and now we have contributions, both theoretical and factual, by sociologists, anthropologists, psychiatrists, criminologists, psychoanalysts, statisticians, anthropometrists, and psychologists. It is not the purpose of this small volume to review all this evidence. Textbooks on the subject exist in rich profusion, and even if I were competent to write still another one, there would be little point in doing so. What I have attempted, rather, has been to relate to this recalcitrant problem of criminality some recent discoveries from the laboratories of experimental psychologists in the hope that the outlines of a new and more realistic picture would emerge.

My failure to discuss in detail the many valuable contributions made by specialists in other fields is not due entirely to ignorance, nor is it due to any lack of appreciation of the importance of their work. I have tried to present to the lay reader a theory which is slowly emerging from many detailed experimental studies of the behaviour of men and animals under strictly controlled conditions. This theory has much to tell us about the antisocial behaviour of some of our fellow men, and it would have made the understanding of this theory much more difficult if I had failed to concentrate entirely on essentials and had allowed myself to be led into excursions into allied fields which, however interesting in themselves, were not strictly germane to my topic.

The theory in question is in some ways the counterpart of the modern views of neurotic behaviour which have been discussed in some detail in *The Causes and Cures of Neuroses*. Both rely on modern learning theory for their foundations and on experimental work in conditioning for their details. A considerable amount of evidence is already available to indicate that while undoubtedly subject to much correction in detail, the views here espoused may not be entirely inaccurate. Suggestive as the evidence is, it is by no means conclusive, and the reader will realize as the theme is developed that what is presented to him is not a set of infallible scientific laws, but rather the outline of a theory based on fairly firm foundations, helped along with specific hypotheses having some basis in empirical fact, and leading to verifiable (or falsifiable) conclusions, at least some of which have already been verified.

It follows that much of this book is concerned with experiments whose relevance to criminality and delinquency is perhaps not apparent at first sight; suffice it to say that what has been included is strictly relevant to our main hypothesis. Some of the discussion is concerned with personality as such, rather than dealing only with the criminal personality; but if the reader comes away with a better understanding of this particularly troublesome concept, he will perhaps be prepared to forgive the writer for extending his treatment of the topic as much as he has.

What, it may be asked, is the point of the theory advanced, and what is the aim of writing this book? Does it lead directly to better methods of dealing with criminals? Does it suggest ways of preventing recidivism? Does it adumbrate treatments of a preventive nature which might lessen the incidence of juvenile delinquency? The answer must be that nothing remotely as ambitious as this is intended. Some suggestions for practical applications of the principles here enunciated are indeed given in the last chapter; but I firmly believe that application should wait upon proof, that if the scheme put forward is found to have some merit when subjected to exhaustive testing, then and only then will it be time to think of basing practical steps of any kind upon it. In the field of neurosis I believe that the time for application has come; in the field of criminality I feel that we are not yet on sufficiently firm ground to do more than try to improve our theories by more exact and well-planned experimental work. New ideas in these fields are often propounded with messianic vehemence; nothing could be more inappropriate in dealing with such very tender plants, which require careful nurturing before being able to stand up for themselves.

There is at the moment only one kind of gain which the reader is likely to carry away from reading this book, and that is a gain in understanding. If the theory advanced here is only approximately along the right lines – and it would not be realistic to hope for anything more – then the reader may gain a deeper insight into the forces which act on criminal and law-abiding citizen alike; he will appreciate the dynamics which impel apparently rational people to act as they do. To me, this insight which modern psychological research has given us is one of the important scientific advances of the century. It is the main burden of *Crime and Personality* to try to share this research with others who – whether as teachers, social workers, law-enforcement officers, parents, or simply citizens – are interested in human behaviour and motivation but have neither the time nor the inclination to keep up with the large and ever-increasing technical literature.

I am indebted to many people for inspiration and help. My debt is greatest to I. P. Pavlov, the great Russian physiologist and psychologist; to C. L. Hull, O. H. Mowrer, and N. Miller, the founders of one branch of modern learning theory; to J. B. Watson, the originator of Behaviorism; and to J. Wolpe, the leading exponent of behaviour therapy. I also wish to thank those of my friends, colleagues, and students at the Maudsley who have carried out empirical studies on adult criminals, recidivists, juvenile delinquents and children with behaviour disorders. Much of this work is still unpublished, but it has had a powerful influence on my thinking, Last, but not least, I am indebted to my wife, who encouraged me to put mouth to dictaphone, and to whom the book is appropriately dedicated.

H. J. EYSENCK
London, England

Crime and Personality

1   Is Human Conduct Predictable?

'How am I to get in?' asked Alice again, in a louder tone.
'*Are* you to get in at all?' said the Footman. 'That's the first question, you know.'

It was, no doubt: only Alice did not like to be told so. 'It's really dreadful,' she muttered to herself, 'the way all the creatures argue. It's enough to drive one crazy!'

ALICE'S ADVENTURES IN WONDERLAND

There is much argument about most of the concepts and words used in psychology. Whole volumes have been written about the definition of such terms as 'instinct' or 'intelligence', or 'emotion', and even now there are many different ideas and views and definitions among psychologists. But of all the terms perhaps none can boast so many different definitions as 'personality'. Almost every writer on the subject has his own definition, his own point of view, his own method of procedure, and his own views as to what the aim of personality research should be. Where there is so much disagreement, it would obviously be unwise to be too dogmatic. Nevertheless, a considerable body of experimental evidence, of empirical findings, and of general theories has been building up in recent years. While this body of evidence can hardly claim the allegiance of all psychologists, we shall give an account of what these major findings are and will not try to go into great detail about the arguments which have surrounded it in the past. The reader must judge for himself whether the point of view taken here is a reasonable one or not.

Let us start with a widely accepted definition of psychology, namely that it is a study of behaviour. Psychologists have given up talking about the 'science of the soul' or the 'science of the mind', not only because these are difficult to define, but also because actual human or animal conduct, or behaviour is all that we can ever observe. This is our field of study, and if we find it necessary later to introduce 'mind' or 'soul' as an explanatory hypothesis we may, of course, be free to do so. But to start out by defining our subject matter in these terms is obviously begging the question, and consequently there is now fairly wide agreement that it is with behaviour, or conduct in general, that we are concerned. The term 'behaviour' is understood in the widest possible way. We do not now rule out from the general conception of behaviour what a person says. Quite clearly, this is something which can be recorded objectively and which has to be taken into account. We will not necessarily take what he says, that is, the content of his pronouncements, as being invariably true, either as a reflection of fact, or even as a reflection of what he himself is experiencing at the time. But we shall integrate it with the other observations we can make, and try to construct a general theory of behaviour in which verbal behaviour will be a part, but only a part. It will not be, as it used to be for psychologists at the turn of the century, the major source of our information about human behaviour.

When the man in the street looks at behaviour in this general fashion, he immediately makes an assumption which may or may not be true, but which has been very much doubted by many modern psychologists. He assumes that there is some kind of underlying basis for a person's behaviour, and that it is this underlying basis, enduring for a long period of time and permeating his activities, which we commonly call personality. Commonsense psychology unhesitatingly describes and explains behaviour in terms of traits, such as persistence, suggestibility, courage, punctuality, absent-mindedness, stage-struckness, being one for the girls, or whatever it might be. Alternatively, the man in the street may posit the existence of types, such as the dandy, the intellectual, the quiet, the sporty, or the sociable type. Even if we agree that these terms may be useful descriptively, they do not help us much in terms of explanation. We call a person sociable because we find that, in many different situations, he behaves in a sociable manner. But it does not help us to account for his being sociable that we can ascribe it to some underlying trait of sociability, because we have only adduced this trait from the very fact of his original behaviour. The same kind of error used to be made with respect to instinct. It used to be said that we have an instinct of self-preservation or of gregariousness or of playfulness. The existence of these instincts was deduced from the fact that we were self-preservative or gregarious or playful. Then, in turn, these instincts were used to explain our self-preservative or gregarious or playful activities. There is a vicious circle here. We are not really explaining anything by introducing such terms as instincts or traits into the discussion.

However, even on a descriptive level, the whole notion of traits, of types and of personality altogether has been very much criticized.[1]* One critic, for instance, has held that 'there are no broad, general traits of personality, no general and consistent forms of conduct which, if they existed, would make for consistency of behaviour and stability of personality, but only independent and specific stimulus-response bonds or habits'. This view, which seems so much in contradiction to commonsense psychology, may at first be quite unacceptable, but we shall see that there is much evidence to recommend it. Even at the commonsense level we may see that there are certain facts which are difficult to reconcile with a general view of traits or types.

Let us take, as an example, Mr Smith, a young man, twenty-four years old, and let us ask ourselves whether he shows a particular trait, say persistence. We look at his pattern of behaviour in a variety of situations. But do we find, in actual fact, that he is equally persistent or non-persistent in all of these? The answer will almost certainly be 'No'. He rather dislikes his monotonous, humdrum job; he works at it only when he is under supervision; normally he shows very little persistence. On the other hand, he is very much involved with a hobby. He likes taking photographs, mounting photographs, and everything connected with photography. Here he shows a great deal of persistence. When it comes to making contacts with girls, going out with them and so on, he is perhaps no different from the average: not particularly persistent and importunate, but also not particularly shy and reticent. He behaves in an average manner. These are just three examples of his behaviour. Should he be called persistent or non-persistent? Is there any point in postulating a trait of persistence and attempting to give him a rating in respect to this trait – either high, low, or intermediate – when quite clearly very little could be predicted from any knowledge of this rating?

Take another example. Here is Captain Brown, who was decorated with the Victoria Cross for his courage in front of the enemy. Can we therefore conclude that he will be a prime example for the trait of bravery, and that he will be brave under all sorts of other conditions? We notice that he is not particularly keen to go to the dentist; in fact, he often lets his appointments lapse and goes only when he is in acute pain. In other situations calling for civic bravery, for instance, he may in fact turn out to be little short of a coward. Although he may believe, for example, that coloured people have equal rights, yet in a group where the majority view is opposed to this, he may not dare to stand up and put forward his opinions. Is he brave, or cowardly, or some degree of both? Again it is not alto-

* References to research work and theoretical views discussed in the text are given at the end of the book.

19

gether clear that the terms have much relevance to his behaviour, or that they help us in predicting how he will behave in different situations. These two examples are brief accounts of the behaviour of actual people. They do not prove anything, of course, but may raise doubts which only experimental evidence can put to rest.

In psychology, this controversy is sometimes known by the names of the two protagonist schools. One is that of *specificity*, putting forward the view that all actions which are performed by a person are specific, separately learned, and do not combine in such a way as to make possible the postulation of traits or types, thus making it unnecessary to postulate any such notion as personality at all. Another group has pinned its faith to the opposite banner, *generality*; they believe that different acts and activities do tend to be bound together in certain broad, general categories which give rise to traits and types; and that the notion of personality is quite indispensable in psychology. We shall see that both these views are, in part, correct and, in part, incorrect; that, in other words, human behaviour is neither as completely general as was thought at first by the generality school, nor quite as disintegrated and amorphous as is held by the specificity school. Before discussing some of the experiments which have been performed to test these two theories, let us consider some of the reasons put forward by the specificity theorists in support of their view.

Essentially the specifists argue that human behaviour is learned. Now there is hardly any doubt that this general proposition is true. Without learning, no behaviour of any kind except the most disorganized reflex behaviour – threshing about of legs and arms, and so on – would be possible. All other behaviour is acquired through learning, and this process of learning usually takes a very long time indeed. How does this learning take place? For many years it used to be thought that it was the result of stimulus-response bonds or connexions. In other words, a particular stimulus is followed by a particular response. If the response is rewarded, a bond is established between the stimulus and the response; and the next time the stimulus occurs, the response will tend to follow. If it is rewarded again, there will be a tendency for the bond to grow stronger, until finally a habit is established. We will not, at the moment, go into the particular details of how this happens, but will only note that the bond is between a specific stimulus and a specific response. If all learning proceeds on this basis, it may be asked, how is it possible for more general traits or types to emerge? The answer, as we now know, lies in a phenomenon sometimes known as stimulus generalization.

Let us start with a very simple experiment, which will be familiar to most people. It was originally performed by Pavlov, the great Russian physiologist. The subject of the experiment is a dog. He is standing on a table and is held in place by a harness. Except for this equipment the room in which the dog is standing is completely empty. The experimenter stands outside the room, watching the dog through a one-way screen, manipulating levers to present stimuli to the dog, and also recording automatically the reactions of the dog. In particular, he is interested in the salivary secretion produced by the animal, which is measured in terms of the number of drops falling into a glass container. One type of stimulus presented to the dog is the sound of a bell. This does not produce any kind of salivation and is known as the *conditioned stimulus* (CS). Another type of stimulus presented to the dog is a plate containing some meat. This evokes very heavy salivation on the part of the hungry dog and is known as the *unconditioned stimulus* (UCS), the stimulus which produces the reaction without having to be connected with any other kind of stimulus. Now the experiment begins. The bell is rung and immediately afterwards the dog is presented with the food. He salivates copiously upon receiving the food and then proceeds to eat it. This pairing of conditioned and unconditioned stimuli is repeated ten, twenty, or more times. Finally, the conditioned stimulus, the bell, is presented on its own; and lo and behold, the dog begins to salivate to the sound of the bell without any meat being presented to him at all. As Pavlov put it, he has become conditioned to salivate to the bell.[2]

In this particular experiment we have a typical example of the stimulus-response bond being formed. But now we can show that this relationship is not quite as specific as might be thought. The bell has a particular loudness and it vibrates with a particular frequency. What would happen if we now presented the conditioned dog with another bell of a different loudness and pitch? The answer is that the response will still be present. It will perhaps not be quite as strong, but it will be much more pronounced than it could have been without the previous process of conditioning. In other words, the conditioned bond between stimulus and response generalizes to other stimuli which have some degree of resemblance to the original one. The greater the resemblance, the greater will be the amount of conditioned response actually forthcoming, although, of course, the word 'resemblance', particularly with human subjects, itself requires experimental investigation and definition.

Here then we might have the basis for a more general personality trait. A person might form a habit of being sociable in relation to one particular person; in other words, he forms a specific stimulus-response bond. But according to the law of generalization, this should generalize from the one person who constitutes a stimulus in this situation to other people, to groups of people, and indeed perhaps to society as a whole. In this way we could imagine the formation of a general trait of sociability on the basis of some form of learning or conditioning. In a similar way, a trait of aggressiveness might arise. We are aggressive in response to one particular stimulus, and this particular response will then generalize to other situations and to other people according to the law of generalization which we have just discussed. There is, therefore, nothing in the literature on learning and conditioning which would necessarily imply that generality was an impossible state of affairs in human behaviour.

However, experimentalists have shown that this generalization is not necessarily very strong or very complete; and it is on some of these findings about what is sometimes called 'transfer of training' that the specificist tends to rely. It used to be assumed in education theory that certain specific acts, learning verses by heart, or doing problems in arithmetic, or writing out French irregular verbs, would, in the course of time, lead to improvement in general abilities or faculties, such as memory, will power, logical ability, and so on. Two very famous American psychologists, William James and E. L. Thorndike showed, in a number of investigations, that this easy assumption had little empirical foundation. When two groups of subjects are equated for their ability in a given task such as learning poetry by heart, for instance, and one group is subsequently subjected to a period of training in memorizing material which might even be closely similar to that on which they had been tested, while the other group was not given any training, then the predicted superiority of the former group over the latter on a repetition of the original task was not observed. For instance, the two groups might have been tested originally on learning five hundred lines of Milton's 'Paradise Lost' and the one group might then be trained on, say, the poetry of Swinburne, or Keats, or Shakespeare. They would then be tested on another five hundred lines from Milton's 'Paradise Lost' and it would be found that the learning on the slightly different task had not benefited the group that had been put through this task at all. Learning is apparently relatively specific. There was no general effect on the hypothetical faculties which such training was supposed to improve. Any transfer effects which might be observed were considered due, not to the action of broad mental faculties, but to the fact that the original and the practised activities had certain elements in common. This theory is known as the 'theory of identical elements'. In Thorndike's words:

A change in one function alters any other only in so far as the two functions have as factors common elements. To take a concrete example, improvement in addition will alter one's ability in multiplication because addition is absolutely identical with a part of multiplication and because certain other processes, e.g. eye movements and the inhibition of all save arithmetical impulses are in part common to the two functions.[3]

The development of personality no less than of linguistic or numerical skill is, therefore, seen as specific training of individual associations, never as generalized improvement of larger mental units or faculties.

Here too, we now know that this very simplified view of specificity of learning is not justified. It has proved difficult to define the very notion of 'element', and it has proved even more difficult to show the alleged 'identity' of these elements. Experimental work has frequently failed to show the theoretically predicted correspondence between improvement after practice and a similarity between original tasks and practice tasks. The position is more complex than was thought, and no simple solution seems acceptable at the moment.

Clearly it would be possible to discuss at great length all these theoretical problems, but, obviously, direct experimental study of this particular problem is needed. As it happens, one of the first, one of the most important, and one of the most large-scale of such studies, carried out in a direct attempt to answer problems of generality and specificity, was one which is also highly relevant to the general theme of this book. I refer to the famous 'Character Education Enquiry' carried out by two American psychologists, H. Hartshorne and M. A. May, towards the middle of the 1920s, and published in three well-known books, *Studies in Deceit*, *Studies in Service and Self-control*, and *Studies in the Organization of Character*. These volumes are still regarded as a landmark which has not been surpassed by later work. As they all are concerned with the development of moral and social impulses, with dishonesty, stealing, lying, and cheating, they will form an excellent introduction to the major part of this book.[4]

Hartshorne and May set themselves the task of discovering any traits of moral or immoral behaviour which might be found in the school children tested in their studies. The first task, of course, was to define the concept of 'traits' in such a way that experimental evidence could be collected in order to throw some light on the existence or non-existence of these traits. They followed Gordon Allport, the American psychologist, in the definition of a trait. Allport wrote: 'Traits are discovered in the individual life – the only place where they can be discovered – only through an inference (or interpretation) made necessary by the demonstrable consistency of the separate observable acts of behavior.' And again:

Traits are not observable; they are inferred (as any kind of determining tendency is inferred). Without such an inference the stability and consistency of personal behavior could not possibly be explained. Any specific action is a product of innumerable determinants, not only of traits, but of momentary pressures and specialized influences. But it is the repeated occurrence of actions having the same significance (equivalence of response) following upon a definable range of stimuli having the same personal significance (equivalence of stimuli) that makes necessary the postulation of traits as states of being. Traits are not at all times active, but they are persistent even when latent, and are distinguished by low thresholds of arousal.[5]

It will be clear from these quotations that the notion of trait is intimately connected with the notion of correlation. Stability, consistency, repeated occurrence of actions – all these terms when translated into more rigorous and operationally definable language refer to co-variation of a number of behavioural acts. What does this mean in everyday terms?

When we postulate a trait of sociability, we mean essentially that if we took a hundred people and put them into ten different situations, all of which were relevant to our notion of sociability, then the person who tended to be sociable in one situation would also tend to be sociable in the others, whereas a person who was unsociable in one would tend to be unsociable in the others also. In other words, his conduct would show a certain degree of consistency. This consistency can be measured mathematically, by means of a *coefficient of correlation*. This simply reduces the whole concept of consistency to a numerical value, ranging from 1 for complete consistency down to zero for no consistency at all. If the person who was sociable in one situation was always sociable in the other situations and if the person who was unsociable in one situation was always unsociable in the others, consistency would be complete and we would talk about a correlation of 1. If, however, we could make no prediction at all from the behaviour of one person in one situation about the behaviour of the same person in another situation, then the correlation would be zero. In actual fact correlations are seldom either zero or 1 but tend to range between these two extremes. Here are a few typical examples to illustrate what is meant by correlation. If you take a hundred people and in each case measure the length of the right arm and also the length of the left arm, the correlation will be very nearly perfect; it will be about 0.98. If you measure the height and weight, the correlation will be very much lower, in the neighbourhood of 0.6 or 0.7. A similar correlation will be obtained between a child's success at school and his performance on a test of intelligence. Correlations between temperament and body build, as we shall see later, tend to be much lower than this; they are rarely higher than about 0.3. What would be the correlation between the order in which horses arrive at the end of a race and the prediction made by an experienced punter? Alas! the correlation is very nearly zero, possibly 0.1, but hardly better than that. And what will be the correlation between what happens to a person during a given week and the astrological prediction made on the basis of his birth date? Well, there the answer will be exactly zero; there is no predictive accuracy attached to this at all. So there you have a rough idea of the range of correlations which you find in various situations, and they will give you an idea of what is meant by correlation. It should be noted, incidentally, that correlations can also be negative. If a person who scores high in one test tends to score low in another, then the correlation will be negative, and it can range all the way from zero to −1.

It follows from our discussion that traits may be defined as a co-variance of behavioural acts; this co-variation thus appears as an organizing principle which is deduced from the observed generality of human behaviour. The observations of this generality are expressed mathematically in terms of coefficients of correlation, ranging from zero, signifying no generality at all, to 1, signifying complete generality. Essentially, Hartshorne and May followed up this notion by constructing a large battery of tests, ratings and self-ratings, administering these to large groups of school children, and then calculating inter-correlations among tests, ratings, and self-ratings. The hypothesis was that if there was any generality of behaviour among the school children, this would show itself by way of positive correlations. We thus have a crucial test of the hypothesis of generality.

The large battery of tests constructed by Hartshorne and May must be described in brief outline now to make intelligible the discussion of the results. They laid down certain general rules to which all tests should, as far as possible, conform. Thus a test situation should be a natural situation as well as a controlled one. The test situation and the method of response should allow all subjects equal opportunity to exhibit the behaviour under investigation. The child should not be subjected to any moral strain beyond the usual, and the test should not be allowed to put the subject and the examiner in a false social relation to each other. The tests should have 'low visibility', i.e. they should not arouse the suspicions of the subject.

Various techniques were found, which conformed to these rules. One of them is the 'duplicating technique'. The child is given any paper-and-pencil type of test; the papers are collected and a duplicate of the answers made in the office. At a later session of the class the original papers are returned and each child is told to score his own paper according to a key supplied. Deception consists in illegitimately increasing the score by copying answers from the key. Other tests make use of the 'improbable achievement technique'. This consists in giving a test under conditions where achievement above a given level is an almost certain indication of deception. Thus when a child is asked to put dots in the centre of a number of irregularly spaced circles on the blackboard with his eyes closed, and he succeeds in doing so well beyond the known capacity of children, the child may be presumed to have peeped.

Still another type is the 'double testing technique'. In this method, the children are tested twice on alternate versions of a given test; on one occasion, conditions permit deception, on the other there is strict supervision and no opportunity to deceive. The difference between scores made on the two occasions is a rough measure of the tendency to deceive, i.e. either to copy answers from the key or to change answers to match the key. It is, of course, essential in this procedure that material be available in two equivalent forms, having the same degree of difficulty at all levels. It may also be noted that, unlike the previous techniques, this one lends itself to showing deception in work done at home as well as in the classroom situation. It also lends itself to testing in another and different context, namely that of athletic contests; the achievement of the child on such activities as 'pull-up' or 'chinning', the 'standing broad jump', or dynamometer and spirometer tests can be measured when the test is given by the examiner and when it is self-administered, the difference noted as evidence of cheating through inflated claims. All these techniques for measuring cheating permit a large number of variations and some of them may be applied in situations quite different from those originally envisaged. Thus the authors found it possible to use tests of this kind in connexion with parlour games and on other occasions when motivation is high and conditions are markedly different from those obtaining at school or in class.

In contrast to these tests, all of which deal with cheating of one kind or another, there are others dealing with stealing and lying. In each case, an opportunity is given for the child to steal or lie under conditions which made it seem unlikely to the child that he could be caught, but which are actually under the control of the experimenter so that a complete check is possible. Thus, for instance, in connexion with the administration of one test, a little box was given to each pupil containing several puzzles, not all of which were used. In each box was a coin, ostensibly belonging to another puzzle which the examiner showed to the children but did not ask them to perform. Each child returned his own box to a large receptacle at the front of the room. It was possible to check which children took the coin before returning the box by a system of numbering and distributing the boxes according to the seating plan of the class. Lying could be detected, for instance, by asking the children whether they had cheated on any of the tests. It was known, of course, whether they had cheated or not; and if they denied having done so, the lie was apparent.

A large number of different populations was studied, coming from different types of schools and institutions, urban and rural areas, and from varied racial backgrounds. All told some 170,000 tests were administered to over 8,000 public school children and almost 3,000 children at private and standardized schools. Attempts were made to find data outside the experimental situation which would throw light on the validity of the techniques employed. Ratings were used and these were found to be reasonably reliable; in other words, one rater tended to agree very much with another, and one rater agreed very much with himself when making the same set of ratings independently a second time. These ratings were made by teachers and others in close contact with the children and knowing a good deal about them.

How about the question of generality now? The nine tests used in this study by Hartshorne and May correlated just over 0.2 with each other. In other words, although there was some correlation, it was relatively slight. However, when all nine tests were taken together as a kind of battery, it was found that they correlated to the extent of about 0.72 with another battery of nine tests similar to those used. This result indicates a considerable degree of generality of delinquent behaviour. Indeed the correlation is not very different from that usually found between different tests of intelligence. One test of intelligence will not ordinarily correlate much above 0.7 with another test of intelligence. The correlations between the behaviour tests and the ratings were also positive and usually in the neighbourhood of 0.4. This is encouraging, because it is not far short of the correlation between intelligence test results and the ratings of children's intelligence by teachers. Indeed it is surprisingly high, because normally children would be only too glad to furnish teachers with evidence of their intelligence, but they would be rather reluctant to furnish them with evidence of their own dishonesty, cheating, lying, and stealing behaviour. Consequently the ratings made by the teachers must inevitably fall far short of perfection. To find that they nevertheless correlated positively with behaviour tests is distinctly encouraging and suggests that there is some validity attaching to both the ratings and the tests.

The same techniques applied to the study of deceitful behaviour were also used in a study of socially approved behaviour. Hartshorne and May defined as socially desirable the tendency to do things for others rather than for oneself, and the tendency to work with others rather than to stand alone, a tendency which they believe, 'passes into and through a stage of cooperation for the sake of organized competition, to a higher level of cooperation for a non-competitive object, the significance of which lies in the relation of the cooperating individuals to one another.' In their attempts to devise test situations they had these two modes of response in mind. Five tests were given, making up a battery called the 'service tests'.

1. *The self or class test.* A spelling contest was set up in which each pupil could compete for one of two sets of prizes, one for the winning class and one for the winning individual. No one could enter both contests. Each had to choose whether his score was to count for himself and help himself towards getting a prize, or count for the class and help the class get a prize.

2. *The money-voting test.* In this test, the class had to decide what to do with some money which might be, or actually had been, won in the previous contest. Scoring was in terms of the altruistic nature of the choice, ranging from, 'Buy something for some hospital child or some family needing help or for some other philanthropy', to, 'Divide the money equally among the members of the class'.

3. *The learning exercises.* This test attempts to measure the amount of drive induced by opportunities to work for the Red Cross, for the class, or for oneself, on a mental abilities test, using as scores gains from the basic, unmotivated score obtained on the first day.

4. *The school kit test.* Each child was provided with a pencil case containing ten articles which came, 'as a present from a friend of the school'. It was then suggested to them that they might give away any part or all of the kit in an inconspicuous way, in order to help make up some kits for children who had no useful or pretty things of this kind.

5. *The envelopes test.* The children were asked to find jokes, pictures, interesting stories, and the like, for sick children in hospitals, and were given envelopes in which to collect them. The number of articles collected by each child was scored according to a complex scoring system.

Various other tests were also tried out, such as the efficiency cooperation test, in which work for oneself in contest with other individuals was compared with work for one's class in an inter-class contest. In the free choice test carried out after the previous one, the choice was given as to whether the child wanted to go on working for himself or for the class.

Again an effort was made to test the validity of these tests by means of ratings. Correlations between the tests were again of the order of 0.2; but when they were all put together in the form of a battery, it was found that this battery correlated with the ratings to the extent of about 0.6. For tests of this kind, this is very high indeed, and shows that there is a considerable degree of generality present in socially desirable behaviour of this kind.

Another battery of tests was constructed in order to measure self control and inhibition. Six techniques in all were tried out. In the first of these, each child had a copy of a story which was read aloud by the examiner up to the climax. The child was then asked to turn the sheets over and write on the back of the last page what he thought the ending of the story would be. The child was thus expected to inhibit the drive to know how the story would end and, instead, take a guess at it. If he chose to guess, he was not told how the story came out. In the second test, a small toy safe with a combination lock was put on each pupil's desk. He was instructed not to touch it for a lengthy period, during which a paper-and-pencil test was given. Self-control consisted of inhibiting the tendency to touch and play with the safe. In the third test, a box was passed to the children containing a peg test as well as five small puzzles definitely attractive to children, with which they were asked not to play. Inhibition consisted of leaving these puzzles alone and concentrating on the major task. In the distraction test, an arithmetic test was set out on a page covered with interesting drawings. Self-control consisted of not giving way to the temptation to look at these. The other tests were similar to those described. Self-control was assessed by ratings in a way similar to the method used for the service and cheating tests. Again, individual inter-correlations of about 0.2 were observed and correlations with outside ratings were again found to be quite reasonable and encouraging.

Hartshorne and May next turned to a study of the relationship between honesty, service, and inhibition, the hypothesis being that these three personality traits tend to be positively inter-related. Correlations of almost 0.4 were discovered among these variables; although this is not high, it seems to suggest that these traits are correlated with each other and define a general tendency towards moral or socially approved behaviour.

We now turn to what is perhaps the most important analysis carried out by Hartshorne and May, their study of integration. Most definitions of personality use this term, although they seldom attempt any adequate operational definition of it. Interpreting the term 'integration' as 'consistency of performance', they argued that the integrated or consistent person gives responses that are organized in such a way that the person's conduct can be predicted.

On an altitude scale then we have excellent or bad characters, but ... they may be depended upon to function consistently on their own level. ... Heretofore we have been placing children on a vertical scale and ranking them high or low. We shall now attempt to place them on what may be called for convenience a horizontal scale and shall arrange them according to the consistency with which they function on their given level. ... Our definition of integration as consistency of performance falls fairly close to a widely used meaning of the term. By *integration* is often intended a certain dependability or stability of moral conduct. Conversely the individual lacking in integration is at the mercy of the varying temptations of every situation. His conduct is inconsistent, undependable, unpredictable or even contradictory.

Hartshorne and May did, in fact, find a distinct relationship between integration and honest behaviour; in other words, honesty was a characteristic which could be predicted from one situation to another: dishonesty, cheating, lying, and so on, the whole range of unsociable or antisocial activities, tended to be unintegrated, unstable and unpredictable. It is interesting, in this connexion, to note that they also found distinct relationships among integration, emotional stability, persistence and resistance to suggestion. These were, of course, objectively measured by means of psychological tests, and the findings are interesting because, in our discussion of criminal conduct, we will notice again and again the lack of persistence and the suggestibility of the criminal, as well as his lack of emotional stability.

I have drawn attention to the high degree of generality which emerges from the data. Hartshorne and May were more impressed with the failure of this generality to be even more apparent than it is. It is true that their correlations tend to be rather low and they are certainly very far from perfect. How can we account for these facts? Let us examine first of all their finding that a child who behaves in a dishonest manner in one situation does not necessarily behave dishonestly in another situation. Their conclusion would be that the trait honesty is not general but specific to the situation. This conclusion rests on the assumption that the two situations made equal demands on the hypothetical honesty of the child – a view for which there is no evidence. A child may fail a difficult item in an intelligence test but pass an easy one; because he passes one and fails on another we do not argue that he is behaving in an inconsistent manner! A child may tell what he considers a white lie but balk at cheating; he may cheat but balk at stealing. To imagine that the existence of a general trait of honesty precludes the existence of degrees of temptation, or of degrees of immorality between one act and another, is quite unrealistic; there is, of course, no such implication in the 'generality' theory. Related to this first point is a second made by Hartshorne and May and by many other writers since. While some children do show the postulated traits, i.e. are always honest or persistent, and while others are consistent in never showing it, i.e. are always dishonest or lacking in persistence, the majority sometimes show the trait and sometimes do not. But the trait is supposedly applicable to only a few cases, i.e., to those who demonstrate it consistently and not to others. By a similar argument it might be maintained that the concept of intelligence is applicable only to those who never fail an item or to those who fail every item. If we conceive of honesty as constituting a continuum, then the most honest should never cheat and the least honest always cheat; intermediate degrees of honesty should be reflected in behaviour, cheating when temptation is strong or when the immorality is rather slight, and not cheating when temptation is weak or the immorality involved is strong. Given the degree of temptation or immorality of the act, we will then be able to predict with as much accuracy for the intermediate child as for the extreme, just as we can predict for the child of average intelligence as easily as for the genius or the dunce, that he will succeed or fail with any given problem.

As a third argument, Hartshorne and May advanced the view that the low inter-correlations among the different tests for each of the personality qualities measured – honesty, persistence, self-control, and so on – do not support the assumption that these qualities exist. Yet, these inter-correlations are in almost every case positive, whereas the specificity theory predicts correlations of zero. While these inter-correlations are admittedly lower than those found between intelligence tests, we must be careful not to compare intelligence tests, composed of fifty to a hundred items, with a single test of honesty or persistence, which would correspond to one item in a much larger test battery for measurement of honesty or persistence, made up of fifty or a hundred such items. We have seen in our discussion of the detailed results of this experiment that reliability and validity values approaching, and sometimes even exceeding, the high values found with intelligence tests, are discovered in Hartshorne and May's own work for such batteries of honesty or self-control or integration tests. Such results are inconceivable on any strict specificity hypothesis, as is the finding that the tests themselves correlate reasonably highly with outside ratings.

In the fourth place, we must take into account the fact that Hartshorne and May used social and ethical concepts as the qualities whose specificity or generality was to be investigated. Even if the chosen qualities had been shown to be entirely specific, it would not follow that because certain socio-ethical qualities lack generality, therefore more genuinely psychological qualities would also be found to be specific. The experiment might be begging the question by selecting the wrong type of quality to investigate. We may find consistency in the habits of those who frequent a library, by observing whether they choose books of fiction, science, history, or poetry; failure to observe such consistency when we direct our attention to the colour of the binding of the books selected does not prove the specificity of the choices!

Finally, the preceding argument appears particularly relevant when children constitute the experimental population, as they did in these studies. Socio-ethical concepts are clearly not innate; they are acquired through social learning. The young child has had insufficient time to integrate the teaching he has received from a variety of sources into some kind of general *set*, some standard which he or she can apply to a variety of situations; hypothetically, integration should be incomplete in the young child and progress as the child advances in age. This is indeed demonstrated in Hartshorne and May's own data, and in later work by other research investigators with adult subjects. These later writers found considerable consistency in the honest and dishonest behaviour of their subjects and even succeeded in predicting their reactions to the tests, on the basis of a short interview. We may, therefore, assert with some confidence that, in part at least, the low correlations found by Hartshorne and May were due to the youthfulness of their subjects. If the investigation were repeated with older subjects, higher coefficients could confidently be expected and have indeed been found.

The argument must not, of course, be taken too far. The proponents of the generality and the specificity positions start out with views which are apparently quite contradictory. Both produce a certain amount of general theoretical support and both find some kind of reasonable argument which may appeal to the man in the street on *a priori* grounds. Investigation demonstrates pretty conclusively that, in the extreme form, both hypotheses are wrong. Conduct certainly is not specific in any extreme sense. There are generalities which can be observed, which can be indexed, and which vary from one type of conduct to another. However, if we so rarely observe such a considerable degree of specificity that conduct is completely unpredictable, the converse is also true. Conduct is rarely as general as had been believed by the early proponents of the generality hypothesis. While conduct is predictable, it is predictable only up to a point; when it is general, it is general only up to a point. Correlations hardly ever reach or even approach .90; they tend to be much lower than this, and even when these low coefficients are corrected, as they can reasonably be, for a variety of imperfections, they still fall far short of unity. We must somehow reconcile the claims of both parties. We find a certain amount of generality in the moral and social behaviour of our subjects, but we also find in it a considerable degree of specificity. We can predict, but our predictions are far from perfect. There is generality, but not complete generality. Both theories are right in what they assert, and wrong in what they deny.

The reader may wonder why we have concentrated so much on a single experimental investigation, and a single theoretical point. The question of generality and specificity is of fundamental importance for our psychological analysis of the problem being examined. Criminologists, sociologists, psychologists, and others interested in these problems have always been at loggerheads about the precise definition of their problem. Some have argued that they are concerned only with crimes, that is, with breaches of the moral and social code of a given society, which are counter to the law and which finally bring the offender to justice. Others have argued that, since the laws differ from one society to another and from one time to another within the same society, there is insufficient unanimity of conception to justify analysing such crimes independently of other transgressions of the moral code. If homosexuality is a crime in England but not in France, then criminologists would be engaged in quite different pursuits on the two sides of the Channel. This, they argue, is absurd.

Clearly, it is difficult on *a priori* grounds to come to any conclusion about this problem, despite its importance. Can we, in our discussion of criminality, include such minor offences of childhood as truancy, temper tantrums, stealing apples, and so on, which do not ordinarily bring the offender into conflict with the law, although occasionally they may? The intervention of the law is such an erratic affair, particularly in modern society, that a reasonable analysis would become very difficult if we had to restrict ourselves entirely to actual law-breakers incarcerated in our prisons.

The generality hypothesis, however, if it were borne out by actual investigation, would allow us to take the other route. We would then be able to look for certain similarities among people who transgress against the rules of their society, whether formalized into law or not, and we could determine systematically the reasons why some people give way to temptation of this type, whereas others do not. We would, in other words, be able to call upon a much wider range of facts to support or contradict any hypotheses we might frame. The fact that there is a certain amount of generality may, therefore, be taken as support for this second view and as justification for the path we have pursued.

We may take the road offender as an example of the kind of prediction which can be made from our notion of generality, and of the kind of data which may be used to support it – or, of course, to contradict it if it should be wrong. It is well-known that, in modern society, a large number of violations of the law are committed by people who drive defective cars, park them in the wrong places, and drive them in an offensive or dangerous manner. These are often considered to be different in kind from the offences normally calling for the intervention of the law: offences like murder, theft, larceny, rape, and so on. Most road offenders are supposed to be otherwise respectable citizens who may have been victims of accidents, momentary carelessness, or simply bad luck. It is possible that this view arises from the very broad generalization that road offences are 'middle-class' offences, whereas the usual run of crimes are committed by working-class people. This is by no means universally true. It is, however, *believed* to be so by many people and this may have determined their views of the situation.[6]

This view is, to some extent, derived from the specificity type of hypothesis. One type of crime, that of the road offender, is specific and in no way related to another type of crime, that of the habitual criminal. Our postulate of generality, however, would lead us to believe the opposite. It would lead us to believe that there is a general tendency for people to break the law, whether in relation to property or in relation to motoring offences, and that, therefore, we would find a distinct relationship or correlation between the two. What are the facts? Fortunately we have available some data recently published by Dr Terence Willett, who examined in detail all convictions for six serious motoring offences which were reported over a two-year period in one of the English Home Counties, 653 cases in all. These 653 offenders appeared in Court charged with one or more of these offences:

1. Causing death by dangerous driving.
2. Driving recklessly or dangerously.
3. Driving under the influence of drink or drugs.
4. Driving while disqualified.
5. Failing to insure against third party risks.
6. Failing to stop after, or to report, an accident.

Willett found that over one-fifth of these 653 offenders turned out to have criminal records for non-motoring offences. Another sixty individuals had no criminal record but were 'known to the police' as notorious or suspected persons. Thus, on the whole, about one in three of the total were far from being respectable citizens who had simply suffered some kind of accident or who had had bad luck. The estimates say that less than one person in ten is likely to be convicted by a criminal court during his life in Great Britain, but the criminal proportion of the road offenders studied by Willett is something like three times the chance expectation.

It is interesting to note that an additional twenty-four per cent of the offenders had previous convictions for motoring offences, so that almost half of the total population had previous convictions of some kind. Of 151 individuals who had convictions for non-motoring offences, it was found that they were responsible for 549 different motoring offences and 610 non-motoring offences, of which only about thirteen could be called trivial. Two out of three in this group had been previously convicted three or more times. Figure 1 shows the percentage of drivers having criminal records in each category of Dr Willett's sample of 653 offenders.[7]

Similar results emerge from a study carried out in Canada by W. A. Tillman and G. E. Hobbs. They compared a group of accident repeaters with two groups of accident-free drivers. Of the repeaters, thirty-four per cent had been before adult courts; of the accident-free group, only one per cent. Of the repeaters, seventeen per cent had been before juvenile courts; of the accident-free group only 1.2 per cent. Eighteen and fourteen per cent of the repeaters, respectively, were known to social service agencies and venereal disease clinics. Of the accident-free group, only one and zero per cent, respectively, were known to these agencies.[8]

The personalities of accident-prone drivers have often been studied in England, in America, in Germany, and in other countries as well, and the result has usually been that abnormally high pro-

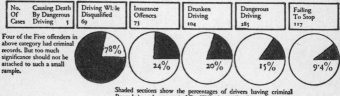

Shaded sections show the percentages of drivers having criminal Records in each category of Dr. Willett's sample of 653 offenders.

FIGURE I

Reprinted by permission of *The Observer*.

portions of people with aggressive, ruthless, psychopathic traits, and also a large proportion of people with neurotic tendencies, are found in this group. As we shall see, these are traits which are also frequently found in criminals in the more usual sense of the term. Again, therefore, we find a certain amount of generality, this time linking personality and socially deviant behaviour. We may conclude our discussion in this chapter by saying that conduct is sufficiently general that we should enquire into the causes of this generality, and that it appears to be related to personality to such an extent that we should enquire into the precise nature of the relationship.

2   The Nature of Personality

'What sort of insects do you rejoice in, where *you* come from?' the Gnat inquired.

'I don't *rejoice* in insects at all,' Alice explained, 'because I'm rather afraid of them – at least the large kinds. But I can tell you the names of some of them.'

'Of course they answer to their names?' the Gnat remarked carelessly.

'I never knew them do it.'

'What's the use of their having names,' the Gnat said, 'if they won't answer to them?'

'No use to *them*,' said Alice 'but it's useful to the people that name them, I suppose. If not, why do things have names at all?'

THROUGH THE LOOKING GLASS

In the first chapter of this book, we have raised the problem of the relationship between criminal conduct and personality. We must now turn to a more detailed discussion of personality, its description and measurement, in order to furnish an answer to our major question in subsequent chapters. First of all, let us look at the methods which are available for studying personality. The first and most obvious one is that of *rating*. This method consists essentially in assigning certain traits to other people on the basis of our observation of them, or of our acquaintance with them. This can be done by calling them sociable or unsociable, or else by rating them in a more complex manner, giving them five points for extreme sociability, one point for extreme lack of sociability, and four, three, or two points, according to various gradations. There are many other ways of carrying out ratings; for instance, it may be done on a graphic scale, in which a mark is put on a line, its position on the line denoting the degree of the trait which is attributed to a given person; or it may be done by having a whole series of sketches available of the very sociable, slightly less sociable, average, unsociable, and the very unsociable person, and then saying which of these sketches is most characteristic of a given person. We all use ratings of this kind, formally or informally, every day of our lives when we talk about other people and call them dominant or suggestible, persistent or submissive, sociable or flighty.

There are many difficulties associated with ratings, and some of these may be mentioned. In the first place, we have a differential understanding of trait names. It is only too obvious, when talking to two persons who undertake to rate others, that their conceptions of terms such as suggestibility, sense of humour, persistence, and so forth, vary widely and that quite contradictory meanings may be associated with the same trait name. This may easily lead to a complete lack of correlation between ratings given by two different judges. On one occasion, I had a hundred patients rated for suggestibility by several experienced psychiatrists. When these ratings were correlated the coefficient turned out to be about zero; in other words, the raters were all rating entirely different things, and one could not, knowing the ratings of one of these psychiatrists, predict how a given patient would be rated by the others. Similar results have often been obtained for other traits. Thus even when such an apparently obvious trait as anxiety has been rated by different observers, all experienced psychiatrists, it has been found that the person rated high in anxiety by one might be rated low in anxiety by another, and average by a third. Even the fact of having had a great deal of experience and training, as all the psychiatrists involved in these studies had, would therefore not seem capable of overcoming this difficulty in all circumstances. It is, of course, possible to reduce the influence of this factor by thorough discussions with the judges about the exact meaning of the terms used; in the absence of such clarification of terms, it is almost impossible to attribute any meaning to the results of rating studies.

Another difficulty is the so-called halo effect. It was observed quite early in the history of psychology, that sets of ratings for different traits in a given person tend to show unduly high inter-correlations and it was soon found that these were due to a general impression of the ratee possessed by the rater. This general stereotyped attitude would then colour all the judgements made of particular traits for a ratee. This stereotyped attitude has been called a 'halo'. Philip Vernon, a well-known British psychologist, has put the matter in this way:

Most commonly, halo consists largely of our general liking for or our dislike of the ratees, for it is usually found that the desirable or admirable traits give high positive inter-correlations and negative correlations with undesirable traits. Doubtless, this has some basis in actual fact; persons of fine character do tend to be high on all good qualities. Others do tend to be weak all round, but one is very liable to exaggerate this and to attribute unwittingly all the virtues to our friends, and the vices to our enemies.[9]

A third factor which makes ratings difficult and unreliable is the unconscious bias which we may have in relation to certain traits. It has been found, for instance, that when a person has a certain trait to a very considerable measure, this may influence his rating of others. If he has insight into his own possession of this particular trait then he will tend to attribute less of it to other people than would normally be their due. If, on the other hand, he lacks insight into his own possession of this trait then he will attribute more of it to others than they could rightfully claim. In other words, supposing that you are very stingy and know full well that this is so, you will then, in judging other people with respect to this trait, call them less stingy than they really are. If, on the other hand, you are very stingy but do not know about this, then you will tend to call other people more stingy than they actually are. This, of course, interferes considerably with the validity of ratings, because different people will show different traits in different degree, and project them onto others in different proportions.[10]

It will be clear from what has been said that a rating cannot be taken strictly as a description of the person rated; it is always an interaction between rater and ratee. As such, it may be used, by appropriate methods of analysis, to throw light either on the ratee or the rater, or on the interaction between the two, that is, the process of rating itself. How this is done may be shown by a very simple example. Suppose we have two teachers, Smith and Jones, who both rate the same hundred essays prepared by the students. The average mark given by Smith is ninety per cent; the average mark given by Jones is sixty per cent. This does not tell us anything about the quality of the essays; it does tell us that Jones is apparently a much more demanding, rigorous sort of person, and that Smith is apparently more easygoing and less demanding. Considerable technical skill is demanded before we can accept ratings as being scientifically admissible evidence for any conclusion we wish to reach.

The second main source of evidence for personality studies comes from *self-ratings*, questionnaires, or inventories. In these, a long list of questions relating to a person's private life is presented to him; each question has following it a 'Yes', a question mark, and a 'No', and he has to underline the 'Yes' or the 'No', whichever is the correct answer to the question, or the question mark if he cannot make up his mind. Questions might be: 'Do you often experience periods of loneliness?' or, 'Do you get rattled easily at critical moments?' or, 'Are you troubled with feelings of inferiority?' Questionnaires such as these may have only a few questions or as many as five or six hundred or even a thousand. Their validity obviously depends on the honesty of the respondent; if he wishes to falsify his replies, it is quite easy to do so.

Questionnaires, too, have their difficulties. In the first place, we have the problem of honesty. Many of the questions we ask might be taken to reflect unfavourably on the subject, and if he wishes to put himself in the best light, he will falsify his answers accordingly. It is possible to guard against this by introducing scales such as the so-called lie scales, which do not form part of the questionnaire which is scored, but which form a separate scale. This scale consists of questions of a mildly defamatory nature which, a person would, in all honesty, be bound to admit to. A question in a scale of this type might be: 'Have you ever told a lie in your life?' If we wanted to put ourselves in the best light we would, of course, wish to say, 'No' to this question. However, there are very few people who would not be forced to answer 'Yes', if they were entirely honest. We might, therefore, consider the answer 'No' to be indicative of a wish to put oneself in the best light and if this tendency was repeated on a large number of similar questions, we might conclude that the questionnaire was worthless because the person completing it had a high 'lie score'.

Another difficulty which arises is 'response set'. It has been found that in certain circumstances people are acquiescent, that is, they may endorse all or a majority of the 'Yes' answers, regardless of the contents of the question; or else they may be contrary, endorsing all or most of the 'No' answers. Some people have a response set for question marks; they are doubtful about their answers in a high proportion of cases and frequently it is impossible to score their replies, because so many question marks are underlined. There are many other types of response set and there are ways and means of measuring these, but nevertheless, they do present a problem to the constructor of questionnaires.

The main problem, however, often presented by questionnaires, is the relative lack of meaning of many questions. Consider the question, 'Do you have frequent headaches?' How strong does a headache have to be to be called a headache? How frequent does it have to be to be called frequent? What is the average number of headaches a person has in our society? How strong are these headaches? It is quite clear that a large amount of interpretation is included in the answer. With exactly the same number and severity of headaches, one person might say, 'Yes', another one might say,

'No' to this question. This excessive degree of subjectivity is obviously difficult to counteract. Does this invalidate the use of questionnaires? The answer to this question is, fortunately, 'No'. We may look on the questionnaire answer in two different ways. We might regard it as a veridical statement of a person's actual behaviour or feeling. As such, we would often find ourselves in doubt as to whether or not a given statement could indeed be taken in this manner. However, suppose that we had available a sample of a thousand neurotic and a thousand non-neurotic persons, and that we administered a questionnaire to them which included the item about the headaches. We might find that, among the neurotics, sixty-nine per cent said 'Yes'; among the normals, only ten per cent. We could conclude from this, not necessarily that neurotics have more frequent headaches or more severe headaches, but that a neurotic person will tend to say 'Yes' more frequently to this question than would a normal person, quite regardless of the number of headaches which both people had at any time of their lives. Suppose we had fifty or a hundred similar questions, for each of which we knew exactly the proportion of 'Yes' answers given by typical normal and neurotic samples. We could, by using these probability estimates, predict whether a given questionnaire belonged to the neurotic or to the normal group. We would do this by simply counting the number of typical neurotic replies and then assessing the probability that the total number was more like that given by a typically neurotic or by a typically normal person. We would not be concerned with the truth or falsity of the answers but simply with their patterning, which we could compare with that produced by representative groups. In this way we may surmount the difficulty of the veridical nature of the answers and nevertheless arrive at a meaningful and useful result. As an example, Figure 2 shows the distribution of scores on a neuroticism questionnaire given to 1,000 normal and 1,000 neurotic persons; the difference in distribution is immediately apparent.[11]

Fortunately, even the veridical nature of answers is not quite as serious a problem as it may appear. It has been shown, in several studies, that if we have judges nominate a group of what appear to them to be highly extraverted persons as opposed to highly introverted persons, and if these extreme groups are given questionnaires of extraversion/introversion, the questionnaire answers are widely separated – so much so, that there is hardly any overlap between them (see Figure 3).[12] This is important, because it shows that there is a considerable degree of agreement between ratings and self-ratings. We have noted some of the objections against ratings, on the one hand, and self-ratings on the other, and we have also shown

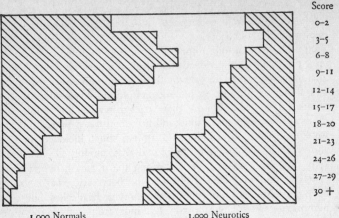

	Score
	0–2
	3–5
	6–8
	9–11
	12–14
	15–17
	18–20
	21–23
	24–26
	27–29
	30 +

1,000 Normals   1,000 Neurotics

Distribution of Scores

FIGURE 2

Distribution of scores of 1,000 normals and 1,000 neurotics, obtained from a neuroticism questionnaire. Note that the modal response for the normals lies in the range of scores from 6 to 8, whereas that for the neurotics lies in the 30+ category. From H. J. Eysenck, *The Scientific Study of Personality*, Routledge, London, 1953.

that these tend to be quite different. Therefore, if there is considerable agreement between ratings and questionnaire answers, then it seems to follow that both must have a considerable degree of validity. Under ordinary circumstances, it is now generally agreed that this is so. Unless people are highly motivated to tell lies, they will, by and large, try to tell the truth on questionnaires of the usual kind. We would not give the questionnaire to someone whom we wished to employ, because he would obviously be forced into the false position of giving evidence against himself, and we would almost expect him to falsify his answers. But if he gives his replies under experimental conditions, knowing full well that the result of the replies which he gives will not be made public but will simply form part of an experimental design, then it seems that we can rely, to a considerable extent, on the truthfulness of his answers.

A third, and most important type of evidence regarding personality comes to us from objective tests. We have already encountered objective tests in the last chapter, and the reader will have admired the ingenuity with which Hartshorne and May tried to overcome

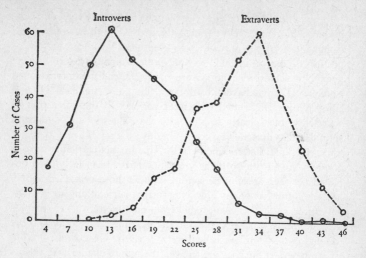

FIGURE 3

Scores on an extraversion-introversion questionnaire of 225 persons described by their friends as introverts; and scores of 225 persons described as extraverts.

the great difficulties of measuring such types of activity as honesty, moral integrity, and inhibition. Many more types of tests are available, and have been used for the measurement of all sorts of personality traits, such as persistence, sociability, fluency, tension, level of aspiration, personal tempo, and so on. We will encounter some of these again later on, and therefore I will not give any detailed description of such tests. Suffice it to say that they often correlate quite highly with other experimental evidence of a person's habitual behaviour tendencies. We have indeed already found some evidence of this in the Hartshorne and May study, and we will find further evidence later on.

How about the results of using these various methods? In the first place, they have given some empirical support to the existence and measurement of certain personality traits. The reader will remember how traits are defined. The essential feature of a trait is the concordance or correlation between different expressions of the same trait. Consequently, when a trait is postulated, we must first of all see whether its different expressions in different contexts correlate with each other. Suppose that we postulate a trait of sociability. We might ask our subjects a series of questions such as these, or have them rated on their behaviour in these situations. 'Can you usually let yourself go, and have a hilarious time at a gay party?'

'Do you like to mix socially with people?' 'Do you usually take the initiative in making new friends?' 'Do you like to have social engagements?' 'Are you inclined to keep quiet when out in a social group?' 'Are you inclined to limit your acquaintances to a select few?' 'In social conversations, are you usually a listener rather than a talker?' 'Do you have difficulty in making new friends?' 'Do you enjoy getting acquainted with most people?' If there is a trait of sociability, then clearly responses to these questions or situations should inter-correlate reasonably highly; if they do not, then we must conclude that specificity is the rule in this particular area of conduct. As a matter of fact, correlations have frequently been obtained between areas of behaviour such as those described above, and the result has nearly always been that correlations are reasonably high, so that we can predict from one question to another. A person who is sociable in relation to one thing tends to be sociable in relation to the others as well and *vice versa*. The correlations are far from perfect but they are sufficiently high to enable us to postulate a general trait of sociability.[13]

It does not follow, of course, because we have postulated a trait, that this trait does, in fact, exist. Suggestibility may present a case in point. It used to be thought that suggestibility was a unitary trait. A large number of different tests were prepared by psychologists to measure this trait, and finally these were administered to a group of subjects. When this was done, it was found, not that all tests correlated to define one single trait, but rather that the tests tended to cluster together in quite distinct groups, defining not one trait of suggestibility but three.

The first of these traits of suggestibility, sometimes called primary or motor suggestibility, is measured in tests such as the following. The subject stands upright, his feet together and eyes closed, his hands hanging down by his side. A thread is clipped to his collar, running back over a wheel to a pointer which moves on a scale. The pointer moves upward whenever the subject sways forward, downward whenever the subject sways backward, thus making it possible for an accurate record to be kept of his amount of body sway. The experimenter then instructs the subject to remain standing, still and erect, with his eyes closed, while he proceeds to talk to him gently in the following manner: 'You're falling, you're falling forward, you're falling forward all the time, you're falling, falling, you're falling forward, you're falling forward now, you're falling, you're falling forward, you're falling forward all the time', and so on. It is noted that quite a number of subjects do begin to sway in response to this suggestion and a certain proportion sway so much that eventually they cannot keep upright any longer, and fall forward and have to be caught by the experimenter. The amount of sway imparted by the suggestion is the measure of suggestibility. Similar tests may relate to the moving upwards or downwards of an arm held out sideways, or to other bodily manifestations of suggestibility.

Another type of suggestibility is called secondary or sensory suggestibility. In testing for this, a suggestion is made to the subject that he will see or hear or feel certain sensations which are not in fact forthcoming; nevertheless, he reports having these sensations. A typical example is the heat illusion. This consists of a very elaborate piece of apparatus, with flashing lights, knobs to be turned, and so forth. The subject is told to hold the grip of a piece of the apparatus which terminates in a metal heading. He is instructed to press this heading against his forehead and he is told that when the machine is on and a particular knob is turned, the metal heading will heat up and he is to report the moment he feels the heat. The first few times that this is done heat is actually produced in the metal heading and he reports this suitably; the next time, however, the experimenter throws a concealed switch, which cuts off the electricity and no heat is produced. Nevertheless, quite a number of people repeat again and again that they experience heat whenever the knob is moved to the position where, on previous occasions, heat had actually been produced. Many similar tests could be mentioned; for instance, you may seat the subject in one corner of the room, instruct him to close his eyes, and tell him to listen for the ticking of your watch. You will be coming nearer and nearer to him and he is to signal the moment he can hear the ticking. The first few times, the watch is actually carried and he reports the ticking whenever he hears it. The next time, the watch is left behind. Nevertheless, a suggestible subject will report the ticking when you have taken the same number of steps as on the previous occasions when the watch was carried, when he could, in fact, hear it ticking. An alternative version of this test might be one in which he is instructed to tell you the moment he can smell a given substance which you are carrying in a glass. The first few times that you go towards him, olfactory substances are put in the glass; then, if only water is carried, a suggestible subject will still report 'smelling' the substance which you are carrying towards him.

A third and quite different type of suggestibility sometimes called tertiary or social suggestibility, can be measured in the following way. First of all, subjects are given a questionnaire relating to certain social and ethical conceptions. After a month or two has passed, they are given another questionnaire, including some of the same questions they answered before. This time, however, after

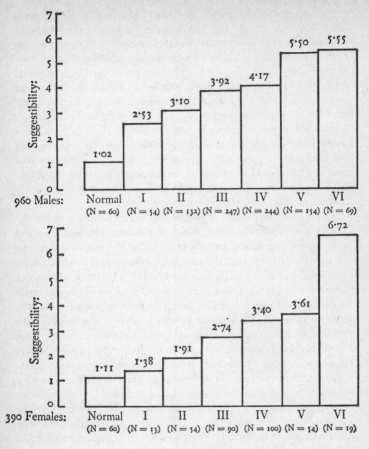

FIGURE 4

Mean scores of normals and various neurotic groups on the body-sway test of suggestibility. The neurotic groups are graded from I (least neurotic) to VI (most neurotic). It will be seen that there is a regular increase in suggestibility with increase in neuroticism, for both males and females. From H. J. Eysenck, *Dimensions of Personality*, Routledge, London, 1947.

each question is put the answer which they are told has been given to this question by someone of very high prestige, such as the President of the United States or a group of Members of Parliament, ministers of religion, or professors. It can then be observed to what extent the subjects will alter their responses to concur with this prestigeful group.

Here we have three different types of suggestibility, all of which fall under the general definition given by the Oxford Dictionary, and which follow popular notions as to the nature of this particular trait. Nevertheless, these three different types of suggestibility do not correlate with each other at all; they are entirely independent. Furthermore, they behave quite differently in relation to other traits and abilities. Thus primary suggestibility is correlated highly with neurotic emotionality (see Figure 4), but not at all with intelligence. Secondary suggestibility, however, is correlated negatively with intelligence (that is, the more suggestible are the less intelligent), but is not correlated with emotional instability. Thus we see that a particular term such as suggestibility may carry several quite separate, meanings and need not give rise to a single specific trait.

We can now measure quite a large number of traits, but it becomes important to note at this stage that personality can be studied at an even higher level of integration. When we look at a group of traits we find that these are not independent of each other. One trait may be correlated with another, giving rise to a higher-order concept. This higher-order concept is the type. The concept of type is, of course, a very ancient one. It probably originated before the time of written records, but for our purpose we will consider it to have entered the scientific field with the writings of Galen. This Greek physician, living in the second century of our era, put forward the view that there were four main types – the melancholic, the choleric, the sanguine and the phlegmatic. These types have become so famous that they are still a part of our everyday language; we still characterize people in these terms and we still retain the essential meaning which Galen gave to these words. He linked these four classical types or temperaments with the 'humours' or secretions of the body, but this part of his theory was so unscientific that it need play no part in our discussion. However, we will have occasion to notice that temperament is in fact related, if not to the humours of the body, at least to the secretions of the endocrine glands, which have taken, in modern times, the part of the ancient 'humours'.

Galen's view of types was one which we might call 'categorical'; he thought that there were really only four types of people – the melancholic, the choleric, the phlegmatic and the sanguine – and that a person was one or the other of these, never a combination of two, or three, or four. The famous German philosopher, Immanuel Kant, who was a follower of Galen and who advocated his system very strongly, also held this view. Many psychologists, even in our own time, believe that typology necessarily implies some such rigid categorical system of classification. However, this is not true. Another, more recent follower of Galen, was Wilhelm Wundt, the famous German psychologist, whose fame rests on the fact that he started the first psychological laboratory in Leipzig in 1879 and is, therefore, often considered the father of modern psychology. He put forward a rather different point of view. According to him, the melancholics and the cholerics were alike in showing very strong emotional reactions, whereas the phlegmatics and the sanguine were alike in showing rather weak emotional reactions. Consequently, he posited the existence of a dimension, or continuum of *strong* as opposed to *weak* emotionality. Similarly, he thought that cholerics and sanguines tended to have emotions which were rather changeable, whereas melancholics and phlegmatics tended to have emotions which were rather firm and stable. Consequently, he posited the existence of another dimension or axis at right angles to the first and independent of it, which he called *changeable* versus *unchangeable*. A person might be assigned any position from one extreme through the centre to the other extreme on either of these two dimensions, and it was the combination of positions on these two dimensions which produced his 'temperament'. If he was extremely strong in his emotions and also extremely changeable, then he might be called a choleric; if he was rather weak and stable, he would be a phlegmatic, and so forth. All possible combinations could occur and there was no question of fixed, unchanging categories. This view of types is much more in line with modern thinking, and it is this view which we will adopt here.

Extensive experimental work has confirmed the essential accuracy of the outline bequeathed to us through Galen and Kant, particularly in the form given to it by Wundt. We no longer talk about the strong or weak emotion; we call this dimension emotionality or neuroticism or stability, in the sense that the person who, according to Wundt, had strong emotions would tend to be a neurotic, unstable, emotional sort of person, whereas at the other end of this dimension, one would find the unemotional, stable, non-neurotic sort of person. The other axis, too, has been renamed, and we now tend to think of it in terms of extraversion and introversion.

These terms were popularized by the famous analytic psychologist, C. G. Jung, but it is an error to think that he invented these terms, for they were in fact current on the Continent for over two hundred years before his time. And it is also an error to imagine that the particular kind of content he gave to these terms is still widely accepted. Insofar as the notions of extraversion and introversion are accepted and acceptable, they derive more from the work of Jung's predecessors; what he added was a very complex system of inter-connected sub-types which are certainly not widely accepted today.

According to Jung, there are two major 'attitudes' or orientations of personality, which are labelled extraversion and introversion. These terms refer, respectively, to the orientation of a person towards the external, objective world, i.e., the extraverted attitude; or the orientation of a person towards the inner, subjective world, i.e., the introverted attitude. Both opposing attitudes are present in each personality at the same time, but usually one of them is dominant and conscious, the other subordinate and unconscious. If a person is predominantly extraverted in his relations with the outer world, his unconscious attitude will be one of introversion. In addition to these attitudes, we have four fundamental psychological functions – thinking, feeling, sensing, and intuiting. As Jung puts it:

Sensation establishes what is actually given, thinking enables us to recognize its meaning, feeling tells us its value, and finally intuition points to the possibilities of the whence and whither that lie within the immediate facts. In this way we can orientate ourselves with respect to the immediate world as completely as when we locate a place geographically by latitude and longitude.[14]

Thinking and feeling he calls 'rational functions'; sensation and intuition he considers 'irrational functions'.

While all four functions are usually present in a given person, one of them is usually more highly differentiated than the others and plays a predominant role. This is called the *superior* function. The least differentiated of the four functions is called the *inferior* function. The latter is repressed into the unconscious, and is expressed in dreams and fantasies. These various systems, attitudes and functions interact with each other in a variety of different ways. One system may *compensate* for the weakness of another system, one system may *oppose* another, or all systems may *unite*, to form a synthesis. As may be seen from this very brief and incomplete outline, Jung has proposed a very complex system of personality description. We shall not discuss it in detail here, because there is very little evidence in favour of any of these suppositions, and because we shall be concerned almost exclusively with the personality dimension of extraversion/introversion. Furthermore, we shall be concerned with this entirely in its overt, conscious, and behavioural aspects, without any supposition that there is a contrary unconscious function or attitude concealed within the person. It would, therefore, be quite incorrect to imagine that what we have to say has very much to do with Jung and his particular system; insofar as the typology discussed here has an historical background, it may be traced back to Galen, Kant, and Wundt, rather than to Jung.

How can we define extraversion and introversion? This can be done primarily in terms of empirical studies, in which we inter-correlate observed traits. We may observe these traits by means of ratings, self-ratings, or objective tests. Whatever we do, the answer seems to be much the same. Below are given typical descriptions of extreme extraverts and introverts; it should be noted that such extreme types as those described will, of course, hardly ever exist. They are, as it were, idealized cases and there is no implication that everyone is either a typical extravert or a typical introvert. Such ideal cases are often useful for stating a general rule or law, and use of them is, of course, made in physics. The first law of motion, for instance, as propounded by Newton, states that a body will continue in its present motion unless acted upon by an external force. In the actual world as we know it, this 'motion continuing unless acted upon by an external force' never happens; it is an ideal case which is merely put in the form of a law, in order to make the symbolic manipulation of data easier. It is in this way that the definitions of extreme extraversion and introversion given below are to be considered.

The typical extravert is sociable, likes parties, has many friends, needs to have people to talk to, and does not like reading or studying by himself. He craves excitement, takes chances, acts on the spur of the moment, and is generally an impulsive individual. He is fond of practical jokes, always has a ready answer, and generally likes change; he is carefree, easygoing, optimistic, and likes to 'laugh and be merry'. He prefers to keep moving and doing things, tends to be aggressive and loses his temper quickly; his feelings are not kept under tight control and he is not always a reliable person.

The typical introvert is a quiet, retiring sort of person, introspective, fond of books rather than people: he is reserved and reticent except with intimate friends. He tends to plan ahead, 'looks before he leaps', and distrusts the impulse of the moment. He does not like excitement, takes matters of everyday life with proper seriousness, and likes a well-ordered mode of life. He keeps his feelings under close control, seldom behaves in an aggressive manner, and does not lose his temper easily. He is reliable, somewhat pessimistic, and places great value on ethical standards.[15]

The relationship between Galen's four temperaments and the results of modern research into the inter-correlations among traits may be seen in Figure 5. In this figure, we must note one important feature. It is possible to plot trait ratings in a two-dimensional diagram in such a way that, when we join each of the particular traits which are plotted, say, anxious and reserved, to the origin (the centre of the circle), then the cosine of the angle between them will give us a correlation between these two traits. When the angle is 90° of course, the cosine is zero and the two traits are independent and have no correlation with each other. When the angle is smaller than 90° the correlation is positive, and the smaller the angle between the two traits the larger the correlation. Where the angle is larger than 90° the correlation is negative and becomes minus one when the angle is 180°. In this way we can, from our knowledge of the inter-correlations between traits, plot the diagram such as that given in

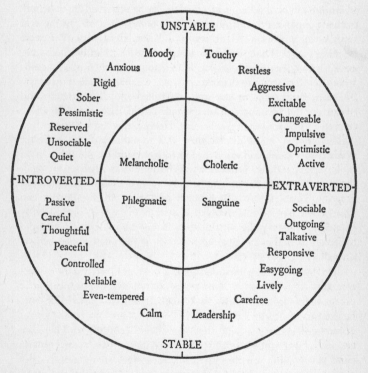

FIGURE 5

The diagram shows Galen's mediaeval personality theory of the four temperaments (inner circle) and the results of modern experimental and statistical studies of personality structure (outer circle). Reproduced with permission from *British Journal of Psychology*, 1963, *54*, 54.

Figure 5. Conversely, once a diagram is given in this form, we can, by simply looking at it, see what kinds of correlations obtain between the different traits which are picture there.

We see from Figure 5 that the choleric tends to be restless, aggressive, excitable, changeable, and impulsive; this is in fairly good agreement with the description of the choleric as pictured by Galen and Kant and Wundt. Similarly, the melancholic tends to be moody, anxious, rigid, pessimistic, reserved and unsociable, which again fits in rather well with the ancient picture of this type. There is a great deal of resemblance in the case of the other two temperaments also, and we can say, on the whole, that the modern and the mediaeval picture fit together remarkably well. This is not surprising. We are dealing, after all, with a description of behaviour and with the kinds of relationships which can be observed by watching other people very carefully. It would be an error to assume that mediaeval writers were fools who did not know what they were talking about. They were very acute observers, highly intelligent, very gifted, and there is no reason to assume that their observations were any less accurate than those which we might make nowadays. Admittedly they were less well-controlled and, in particular, did not have the advantage of mathematical calculations such as those involved in correlation coefficients. However, when we are dealing with only two major dimensions, such as stability or emotionality on the one hand, and extraversion/introversion on the other, then this particular defect is not nearly as noticeable as when we are dealing with a much larger number. The human mind is not a very efficient calculating machine but it can cope with the limited and restricted correlations involved in such an analysis. Consequently it does not seem quite so strange as it might appear that Galen did succeed so well in anticipating the most modern description of personality.

Having become acquainted with a very general system of personality description, we turn to the more specific classification of neurotic disorders within this system. It is well known that psychiatrists tend to group patients into syndromes, that is, clusters of correlated symptoms, and diagnose them accordingly. There are many such diagnoses of different types of neurosis, from hysteria and psychopathy on the one hand, to anxiety states, reactive depressions, obsessive-compulsive states, and so forth, on the other. These diagnostic categories are occasionally useful, but they have one important defect. They are essentially categorical systems of classification, analogous to that advocated by Galen and by Kant, and they do not make use of the much greater flexibility which is possible with a dimensional system such as that advocated by

Wundt and Jung and used above in structuring the field of human personality. Medical men usually classify diseases into quite definite entities, such as malaria, or typhoid, or cancer, or tuberculosis; these are indeed disease entities in the sense that they are caused by different organisms, that they show entirely different symptoms, that they can be treated by entirely different types of medication and that their outcomes typically are different one from the other. None of these facts is true in relation to the neuroses. Neurotic disorders are not clearly separated one from the other; they do not normally call for different methods of treatment; they do not normally end differently; and they do not present the kind of categorical differentiation that is common in physical medicine. This is shown most clearly and obviously when we look at the problems of diagnosis which face the psychiatrist. Admittedly, physical medicine, too, knows its errors of diagnosis, but at least there is a fair degree of reliability in the diagnosis of tuberculosis, say, or cancer. But there is very little such reliability in the diagnosis of neurotic disorders. When the same group of a hundred neurotics is diagnosed independently by a number of experienced psychiatrists, the agreement between them on the particular label used to describe a given neurotic is very little better than chance, and disagreement is far more apparent than agreement. This experiment has been done a number of times and the outcome is always very much the same. These categorical labels simply do not work they do not give us a reliable, let alone a valid, picture of the neurotic symptomatology with which we are dealing. A dimensional kind of system might be much more appropriate to this type of material.[16]

At about the turn of the century, the essential clue to this problem was given by the famous French psychiatrist, Pierre Janet, who argued that the neurotic disorders fell essentially into two main groups. One of these he called the *psychasthenic* group, the other he called the *hysteric* group. In the psychasthenic group we find the anxiety states, the depressions, the phobic fears, the obsessive and compulsive habits; in the hysteric group we find a variety of personality disorders, histrionic behaviour, memory lapses, paralysis, blindness, and other apparently physical disorders having, however, no anatomically observable cause. Jung accepted this differentiation and suggested that extraverts tended to develop hysterical symptoms when ill, whereas introverts tended to develop psychasthenic symptoms. This observation has been a very useful and fruitful one indeed and psychology owes a debt of gratitude to Jung for this discovery, which has been amply verified by later workers.[17]

There are one or two changes which modern writers might make in this system. The term 'psychasthenia' has a certain obsolescent ring, particularly in view of several erroneous theories associated with it, and it is not commonly used nowadays. We may call this whole group of mood disorders the *dysthymic* group of disorders, to emphasize that they are largely concerned with overt anxieties and depressive and other emotional reactions. On the other hand, it has been found that even more extremely extraverted than the typical hysterics are the so-called psychopaths. This is an extremely interesting group of people and, because they are so very relevant to the main theme of this book, we shall discuss them now in more detail.

We may get some notion of what the term 'psychopath', or 'sociopath', means when we realize that it is often used interchangeably with the term 'moral imbecile'. Here is one description of the symptoms typically found in a person diagnosed as a psychopath. The term is used to designate those individuals

... who have manifested considerable difficulty in social adjustment over a period of many years or throughout life, but who are not of defective intelligence nor suffering from structural disease of the brain or epilepsy, and whose difficulties in adjustment have not been manifested by the behavioural syndromes which are conventionally referred to as neuroses or psychoses. Among the symptoms often stressed are defects of emotional control, inability to profit from experience, impulsiveness, lack of foresight, inability to modify infantile standards of conduct, lack of self-reliance, unsatisfactory adjustment to the group, inability to withstand tedium, and irresponsibility of character. The psychopath can usually verbalize all the social and moral rules but he does not seem to be able to understand them and to obey them in the way that others do. The American psychiatrist, Cleckley, has called this the 'mask of sanity'.

The California psychologist, H. G. Gough, has given a summary of the characteristics of the psychopath in more psychological terminology. According to him, psychopaths are characterized by an over-evaluation of the immediate goals as opposed to remote or deferred ones; unconcern over the rights and privileges of others when recognizing that they could interfere with personal satisfaction in any way; impulsive behaviour, or apparent incongruity between the strength of the stimulus and the magnitude of the behavioural response; inability to form deep or persistent attachments to other persons or to identify in inter-personal relationships; poor judgment and planning in attaining defined goals; apparent lack of anxiety and distress over social maladjustment and unwillingness or inability to consider maladjustment as such; a tendency to project blame onto others and to take no responsibility for failures; meaningless prevarication, often about trivial matters in situations where detection is inevitable; almost complete lack of dependability and of willingness to assume responsibility; and finally, emotional poverty. None of these attitudes or characteristics, taken alone, would be crucial, but, when seen to converge in a particular person, they constitute strong evidence of psychopathy. Nor is any of these factors explicitly dependent on illegal or asocial behaviour, although they may easily be inferred from such behaviour. The person may be characterized by the above factors, that is, he may be psychopathic, and still not be institutionalized or guilty of illegal acts; on the other hand, the psychopaths would be expected to contribute more than their share to the delinquent and criminal population.[18]

It would be an error to identify the psychopath and the criminal; there are many criminals who are not psychopaths; equally, as we have seen, there are many psychopaths who are not criminal. One reason for this is, of course, that what a psychopath does, although it may be criminal, is quite frequently not reported to the police. As an example, we may take one particularly horrible psychopathic murderer, who was caught when he savagely assaulted, tortured, and finally killed a young girl. After his trial had begun, it came out that he had, on many previous occasions, seduced or raped young girls of his acquaintance, had beaten them, tied them up, and tortured them in other ways; yet, throughout the years, none of these girls had complained to the police. There are many possible reasons for this. A typical working-class girl may be afraid of going to the police; she may feel ashamed of what has happened and not want this to be known, or to come out in a particularly salacious form during a trial, and be reported in all the newspapers. She may even feel some kind of guilt about having agreed to the first few steps in this long road down the path of debauchery. Whatever the reason, this particular psychopath 'got away with murder', as the phrase goes, at least until he did, in fact, commit a murder, bringing the forces of law into the case. Nevertheless, much of the lying, stealing, sexual delinquency and aggressive behaviour in which the psychopath indulges tends to go unpunished, either because no complaint is made to the police, or for various other reasons. One of these reasons, in particular, is that the psychopath tends to be a bird of easy passage; he seldom stays in one place long. When he has wreaked his havoc he will be quickly gone and difficult to locate, particularly as he may change his name and his assumed background.

As we shall see later, the psychopath presents the riddle of delinquency in a particularly pure form, and if we could solve this riddle in relation to the psychopath, we might have a very powerful weapon to use on the problem of delinquency in general. This will be our task in later chapters. Let us now, first of all, look at the evidence and see whether the psychopath, together with the hysteric, whose antisocial behaviour tends to be milder than that of the psychopath, does indeed tend to be extraverted in his personality, as opposed to the dysthymic group of disorders at the introverted end of the scale. Figure 6 shows the position, with respect to a particular questionnaire, of various neurotic groups in relation to each other. It will be seen that, as predicted, the psychopathic is indeed the most extremely extraverted group, followed by the hysteric; whereas, on the introverted side, we have the anxiety states, the obsessive-compulsive groups, the phobics, and the reactive depressions. We may therefore say, looking back at Figure 5, that the psychopath and, to

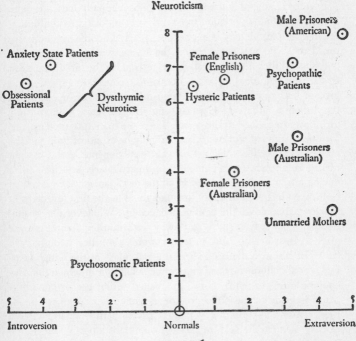

FIGURE 6

Neuroticism and extraversion-introversion scores of various neurotic and criminal groups. Note the high degree of introversion of neurotic groups and the high degree of extraversion of criminal and psychopathic groups. Note also the high degree of neuroticism of both neurotics and criminals.

a lesser extent, the hysteric, are extreme versions of Galen's choleric type, whereas the dysthymic groups are extreme versions of his melancholic type. Not all neurotics, of course, belong to either of these two large groups; a very large number of them lie in between, being neither particularly extraverted nor particularly introverted.[19] This, of course, should not surprise us. We are dealing with a dimension ranging from one extreme to the other, where the majority of people would be expected to lie somewhere between the extremes, just as, on the dimension of intelligence, the majority of people are neither geniuses nor mental defectives, but have I.Q.s between 90 and 110. Not all neurotics, therefore, are clearly either dysthymics, or hysterics and psychopaths; many of them will lie in the middle, having some symptoms apparently pertaining to either group. It is for this reason that the categorical diagnosis of neurotic disorders is so difficult and so pointless. It is much better to recognize the absence of discrete categories and to assign each person a particular position on the continua of neuroticism or emotionality on the one hand, and extraversion/introversion on the other.

Having introduced our general descriptive system of personality and some of the terms, which we shall use later on, we next turn to a consideration of some of the important underlying factors in the creation of the criminal. We will then try, in later chapters, to link personality description with the origins of criminality.

3 The Mark of Cain

So she set the little creature down, and felt quite relieved to see it trot away quietly into the wood. 'If it had grown up,' she said to herself, 'it would have made a dreadfully ugly child: but it makes rather a handsome pig, I think.' And she began thinking over other children she knew, who might do very well as pigs.

ALICE'S ADVENTURES IN WONDERLAND

Throughout history, one of the assumptions that many people have made about crime is that it is committed by people who are born criminals; in other words, they have a curse, as it were, put upon them from the beginning. It is not a question of environmental influences determining what they were going to do; they were 'born bad'. Consequently, whatever society may do, these people will eventually commit criminal acts. The mark of Cain, as it were, is upon them.

In modern times, the main exponent of this view has been the Italian anthropologist, C. Lombroso, who put forward the view that the criminal is born and not made, and that each criminal could be distinguished from non-criminal people by the 'stigmata'; in other words, certain physical abnormalities which would be found only in criminals and which would be found in practically all criminals. This view was never widely held, although it was very well-known on the Continent and in America. When it was disproved, however, many people believed that what had also been disproved was the general proposition that heredity played an important part in the causation of crime. This, of course, did not follow. Lombroso had put forward a particular theory as to the possible role of heredity in crime; and the fact that this particular theory had been disproved threw no light at all on the wider question of the importance of heredity to crime.

The first to attack this whole problem in a truly scientific manner was Professor Johannes Lange, in his book *Crime as Destiny*. This was published in 1928, when Lange was physician-in-chief at the Munich Hospital and departmental director of the German Experimental Station for psychiatry in Munich.* In it, he studied the careers of a large number of criminal twins, some of them identical, others fraternal. Before we can discuss his book in detail we must first look at the particular method, the twin method, which he used for deciding on the importance of hereditary features in the causation of crime. The first to point out the value of twins for genetic studies was Sir Francis Galton, a cousin of Charles Darwin, who was born in 1822, and who was one of those versatile, amateur geniuses who seem to have been so commonplace in the England of Queen Victoria. He was a well-known explorer; he was one of the first people to introduce scientific method into meteorology; he pioneered the use of statistics, particularly correlation coefficients, in psychological and social research; he was the first to point out the vital importance of fingerprints in relation to personal identity; he was a founder of the science of eugenics: and he investigated the causation of human behaviour in terms of genetic factors by means of the method of twins. It was already known in his time that there were two different types of twins. In one type, each twin is the product of a separate female germ cell or egg, both being separately impregnated by male germ cells or sperms. With the other type of twins, both individuals are derived from the same egg, which is impregnated by a single sperm, the egg splitting up later in the process and developing into two separate individuals. Twins which are the product of separate eggs are sometimes known as fraternal or 'dizygotic' twins. Twins which are derived from the same egg are often referred to as identical or 'monozygotic' twins. In the latter case, the twins are always of the same sex. Galton noted that many twins of the same sex were alike from birth and tended to remain alike in their height and girth, their behaviour, their temperament, and even in the diseases to which they fell prey. He considered that these twins must have been derived from a single egg and, therefore, must be identical with respect to heredity. Twins of unlike sex, however, tended to be much more unlike each other in these respects, as were a proportion of like-sex twins. These early notions of Galton's have been fully confirmed since, and it is relatively easy nowadays to diagnose a given pair of twins as identical or fraternal. What we look for are similarities in respect to certain features which are known to be inherited, such as blood group, fingerprints, and so forth. When these are congruous, probability is high that the twins are identical. When these are different, it is practically certain that the twins are not identical but fraternal.

*A translation into English was published in 1931 by Allen & Unwin, of London; I am indebted to them for permission to quote and summarize relevant portions of the book in this chapter.

Identical twins tend to be relatively rare. They occur all over the world at a rate of between 3 and 4 births in a thousand. Furthermore, the occurrence is relatively independent of the age of the mother, and there is no tendency for this type of twinning to run in families. Fraternal twins occur in quite a different manner. The incidence varies considerably from country to country. For instance, fraternal twins are much more common in Europe than in Japan, where two-thirds of the twins are identical. Fraternal twins occur more frequently as mothers get older, rising to a maximum when mothers are between thirty-five and thirty-nine years of age. Furthermore, this type of twinning very markedly runs in families. The proportion of all twins born which are identical and fraternal can be established by examining the proportion of twins of like and unlike sex respectively. Identical twins, as we have seen, must always be of the same sex, whereas only half of all fraternal twins are of like sex. We can, therefore, find the number of identical twins in any particular group by subtracting the number of unlike-sex twins plus an equal number of like-sex twins from the whole. When this method, which was first suggested as early as 1874 by the French mathematician, Bertillon, is applied to twins in Western Europe, we find that about a quarter of all twin pairs are identical.

How can we use the existence of identical twins, who share a completely common heredity, and the existence of fraternal twins, who share heredity only to the extent of fifty per cent (that is to say, no more than ordinary siblings, or brothers and sisters not born at the same time)? To answer this question, let us take characteristics for which differences between one person and another are largely due to genetic factors and where, therefore, the resemblance of the identical twins will be practically complete. We will expect that the resemblance of fraternal twins will be considerably less because, as we said before, they share heredity to a markedly lesser degree. Consequently, there will be a marked difference between identical twins, who should show this trait in pretty much the same degree, and fraternal twins, who should share it to a much smaller extent.

Let us next take characteristics for which the differences between one person and another are, in the main, due to environmental influences and experience. Here the greater genetic resemblance of identical twins is irrelevant and they will be no more and no less alike than will fraternal twins. The really interesting point, of course, arises when we are dealing with characteristics in which differences may be due to both genetic and environmental differences. Here we would expect that identical twins would be more alike than fraternal twins but, nevertheless, would fail to resemble each other in every detail. We would then be able to get some idea of the importance of hereditary factors, by comparing the relative similarity or concordance of the identical twins as compared with the fraternal twins. If concordance or similarity was pretty much the same in both cases, then we would conclude that hereditary causes were relatively unimportant. If the differences were reasonably marked, we might conclude that heredity had some fairly important function. If the differences were very strong indeed, then we would conclude that heredity played a very important part. Thus, by examining identical and fraternal twins respectively, with regard to some standard of conduct, we can arrive at conclusions about the influence of heredity and environment on their behaviour in relation to this particular standard. There are, of course, certain difficulties which arise, and there are certain criticisms which may be made. We will deal with these later. For the moment, let us return to Lange and his investigation of criminal twins.

In his book, Lange gives the following information about his method of procedure.

The material was provided by the records of the Institute for Criminal Biology. Furthermore, at our request, the Bavarian Ministry of Justice ordered that all prisoners in Bavarian prisons who were twins should be reported and examined from the point of view of criminal biology. In addition, we also asked for such prisoners as had twins among their brothers and sisters who might also be of an age to be sentenced. Finally, I looked among the psychopathic patients of the Genealogical Department of the German Institute for Psychiatry for twins who had been imprisoned. I also asked all twins whom I met in the course of my hospital duties for criminal records. All those twins who fulfilled the above mentioned conditions were taken as subjects. First of all, the criminal records of the subjects themselves and of their twins were examined. Then I interviewed those twins who were still in prisons. We then went into the degree of resemblance and the life stories of all the subjects. Police records and sentences were, of course, examined at the same time. These were put at my disposal as well as other ordinary official documents. On various other pretexts, I got some of the criminal twins to come for interview to my consulting room. Others I visited at their homes in different cities.

Thirty-seven pairs of twins were discovered and investigated in this way. These pairs included fifteen identical and twenty-two fraternal couples. In two cases of identical and five of fraternal, neither twin had been in prison. These were pairs discovered among the brothers and sisters of ordinary prisoners and as they had nothing to do with the problem at hand, they may here be disregarded. We are then left with thirty pairs, thirteen identical and seventeen fraternal twins, one of whom, that is to say the subject of the first investigation, had been imprisoned. Among the thirteen identical pairs, the second twin had also been imprisoned in ten cases but had remained clear of the law in three. Among the seventeen fraternal pairs, the second twin had also been imprisoned in two cases, whereas in fifteen cases he had remained clear of the law. *This leads us to the following conclusion: as far as crime is concerned, monozygotic twins on the whole react in a definitely similar manner, dizygotic twins behave quite differently.* Lange concludes that if we attach importance to the twin method of investigation, we must admit that, as far as the causes of crime are concerned, innate tendencies play a preponderant part.

Lange went on to compare the criminality of ordinary brothers and sisters with that of dizygotic twins. As he points out: 'If we found that among dizygotic twins both were punished more often than happened on an average among ordinary brothers and sisters, we should have to allow for the influence of environmental conditions more or less according to the degree of difference between expectations and the facts discovered.' In other words, what he is saying is that ordinary brothers and sisters should be criminal just about as frequently as dizygotic twins, because in both cases the contribution of heredity is pretty much the same. If it were found that dizygotic twins were both criminal in a higher proportion of cases, then that might be due to the fact that being a little more similar, being born at the same time, and so forth, the twins were treated more alike by their environment and, therefore, both had a better chance of being criminal or being free of crime. In that case we would, therefore, have to allow that environment has contributory effects. But Lange's comparison shows that this is not so. He concludes that 'In the case of crime in dizygotics the similar environment plays only a very small part.'

Lange gives a very large number of detailed case histories, to enable the reader to see to what extent the two twins in each case are similar in their criminal behaviour. Let me quote one or two of these as an example of the sort of thing Lange presents. Here are two brothers, Adolf and Auguste. The father was a rather bad-tempered man, who treated them roughly. He was serious, quiet, depressed and a very intelligent and industrious person. The mother was quiet, good, kind and warm-hearted. She adored the twins and always took their part against the father. The children were devoted to her. Neither of the parents nor the five brothers and sisters of Adolf and Auguste had ever been in conflict with the law. They were slightly nervous people but got along in life and were kind to their unfortunate brothers. Adolf was born one hour earlier than his twin and was always a little weaker and more delicate. Auguste was the more intelligent; he got through school easily in spite of his laziness. But Adolf, in those days at least, was the better boy. Auguste was always very quickly attracted to bad characters. Both twins were selfish, excitable, quarrelsome, and they could not get along with one another. If they were left alone for a few minutes they were sure to fight. In spite of the poverty of their home and the strictness of their father, both the twins had happy memories of their childhood. They loved their mother and had much respect for their father.

At the age of fourteen, Auguste was sentenced to five days imprisonment. He had broken into a building site with another boy and stolen iron material. When discovered, he threw away the sack containing the stolen goods, told various lies, but finally confessed. Later on, he was sentenced several times for theft and once for breach of domestic peace. A little later, when wandering about on the open road with a friend, he met a girl of twelve whom he suddenly attacked, on the ground that she had 'laughed cheekily at his prison shoes'. He threw her down, pulled up her skirts, and tore a little necklace from her neck. The friend objected and he let the struggling girl go, but then, with his friend, he went and pawned the necklace for a pot of beer. In court he admitted the theft and also pleaded guilty to a sexual offence against the girl. After discharge from prison he was arrested for begging on the high road. Other sentences followed. He had stolen a bicycle and in spite of pleading innocence, the court considered him guilty. There followed several cases of breaking and entering, burglary, and gang crimes. During the revolution, he belonged to the Red Army, though he did not commit any deeds of violence. Afterwards, however, he again stole a bicycle and was sent to prison for four years. After his release he was apprehended for receiving stolen goods. When he came out of prison he resumed his old games, becoming involved in another series of small burglaries. This man, now thirty-eight years of age, had, since his fourteenth year, spent seventeen years and ten months behind prison bars, sixteen years since the age of twenty. In the last eighteen years he had not had two whole years of freedom.

Adolf managed to keep out of prison for a few years longer than his brother, apart from a detention at the age of fourteen for stealing wood. He finished an apprenticeship with a master painter, although he once ran away from him. At sixteen, however, he was involved in two criminal prosecutions. He and a friend had been stealing items of little value whenever they got the chance. Then followed a whole series of sentences for begging. Finally, there was sentence of one year's imprisonment for having acted as 'look-out' during a big warehouse robbery. Adolf then continued with a career of vagrancy, but not before he had again been imprisoned for three months for stealing wood. For a while he worked steadily in Switzerland but was then called for military service. Apart from being confined to barracks for eighteen months, he was no serious trouble there, although very soon afterwards he was involved in a series of suspicious situations. It was alleged that he had stolen a large number of bicycles, as well as money, paint, and moulds from his workshop. At the same time, Adolf had to pay up under a paternity order made against him. After the war, he got several heavy sentences in a short period, as well as having an affair with his brother's mistress, while his twin was in prison. He also took part in a robbery with violence. With another hopeless criminal, he had attacked a lonely woman and cruelly ill-treated her, until she revealed where her money was hidden.

Lange sums up their careers by saying:

Both brothers are professional thieves and burglars, whose crimes, in so far as we know them, are of a pretty similar character. We must assume, in view of Adolf's various confessions in prisons, that several of them have probably not come to light. Both of them began stealing and housebreaking at a very early age. Auguste's offence against decency in his seventeenth year may have been due to puberty, as he informed me that his sexual life began at about this time. Later he certainly did not repeat similar brutalities. Both Adolf and Auguste proved by their elaborate burglaries – Adolf breaking into a private house, Auguste into a theatre – that they were real professionals at the game. When undergoing sentence, both are exceptionally difficult owing to their excitability and their emotional behaviour. They are both full of grievances, quarrelsome, provocative, and paranoid. Both start rows: in 1914 Auguste was known to tremble with rage, Adolf still does today. Both have had attacks of hysteria, Auguste probably as a schoolboy, Adolf later on. Both are always complaining of physical ailments which examination fails to reveal. They are never satisfied with their medical treatment. They complain of being incompetently or unfairly treated, get cheeky and disobedient, so that occasionally both have to be reported by the doctor for punishment. They both suffer under detention and get more excitable. They constantly express themselves on the same subject in the coarsest manner, and throw about open and veiled accusations, exaggerations and suspicions.

Next let us have a look at two sisters, Antonie and Amalie. These two sisters are now thirty-one years old and have always been extremely alike. They are now stout jolly women, but not of an altogether happy disposition. When they have bad luck they are at once deeply affected; they become depressed, contemplate, or at any rate threaten, suicide. The father was a very decent man, though strict with them; their mother was kind. There are ten other living children, all clearly respectable, and the twins got along well with them. Both were quite good at school, although they were rather careless. They ran away from home on several occasions, and when they were sixteen years old, it became necessary to apply for them to be put away under compulsory official supervision. Towards the end of 1912 they ran away from home and at first went into service. However, they soon left, only to wander about without employment, living immoral lives. When they returned home at the beginning of April, they had grown quite degenerate. They both ran away again on April 27th, and on April 29th their father fetched them home. On the very same day they again slipped through their parents' fingers. Soon after that Amalie was admitted to a hospital for treatment of a venereal disease. Both twins had frequent promiscuous sexual intercourse and were so far corrupted that their parents were unable to reform them or protect them. After discharge from the reformatory, they separated, but both went on living immorally. Antonie became pregnant and married a man other than her seducer in order not to have an illegitimate child. Some of her later children were her husband's, but she also named various men as the fathers of the first three or four children. Among these fathers was a brother of her brother-in-law. Her marriage was extremely unhappy and Antonie consoled herself with other men, often leaving her husband. Amalie married much later but led much the same sort of life as her sister. She had one lover after another. In addition, both sisters had mysterious conflicts with the law regarding thefts and other types of crime. Antonie was also served with a warrant and sentenced to two months' imprisonment for procuring. Lange sums up the history of these two girls by saying:

It is unnecessary to stress the extreme resemblance of the social behaviour of these twin sisters. A constant sexual urge and lack of self-control decided their destinies, which only outwardly are a little different from one another. Whatever other guilty acts they may commit will be closely allied with their sexual life.

One more illustration will suffice; the brothers Maat. They come from an excellent family; both are extremely nervous and suffer from a variety of neurotic symptoms. They were very difficult to bring up; all sorts of treatments were tried, for longer or shorter periods, but neither of them seems to have benefited very much. They are cold, egocentric beings without any human affections, without sympathy, respect, or affection for their parents or anyone else. Both are extremely anxious for their own safety and callous to anyone else. Both were sexual inverts. They had relations with people of their own sex from puberty onwards and indeed, both had been kept, for as long as he could afford it, by a homosexual friend. Lange points out that,

Mutual influence had certainly no effect on inversion. They spoke with revolting tactlessness and lack of ethical sensibility, quite frankly and unashamedly, of the most dreadful incidents. But all questions with regard to common sexual experiences, mutual masturbation, common seductions, etc., were answered with emphatic negatives. It was only after each brother had independently recognized his tendency that they discovered their similarity in this respect and used their common ability to support themselves by their perversity. Other members of the family do not show the same tendency. It was not possible to ascertain common experiences at home which could have turned the Maats in the direction of inversion.

The reader may wonder what the professional geneticist would make of the material provided in Lange's book. J. B. S. Haldane, a world-famous geneticist and at that time a member of the Communist Party of Great Britain, wrote a foreword to the book. His opinion is important, not only because of his professional competence, but because, as a Communist, he might be expected to be prejudiced against any kind of hereditary hypothesis. He says: 'An analysis of the thirteen cases shows not the faintest evidence of freedom of the will in the ordinary sense of the word. A man of a certain constitution, put in a certain environment, will be a criminal. Taking the record of any criminal, we could predict the behaviour of a monozygotic twin placed in the same environment. Crime is destiny'.

The reader may wonder why not all identical twin pairs are, in fact, concordant. If indeed crime is destiny, then why are there individual exceptions? There are several answers to this. When we examine the two undeniable cases of monozygotic pairs where only one was a criminal, we find that in each case the criminal brother had suffered a severe head injury. In another discordant pair, one but not the other of the twins suffered from goitre, a disease which undoubtedly alters the character. We shall see later that brain damage has an effect on the normal person which essentially displaces that person's character in the direction of greater extraversion. Goitre and the associated hormonal upsets in the nervous system may work in a similar direction. We see then that in discordant cases there has been a definite interference with the intact nervous system of one twin, possibly leading to crime. These exceptions, then, may be only apparent and not real. As Lange says:

In at least two out of three cases, the criminal twins, and they alone, have suffered serious brain lesions; it is possible to conclude the crimes in question were actually among the consequences of the lesion. In the case of one, a murderer, we were almost certainly dealing with a traumatic epileptic, who committed his dreadful deed when in a pathological condition. The other, a miserable invert, was not only mentally different from his twin, but revealed the physical signs of his abnormal sexuality. The cause of these differences between the twins was obviously a serious birth injury, the marks of which both still bear to this very day.

How about the concordant dizygotic pairs? How can we account for the fact that although these were not identical with respect to heredity, they did commit similar crimes? In the case of one pair, Lange points out that he could not help suspecting a common hereditary venereal infection. 'If this was a fact, it might be that we were not dealing in this case so much with innate tendencies to crime as with the results of considerable brain lesions, which, as we know, often predispose to antisocial behaviour.' Here then, we have some possible reasons suggesting why identical twins may not always act in an identical manner and why fraternal twins may both succumb to crime. There are, of course, one or two other causes for this which may be worthy of comment. In the first place, investigators are human and may make errors. It is not always possible to discover whether a given person has or has not committed a crime. Thus, we may have one twin who is known to be a criminal, but we may not, in our investigation of the other twin, discover that he also has committed a crime. The crime may have been committed, say, in a different country, the records of which are not available to us. Or the crime may have been committed in the same country but the records may have been destroyed during the war, during a revolution, during a fire, or in some other way. This may result in the identical twin pair being recorded as discordant, when in fact no discordance exists. Another difficulty that arises is, of course, that crimes may be committed but are not always brought home to the person responsible for them. One twin might commit a crime, be caught, and be sentenced to prison; his identical twin may commit the same crime and get away with it. If that were so, then these two twins would be regarded as discordant, when in fact they should be recorded as being quite alike. When we realize the seriousness of these difficulties, it is surprising that Lange found concordance rather than discordance in so many cases. In other words, we should not expect to find a hundred per cent concordance even under the most favourable conditions.

Lange's revolutionary study aroused a great deal of interest, of course, and a number of people repeated his work in an attempt to verify his conclusions. Some found results even more in favour of hereditary bases for criminality than Lange had done. Legras, for instance, found a hundred per cent concordance in his identical twins, and no concordance at all in his fraternal twins. Most other students, however, such as Kranz, Stumpfl, Rosanoff, and Borgstroem, have found results which were similar to Lange's but perhaps not quite as impressive. By now, something like 225 pairs of twins have been studied, in each of which one was a criminal. Of these, about equal numbers were monozygotic and same-sex dizygotic twins. The overall finding is that just about twice as many monozygotic as dizygotic twins are concordant. In other words, when one twin is criminal, then among identical twins the other one has twice the chance of also being a criminal that he would have if the twins were fraternal. These results, then, strongly support Lange, although they perhaps do not enable us to say quite as firmly as he did that crime is indeed destiny.[20]

So far we have been dealing with adult criminals. Similar figures are also available for juvenile delinquents and for children with behaviour disorders. Sixty-seven pairs of juvenile delinquent twins have been studied, and here the concordance is eighty-five per cent for identical twins and seventy-five per cent for fraternal twins. In 107 pairs of twins, where one was found to suffer from one of the childhood behaviour disorders, there was an eighty-seven per cent concordance for identical twins and only forty-three per cent concordance for fraternal twins. In other words, for children, the figures are very similar to those for adults; for juvenile delinquents the evidence in favour of determination by heredity is less impressive. It should be remembered, however, that the figures for juvenile delinquents were all collected by one person, so we would want to have a further check on this before arriving at any conclusion.

There are some figures, too, on homosexuality and on alcoholism. These, of course, are not crimes in the ordinary sense, but they are often associated with criminality, and in some countries, of course, homosexuality is in fact punished by the law. Here the figures are as follows. For homosexuality we find that in sixty-three pairs of twins there is a hundred per cent concordance for monozygotic twins and only twelve per cent concordance for dizygotic twins. For alcoholism there are eighty-two pairs, and concordance is found in sixty-five per cent of monozygotic and in thirty per cent of dizygotic twins. Again, the evidence is very strong that homosexuality in particular, and alcoholism to a lesser extent, has a very marked hereditary component. These figures are shown in Table 1.

What can we conclude from these data? In the first place, of course, they do demonstrate, beyond any question, that heredity

TABLE I

Concordance of identical and fraternal twins respectively for various
types of criminal, antisocial, and asocial behaviour

	Number of twin pairs	Identical	Fraternal	Proportion concordant	
				Identical	Fraternal
Adult crime	225	107	118	71	34
Juvenile delinquency	67	42	25	85	75
Childhood behaviour disorder	107	47	60	87	43
Homosexuality	63	37	26	100	12
Alcoholism	82	26	56	65	30

plays an important, and possibly a vital part, in predisposing a given individual to crime. As we have seen, the probability that a criminal's twin will also be a criminal is about twice as high if they are identical twins as it is if they are fraternal twins. Looking at the concordance figures, it should be kept in mind that fraternal twins are not unrelated; in other words, we would expect to find as much concordance among them as among pairs of brothers and sisters born singly. It is only in comparison with identical twins that we expect relatively less concordance among fraternal twins. We must next consider some of the reasons why the empirical figures are not in perfect agreement with those predicted. We must also consider whether these discrepancies would lead to an over- or under-evaluation of the contribution made by heredity.

We have already considered some possible reasons why the figures for identical twins are more nearly as predicted. We considered the case of brain damage, which may affect one twin, making him criminal, but not affecting his co-twin; we also considered the possibilities of common disease processes which might affect two fraternal twins. We looked at the difficulties involved in tracing twins, and the possibility that crimes committed by co-twins may not have been detected. All these causes, of course, work against the hypothesis we are considering and, insofar as they have any validity at all, it must be considered that these empirical concordance figures represent under-estimations rather than over-estimations of the role of heredity.

Since the evidence is so conclusive and reproduced by so many different investigators in different countries, and since it agrees so much with what might be called the common wisdom of the ages, one might expect that common acceptance had been accorded to it, and that any textbook of criminality would give pride of place to these findings. This is not so, however, and it is interesting to consider for a moment why these findings have been largely disregarded. One reason for this may lie in the climate of opinion which prevails, particularly in the United States and in the Soviet Union. In both these countries there is a strong belief in what one might call the technological or manipulative outlook on life. In both countries, there is a widespread belief that almost anything is possible to the person with technical knowledge who is determined to effect certain changes. This is obvious, as far as the external environment is concerned, and there is a great deal of evidence that much can be done. But when we come to the manipulation of people, it must be said that this manipulative outlook is very much less promising. As far as our knowledge goes, at least, we may say that our success in manipulating people lags far behind our success in manipulating material circumstances. It is doubtful whether our educational systems are any more successful than those which prevailed two thousand years ago. As far as our treatment of neurotics is concerned it is doubtful whether our modern methods are in any way better than those which have been current throughout the centuries. As far as our treatment of criminals goes, too, it is very doubtful whether there have been any advances during recent centuries which would make it likely that the number of crimes committed would be less or the proportion of recidivism smaller than it was, say, in 1500 A.D., or 500 A.D., or even 1000 B.C. Nevertheless, the belief is strong that we can do almost anything, provided we find the right manipulative method, and anything that sets bounds to this, as heredity is conceived to do, is, therefore, anathema.

This general attitude is often supported by reference to political notions. It is said that all men are born equal and it is deduced from this that indeed all men have the same innate ability, the same good or poor degree of personality, the same propensity to crime, and so on. This, of course, is a misinterpretation of the old saying. What it means is simply that all men are equal before the law, and that they should be regarded as having equal value from the spiritual point of view. It does not say anything whatsoever about their strength, their health, or other features in which they may differ from each other, and in which, as we know perfectly well, they do in fact differ. However, the fact that this is a misunderstanding has in no way lessened the impact of the saying on the great majority of people who are strongly convinced that any innate differences in ability or in propensity to crime would set some kind of limit to the working of modern democracy.

It is curious that much the same kind of attitude should be common in the Soviet Union. Here, of course, the emphasis is somewhat different. It is believed that society can make a new man, a Soviet man, who will be, in all respects, vastly superior to the bourgeois man who is bred in the capitalist world, and again there is a resentment against any forces which may seem to set bounds to this human perfectibility and to the power of the state to create man in its own image. As is well known, this general belief has, in the Soviet Union, led to interference by the state in the affairs of academic research workers, their freedom to carry out research, to publish and to freely communicate their results, and to criticize the the edicts of the state. We have the sad picture of a genetics which is governed, not by the facts of research, but rather by the presuppositions of a political élite.

In the West there has also been a tendency for religious views to interfere with the acceptance of these facts. It is often held that responsibility and the notion of free will fly out the window once determination by hereditary forces is admitted of such things as personal conduct, crime, and so forth. This argument, as well as the preceding ones, is, of course, a rather weak one. It argues essentially that we would like things to be a certain way and that, therefore, things *must* be that way. This is not a scientific way of looking at things. It has often been found that human desires go counter to the facts of nature. In such cases there has been a tremendous battle before the facts won and human beings rearranged their ideas to fit in with the facts. One obvious example, of course, is the old battle about the position of the earth. Was it, in fact, the centre of the universe, with the sun and the stars and the planets revolving around it, or was it rather a minor planet circling around the sun? In the end, of course, the Copernican view won and we know now that the earth is indeed only a minor planet and not the centre of the universe. A similar battle was fought by Darwin over the facts of evolution; we realize now that man was not created separately but has developed from earlier forms of animal life. Similarly, it seems obvious that the facts of the case must win in relation to the determination of human conduct by hereditary forces.

One possible reason why people tend to oppose the view which accords a high place to the forces of heredity is that the belief in heredity seems to generate what is sometimes called 'therapeutic nihilism'. In other words, it is believed that because heredity produces certain effects it is therefore impossible for us to do anything about them; heredity sets definite limits to our powers of manipulation. This is not always true; quite the opposite is sometimes the case. It may be that through our investigations of heredity we have learned much which enables us to control the phenomena with which we are dealing. One example may serve to make this point.

There is a well-known disease called phenylketonuria, which affects about one child in forty thousand in England. This disorder causes mental defects, and it has been found that about one in every hundred patients in hospitals for severely mentally handicapped children suffer from phenylketonuria. This disorder is known to be inherited and it is, in fact, due to a single recessive gene. It was first recognized by a Norwegian doctor, Foelling, in 1934. The great majority of children suffering from it have a level of mental performance which is usually found in children half their age. These children can be distinguished from other mentally handicapped or from normal children by testing their urine, which yields a green-coloured reaction with a solution of ferric chloride, due to the presence of derivatives of phenylalanine. Here we have a perfect example of a disorder produced entirely by hereditary causes, where the cause is simple and well understood, and where the presence of the disorder can be determined with accuracy.

Is there reason to believe that 'therapeutic nihilism' is called for? Definitely not. However, we must go on to demonstrate in what way the gene actually produces the mental defect. It has been shown that children affected by phenylketonuria are unable to convert phenylalanine into tyrosine; they can only break it down to a limited extent. It is not clear why this should produce mental deficiency but it seems probable that some of the incomplete breakdown products of phenylalanine are poisonous to the nervous system. Phenylalanine, fortunately, is not an essential part of the diet, provided that tyrosine is present in the diet. It is possible to maintain these children on a diet which is almost free of phenylalanine, thus eliminating the danger of poisoning to the nervous system. It has been found that when this method of treatment is begun in the first few months of life, there is a very good chance that the child may grow up without the mental handicap he would otherwise have encountered. In other words, by understanding the precise way in which heredity works, and by understanding precisely what it does to the organism, we can arrange a rational method of therapy which will make use of the forces of nature, rather than try to counteract them. As we shall point out later in this book, it is precisely by this kind of approach that we can hope to overcome some of the dangers and difficulties which are ever-present in our criminal population. [21]

We have, so far, dealt with objections to the notion that criminality, or the predisposition to criminality, is inherited. These were not entirely rational and could not in fact be considered reasonable arguments against the evidence. But there is one very powerful argument which must be mentioned. This argument relates to the fact that it is very difficult to demonstrate any feasible mechanism for the inheritance of criminality. What is meant is essentially this. We can conceive of nervous structures of various types as being inherited through the ordinary process of Mendelian genetics; even though our understanding of these processes is incomplete. But how can we imagine that some kind of psychological or social or even religious propensity such as criminality can be inherited? What kind of structure can be imagined to underlie such a type of conduct? After all, criminality is a social concept, not a biological one. Indeed, what is criminal in one country may not be criminal in another; homosexuality is a crime in some American states but not in Germany. Similarly, what is a crime at one time may not be at another. It is a crime to kill people but only in peace time; during war time, it becomes a citizen's duty to kill others. We can understand how these differences come about and we can adjust our conduct accordingly. But what is so difficult is the postulation of some kind of gene, chromosome, or other structure, which could be the physiological or neurological basis for differences between the criminal and the non-criminal kind of person. This difficulty has prevented many people, who might otherwise have accepted the evidence, from doing so. It is the purpose of this book to put forward a theory which may overcome this difficulty.

Before turning to this task, however, we must consider one other objection which has been quite widespread, although it has, in fact, very little basis. Most people are familiar with at least some of the ideas of Mendel, who is often called the originator of modern genetics. He experimented largely with discrete characters in peas, such as tall versus short, wrinkled versus smooth, and so on. In other words, he was primarily concerned with *discrete* differences by which each individual plant or animal, could be regarded as having either one characteristic or the other. Psychological data are rarely discrete. We cannot regard people as being either intelligent or dull. When we measure their intelligence quotients, we find that they tend to order themselves in a continuous distribution, usually bell-shaped, the great majority of people having I.Q.s in the neighbourhood of 100, with fewer and fewer at each value, moving outward in either direction; that is to say, only a very few people have I.Q.s above 150 or below 50. As we approach the means the frequency becomes greater, so that about 50 per cent have I.Q.s between 90 and 110. At first sight it seemed impossible to reconcile the laws of Mendelian genetics with these continuous distributions. Indeed, dispute arose between the Mendelians and what are sometimes called the biometric geneticists, those who were interested in the inheritance of characters which showed a continuous distribution. The biometricians originally regarded continuous variation in the character which was observed as implying continuous genetic variation, whereas the Mendelians seem to have considered discontinuous genetic variation as incompatible with anything but the most obviously discontinuous somatic variation. Both Mendelians and biometricians agreed that, whichever hypothesis was nearer to the truth, the hereditary determination of continuous or graded traits was quite incompatible with the segregation of discontinuous units postulated by the Mendelian theory. This view is still held by many psychological writers who have not kept up with recent advances in genetics. The one point on which the two disputants happened to agree has been shown repeatedly in recent years to be invalid. There is no reason to believe that there is any incompatibility between psychological traits which are continuously distributed and Mendelian genetics. It would take us too far afield to go into the details of the reasons for this, or to describe in detail the methods now used for analysing continuous data. Suffice it to say that among professional geneticists there is no longer any doubt on this point.[22]

Criminality is obviously a continuous trait of the same kind as intelligence, or height, or weight. We may artificially say that every person either is or is not a criminal, but this would be so grossly oversimplified as to be untrue. Criminals vary among themselves, from those who fall once and never again, to those who spend most of their lives in prison. Clearly the latter have far more 'criminality' in their make-up than the former. Similarly, people who are not convicted of crimes may also differ widely in respect to moral character. Some may in fact have committed crimes for which they were never caught or, if they were caught, perhaps the court took a rather lenient view. Others have never given way to temptation at all. From a rational point of view, therefore, we cannot regard criminals as being completely distinct from the rest of the population. They simply represent the extreme end of a continuous distribution, very much as a mental defective represents the extreme end of a continuous distribution of intelligence, ranging upward through the average to the very high I.Q. of the student or even the genius.[23]

Nothing that has been said so far should lead the reader to imagine that environment plays no part at all in the causation of crime. None of the authors so far mentioned, from Lange onward, would subscribe to such a view. The very notion of criminality or crime would be meaningless without a context of learning or social experience and, quite generally, of human interaction. What the figures have demonstrated is that heredity is a very strong predisposing factor as far as committing crimes is concerned. But the actual way in which the crime is carried out, and whether or not the culprit is found and punished – these are obviously subject to the changing vicissitudes of everyday life. It would be meaningless to talk about the criminality or otherwise of a Robinson Crusoe, brought up and always confined by himself on a desert island. It is only in relation to society that the notion of criminality and of predisposition to crime has any meaning. While recognizing therefore, the tremendous power of heredity, we would by no means wish to suggest that environmental influences cannot also be very powerful and important indeed.

What will be suggested rather is that without an understanding of the way in which the innate criminality, the predisposition of the person to commit a crime, is translated into reality, it will be very difficult, if not impossible, to carry out investigations into the environmental influences which determine criminality or lack of criminality in a given person. It will be argued that purely statistical studies, such as those which have customarily been carried out by sociologists and others, in an attempt to correlate such items as absence of the father, absence of the mother, poor conditions of upbringing, lack of home life, and so forth, with criminality, while interesting, lack any great causal importance because it is difficult to see just precisely how these various factors exert their influence. It is hoped that, by relating these factors to a general theory which also accounts for the way in which the hereditary causes work, we shall be able to produce a more satisfactory picture of the whole complex of causes which produce criminal behaviour in our modern world.

4 The Biological Roots of Personality

'I didn't know that Cheshire cats always grinned; in fact, I didn't know that cats *could* grin.'

'They all can,' said the Duchess; 'and most of 'em do.'

'I don't know of any that do,' Alice said very politely, feeling very pleased to have got into a conversation.

'You don't know very much,' said the Duchess; 'and that's a fact.'

ALICE'S ADVENTURES IN WONDERLAND

In every science we have descriptive and causal aspects; in physics, for instance, we have *kinematics* and *dynamics*. First, we have the actual description of the paths of the planets around the sun; then, following that, we have the dynamics of Galileo and Newton to paint a causal picture of just why these planets behave as they do. In other words, description of what happens is followed by attempts to force these descriptions into a connected network of causal laws. Much the same, of course, is true in psychology. We have, in the second chapter, given a descriptive framework of personality, and we have shown some evidence that psychopaths and psychopathic criminals belong in one particular corner of this framework namely that part of it which combines high extraversion with high emotionality.

But from the scientific point of view, of course, this is not enough; it does not enable us to make predictions, and it does not enable us to understand why the behaviour of the criminal is as it is. Neither is it sufficient to say, as we did in Chapter 3, that heredity plays a very large part in his behaviour. This is not sufficient because it does not enable us to test or to make up any specific hypotheses about the *reasons* for the behaviour which we observe. Simply to ascribe it to hereditary causes may be true as far as it goes, but it clearly is not sufficient. We must go beyond that and try to anchor our dimensions of personality in a framework of causal relations. The present chapter is concerned with the description of such a framework. While it is not fully developed, it will give the reader some idea of modern thinking about these problems.

Consider, first of all, the problems raised by the emotionality, stability, neuroticism dimension, i.e. that dimension which, according to Wundt, deals with the strength or weakness of emotional reactions. The roots of this dimension in the biological nature of the organism are fairly clear. There is, in all mammals, a particular and relatively separate part of the nervous system, the so-called *autonomic nervous system*, which is set apart almost specifically for the creation and transmission of emotional impulses (as well as the maintenance of bodily functioning generally). This system, which evolved very early in man's history, is not, by and large, under voluntary control; hence the name 'autonomic'. It deals with a great variety of activities of the organism, of many of which, in the ordinary course of events, we are not aware. It regulates our heart beat, for instance; it regulates our breathing when we are asleep, as well as when we are awake; it changes the size of the pupil in adaptation to light; it governs our digestive processes, as well as the secretion of saliva into our mouths; it regulates the size of the arteries and veins through which our blood courses. It has many effects of which we are introspectively quite ignorant; thus, for instance, our skin presents a certain resistance to the passage of an electric current, and when we are emotionally aroused, this resistance suddenly drops, probably due to the fact that we tend to perspire a certain slight amount and perspiration is a good electrolytic substance. The autonomic system, then, is concerned with a large variety of bodily processes, of many of which we are not aware.

The autonomic system essentially consists of two antagonistic parts, the sympathetic and the parasympathetic systems. Essentially the sympathetic system is one devoted to fight or flight reactions; in other words, it is an emergency system, the main purpose of which is to gear the organism to the greatest possible efficiency in flight or flight. It stops the digestion, to make more blood available for use in other parts of the body; it increases the rate of respiration to make more oxygen available; it dilates the pupil of the eye to enable the organism to see better; it causes sweating of the hands to enable a person to grasp his opponent more effectively; it causes the heart to beat faster, to make the blood rush through the body more quickly. These are only some of the reactions of the sympathetic system, but it will be obvious that they are the kinds of reaction of which we tend to be dimly aware when we are very angry or very much afraid. Anyone who has ever experienced one of these strong emotions will remember the rapid intake of breath, the strong beating of the heart, the feeling of heat in the skin as the blood rushes through the veins and arteries, and other associated sensations.

The parasympathetic, on the other hand, is a kind of vegetative or maintenance system. It tends to counter-balance the action of the sympathetic system. It slows down the heart, it slows down the rate of breathing, it causes digestion to proceed unhampered; it is, in all essentials, a quiescent, energy-conserving kind of system which enables the organism to pursue its functions uninterrupted. It would appear, from what has been said, that the person who is subject to strong emotions, even under conditions which would not call forth such strong emotions in the normal person, has been endowed, probably by heredity, with an autonomic system, the sympathetic branch of which is particularly strongly reactive to external stimuli. There is much evidence in the literature to suggest that this is indeed so. We will deal later on with the problem of heredity and the degree to which personality dimensions are indeed based on hereditary factors. Let us note here simply that when studies are made of identical and fraternal twins, involving the recording of sympathetic reaction to various forms of stress, whether physical, such as thrusting one's hand into a bucket of ice water, or mental, such as performing certain tasks under stress, then identical twins are found to be much more alike in the strength of their reactions than are fraternal twins.[24]

However, simply equating emotionality and the autonomic system poses certain problems which must be faced. One major problem concerns what is sometimes called 'response specificity'. It will be recalled, from our discussion in the first chapter, that throughout psychology and the description of personality and conduct, there is a running argument between those who believe that reactions tend to be *specific* and those who believe that they tend to be *general*. What we have said so far may give the impression that the sympathetic system acts as a whole: that, therefore, generality prevails. This, however, is by no means true. There is a considerable degree of specificity in the reaction of the autonomic nervous system. Thus some people react to stress specifically by speeding up the heart beat rate. Others react more markedly by speeding up respiration. Others again may react more by tensing the muscles, a reaction which is usually an accompaniment of sympathetic action. A person who reacts in one of these ways does not necessarily react in the others as well; that is to say, a person who reacts by tensing his muscles may not show any change in his heart-beat or in his breathing. Conversely, a person who reacts specifically by changes in his heart-rate may not react by tensing his muscles. Thus the nervous or emotional reaction of a person may be fairly specific.

Indeed, specificity may go even further than that. We have spoken of the tensing of the musculature as a typical autonomic reaction. However, here again, specificity often prevails. Thus, under stress, a person may react by tensing his frontalis muscle, that is, the muscle in the forehead, but not the muscles in his arms or legs. Another may react by tensing the muscles in his back, but not those in other parts of his body. Specificity, therefore, seems to be fairly widespread, though not complete; there is undoubtedly a tendency for different types of reactions to be inter-correlated. This means that a person who tends to react vehemently to stress with one of these many systems tends to react, on the whole, with the other systems as well. However, these correlations are not very high; indeed, they tend to be quite low and, without taking specificity into account, we might get an entirely distorted picture of a person's reactivity.

This fact of specificity is very useful to us because it gives us an explanation of the reasons why different neurotics seem to manifest quite different reactions to the stresses which produce a neurosis. For instance, we find that the person who, in the experimental situation, tenses his frontalis muscle, is the person who, when confronted in his everyday life with stress, develops neurotic headaches. Similarly, the person who, in the laboratory, reacts with tensing of the back muscles, tends to be the person who, in everyday life, suffers from backaches whenever he is faced with stress and unpleasantness. The person who, in the laboratory, tenses his arm muscles, tends to be aggressive when confronted with stress in everyday life; the person who, in the laboratory, shows acceleration of the heartbeat, will tend to complain of symptoms connected with the heart, whereas the person who, in the laboratory, shows reactions of the breathing apparatus, will complain about those when confronted with trouble in his private life. Many of these everyday reactions, when presented to a doctor, turn out to be psychosomatic disorders, which seem so mysterious when first encountered, but which become quite intelligible when reduced to their biological reality.

No more will be said about the basis of emotionality or stability as a personality variable; what we have said must suffice to give the reader a general idea of the kind of biological reality underlying behaviour. We shall be more concerned with the extraversion/introversion dimension because, as has been mentioned before, it is much more closely related to social, as opposed to anti-social behaviour. Unfortunately, the story is more complicated and will require a considerably longer discussion. It is also, however, more interesting, and there is available a great deal of experimental evidence, some of which will now be cited.

Before we discuss extraversion and introversion in detail, let us have a look at two concepts which play a very large part in modern psychology. They were originally introduced by the great Russian physiologist, I. P. Pavlov, the originator of the concept of conditioning, and they have assumed a very important role indeed in our speculations. These are the concepts of excitation and inhibition. The concept of excitation, from some points of view, is probably the easier one to understand; it simply means that some incoming stimulus has succeeded in firing the neurons which link the sensory surfaces to the cortex, and that this now stimulated neuron passes on its excitation to other neurons through a system of links, or synapses as they are known, which connect the different neurons throughout the body. Without such excitation and conduction, no learning, in fact no behaviour, could take place. It is, therefore, absolutely fundamental for all our activities. It might be thought, at first blush, that we can account for individual differences in such activities as learning or performance on a given task by hypothesising that, for certain individuals, there was less excitation than for others, and that consequently some were better than others at these particular tasks. This, however, is not true. It has been found essential to postulate also a concept of inhibition, the function of which is to counteract excitation.

Why did Pavlov find it necessary to postulate inhibition? Consider, further, some of the experiments he did with his dogs, which had been conditioned, as we described in an earlier chapter, to react with salivation to the sound of a bell. Suppose that a dog had been so conditioned, and suppose that we now wanted to remove this conditioned reflex; how would we set about it? Pavlov showed that a conditioned reflex can be extinguished by simply presenting the conditioned stimulus – that is, the bell in this case – without ever pairing it again with the unconditioned stimulus, the plate of meat. When this is done a sufficient number of times the salivation rate goes down until finally the dog ceases to salivate altogether to the bell. Can we account for this by saying that the dog simply forgets, or that he loses the excitatory potential which has been built up in him through the process of conditioning? The answer seems to be 'No'. Suppose we bring him back the next day after his conditioned salivary reflex has been extinguished, put him in the stand again, and present him once more with the unconditioned stimulus. The day before, he had not responded to this at all; the response had been completely extinguished. Now, however, he does respond, almost as well as ever. We can extinguish the response again and we find that this time it takes a much shorter time; but even after the response has again been extinguished, when we bring the dog back the next day, the response will be there again, rather less marked than before but still relatively strong. It takes quite a number of repetitions, on separate days, before no response whatsoever is shown on the next occasion. Pavlov accounted for this recovery of the reflex by saying that during the building-up and during the evocation of a conditioned reflex a certain amount of inhibition is built up, and that this dissipates during rest. Thus the inhibition which has been built up during the extinction procedure adds its bit to keep salivation down. However, during the night this inhibition dissipates, and on the next day salivation occurs again.

There is another way in which we can demonstrate the same point. Suppose we take human subjects and condition them to respond with the closure of the eyelid to an auditory stimulus which is transmitted through earphones. This sound is the conditioned stimulus; the unconditioned stimulus is a puff of air delivered to the cornea of the eye. Suppose now that we pair the sound and the puff of air a number of times. We soon find that conditioning occurs and that the organism blinks to the sound alone, without needing the puff of air. Figure 7 shows the results of such an experiment in eye-

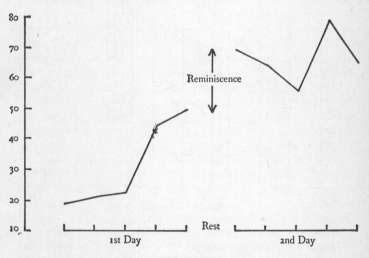

FIGURE 7

The diagram shows the increase in number of conditioned responses which occurs after rest, through the dissipation of cortical fatigue or inhibition during rest. This phenomenon is called 'reminiscence'. Each point represents a mean of five trials on the eyeblink conditioning apparatus. Drawn by the author from data given by D. A. Grant and E. B. Norris, *Journal of Experimental Psychology*, 1947, *37*, 429.

blink conditioning. During the first day, a certain level of reactivity is produced in our experimental population. Now, according to Pavlov's theory, the evocation of the conditioned stimulus and the whole process of building up the association produces a certain amount of inhibition, which keeps down the rate of reaction. This inhibition should dissipate during the night, so that when we return to our subjects on the morning of the next day and start conditioning them again, they should start, not at the level at which they left off the day before, but at a somewhat higher level. Now, as Figure 7 shows, this is indeed the case. This improvement during rest has been given the technical name, 'reminiscence'. The existence of this phenomenon, which has been reported under a great variety of circumstances and with many diverse tasks, is probably the best argument in favour of such a theory of inhibition as that mentioned here.

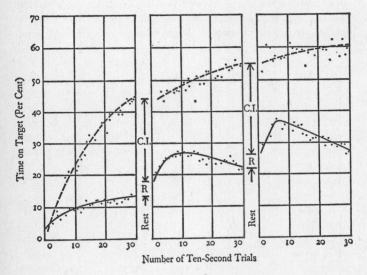

FIGURE 8

Pursuit-rotor performance under conditions of spaced practice (top curve) and massed practice (bottom curve). Each point represents the average time-on-target during a ten-second period. The 'spaced-practice' group was allowed a thirty-second rest between ten-second trials; the 'massed-practice' group was not. Both groups were given two ten-minute rest periods. The improvement in performance shown by the 'massed-practice' group immediately following the ten-minute breaks is called reminiscence (R). Note that no reminiscence is found in the 'spaced-practice' group. Reproduced by permission from *Scientific American*.

Figure 8 shows another example of reminiscence, as well as a further deduction from this general hypothesis. Suppose that we take a rather different task from the eye-blink conditioning one which we discussed a moment ago; in this task, the so-called pursuit rotor, we are dealing with a bakelite disc rather like the turntable of a gramophone, into which is inserted a small metal disc about half an inch across. The bakelite disc, with the small metal disc set in its surface, rotates at a speed of about sixty revolutions per minute, and the subject, holding a metal stylus in his hand, is required to try to keep the stylus in contact with the rotating metal disc. This is a rather difficult task and most people are able to keep the stylus in contact with the disc for only about five per cent of the time when they have had no experience with this kind of task. Time on target during each successive ten-second period, expressed in per cent, is recorded. For purposes of this experiment, we can vary work and rest periods in two different ways. In one arrangement, called 'massed practice', the ten-second periods are consecutive and there is no rest between them at all. The subject continues working on the pursuit rotor for a period of five minutes. He is then given a ten-minute rest, followed by a second five-minute work period, and then another ten-minute rest. After that, there is a final, five-minute work period. Another group of subjects perform under conditions sometimes referred to as 'spaced practice'; these subjects work for ten seconds and then have a thirty-second rest, work again for ten seconds and have a thirty-second rest, and so on. They also are given, at the appropriate moment, a ten-minute rest pause, then go on working, have another ten-minute rest pause, and go on working again, until they have worked for as long a period of time as the other group.

According to the theory of inhibition, we would expect the group given spaced practice to do very much better than the group given massed practice, for this reason. Inhibition is expected to build up in both groups, but it should be dissipated during the thirty-second breaks given the spaced-practice group after every ten seconds of practice. No such dissipation should take place in the massed-practice group, who would not have a chance to dissipate their inhibition until each ten-minute rest break. Thus, as in the case of the eye-blink conditioning, we would expect the massed-practice group to show reminiscence; that is to say, we would expect them to have a better score after the rest pause than immediately before. That this is so may be seen in Figure 8. The spaced-practice group, having never accumulated very much inhibition, should not show any reminiscence, and it may be seen that in fact they do not. Furthermore, it will also be seen in Figure 8 that they perform at a very much higher level almost throughout the experiment than does the massed-practice group. We may conclude from this that some such notion as 'inhibition' is indeed required by our data.

Where in the nervous system does this inhibition occur and how can we conceptualize it? It would seem, from much evidence that has been collected, that this inhibition is a property of the cortex, the brain itself, and that it is a kind of neural, or cortical fatigue. It is important to distinguish it from muscular fatigue which, of course, is something quite different and does not occur in the kind of task with which we are dealing here. This cortical fatigue is sometimes said to have the status of a *negative drive*. The notion of drive is a very fundamental one in psychology; it corresponds to what is sometimes called motivation in everyday life. We do things, we perform tasks, only because we are motivated to do so, and the stronger the motivation – other things being equal – the better we will tend to do the task. Obviously fatigue may be conceptualized as a kind of negative drive – a drive not to carry out the task, not to go on with it, but rather to 'sit down and rest'. Performance, therefore, will be governed by the amount of positive drive or motivation under which we are working and the amount of negative drive, cortical fatigue, or inhibition which we have accumulated.

We may link this notion of inhibition as a negative drive with a general law which is widely accepted in psychology. This law may be stated in many different ways, but perhaps we may state it most simply in the form: performance equals habit $\times$ drive. Let us look at this law in the simplest possible case. Supposing we find a person playing tennis or indulging in some other sport. Clearly the excellence of his performance will depend upon two things. It will depend, in the first place, on his drive; the more highly motivated he is to play well, the better his performance will be, on the whole. It also depends, of course, on his experience and on the amount of practice that he has previously put into the task, on the length of time he has been playing, and so on. In other words, it will depend on the system of bodily habits which he has built up during the past. If he has taken up the game only recently, then these habits will be rather weak and many of them will, in fact, be incorrect habits. If he has been playing for a long time, and has been well-taught, he will have the correct habits, and they will be quite strongly developed. His actual performance will be a function of both these variables; the stronger the drive, and the more highly developed the habits which are necessary for carrying out his task, the better his performance will be. Where does inhibition fit into this picture?

The answer, of course, is this. If a person is carrying out a task, particularly under conditions of massed practice, then inhibition will continue to accumulate. Being a negative drive, it will subtract from the positive drive under which the organism is working. And, finally, when inhibition builds up to such an extent that it is equal to the positive drive under which the person is working, he will simply cease to work altogether, because now drive is equal to inhibition, and drive minus inhibition equals zero. If we put this into our general formula it will read: performance equals habit $\times$ zero. Habit $\times$ zero – or indeed, anything multiplied by zero – is, of course, zero and, therefore, performance will cease. We will be confronted with what is sometimes called a block, or an involuntary rest pause, in performance. Do such blocks actually occur? The reader may like to devise a very simple experiment. Simply tap, as fast as you can, with the index fingers of your right and left hands on the edge of the table, trying to maintain a rhythm. After a very short time, you will find that one or the other of your fingers will cease to obey your will; it will suddenly take an involuntary rest pause on its own, disrupting your performance and making it impossible for you to continue. This involuntary rest pause is quite brief. It is not a question of muscular fatigue, because the amount of muscular energy expended is minimal. Nevertheless, you will find that you are quite incapable, for a period of perhaps half a second to a second of bringing the behaviour of your fingers under your voluntary control. During this involuntary rest pause, inhibition will dissipate, and when the involuntary rest pause is over, you will again be able to go on tapping at the same fast rate. The theory says that whenever you are performing a task under conditions of massed practice, as fast as you can, involuntary rest pauses will occur, enforced as they are by the build-up of inhibition. During the rest pause inhibition will dissipate and allow performance to continue, until another involuntary rest pause occurs because of a renewed build-up of inhibition. Performance will, therefore, be an affair of stops and starts, very much as indicated in Figure 9.

You may protest that, under ordinary conditions, this does not happen. That, of course, is perfectly true. We seldom perform under conditions of massed practice for a very long period of time at a maximum rate. We have learned to adapt our performance to the build-up of inhibition and usually perform at such a rate and in such a way that build-up of inhibition does not take place to the extent that it enforces involuntary rest pauses. However, under experimental conditions, it is very easy to produce involuntary rest pauses and to demonstrate conclusively that they occur. We shall encounter several examples of this later on in the chapter, when we will try to show that the occurrence of involuntary rest pauses is

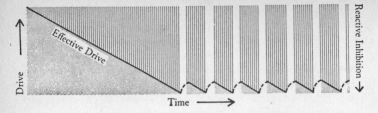

FIGURE 9

The effective drive under which a person is working decreases as inhibition increases and cancels drive. When drive equals inhibition, effective drive reaches zero and an involuntary rest pause occurs (blank vertical space in the chart). During this rest pause inhibition dissipates and performance resumes, only to decline again. Reproduced by permission from *Scientific American*.

very closely associated with different types of personality. For the moment, let us merely note this theoretical tie-up between the growth of inhibition and the occurrence of involuntary rest pauses.

We have so far spoken about a form of inhibition which is sometimes called temporal or internal inhibition, referring to inhibition in the transmission of a nerve impulse, set up by the passage of nerve impulses along the same channel a little earlier. There is also, however, another kind of inhibition, sometimes called spatial or external inhibition, which depends rather on the excitation of a different channel of transmission, inhibiting the passage of impulses along another channel. An example of this is seen in a well-known type of investigation which is often carried out to determine whether or not a person is brain damaged. The experimenter instructs the patient to close his eyes; he then touches his hand and asks the patient to notify him whenever he feels the touch. The patient has no difficulty in doing this. The experimenter touches the patient's forehead and again the patient has no difficulty in notifying him of the touch. The experimenter then touches the forehead and the hand simultaneously and, instead of feeling two touches, the touch on the hand is inhibited through spatial inhibition by the touch on the forehead, and the patient reports only one touch. This is a rather gross form of inhibition which is found almost exclusively in cases of brain damage and in some cases of hysterical neurotic disorder. However, the experimental situation can be manipulated in such a way that normal persons also become subject to spatial inhibition. Indeed, it is probably this form of inhibition which gives rise to what is sometimes called distraction; that is to say, the inhibition of one incoming impulse by another.

One of the most recent demonstrations of this fact is a method of reducing pain during childbirth and during dental treatment, which has been given the name 'audio-analgesia'. This method of increasing tolerance for pain essentially makes use of the device of stimulating the patient with sound at the same time he is exposed to the painful stimulation. This method works quite well with some people, although not with others, and there is evidence to suggest, as we might have expected on the basis of our general theory, that extraverted people show greater spatial inhibition and therefore are more susceptible to audio-analgesia than introverts.

We are now in a position to state the fundamental postulate which links inhibition and excitation to personality. It may be stated in several different ways, but perhaps the clearest and the simplest is this. People differ in the rate of build-up of inhibition, the strength of inhibition which is tolerated, and the speed with which inhibition dissipates. In particular, extraverts build up inhibition quickly, show high degrees of inhibition, and dissipate inhibition slowly. Introverted people, on the other hand, build up inhibition more slowly and to a lesser degree, and dissipate it more quickly.* We may add, parenthetically, that the opposite may be postulated for excitation; namely that introverts develop excitation more quickly and strongly, extraverts more slowly and weakly. However, we shall here be concerned mainly with experiments making use of inhibition and will, therefore, not go in any detail into the question of excitation. Clearly it will often be quite difficult to demonstrate whether a particular effect is due to low excitation or to high inhibition, because both these influences would produce very much the same effect.

We must now ask ourselves two questions. The first one is, of course, whether this postulate is true. What evidence is there to link extraversion with inhibition? The other question to which we must turn, if the first one can be answered in the affirmative, is: just how is the pattern of behaviour that we call extraversion, related to this rather mysterious concept of inhibition? Can we deduce the one from the other?

The most clear-cut demonstration of the relative incidence of inhibition in extraverted and introverted groups is given in an experiment conducted in my laboratory by a young Swedish student, Dr I. Spielmann. She used a total of ninety subjects, who were given

* We may note here a possible source of confusion. *Cortical inhibition* is stronger in extraverts, but this should not be confused with *inhibited behaviour*, which is characteristic of introverts. Cortical inhibition, to put it crudely, inhibits the higher centres, whose major role is the inhibition of outgoing, instinctual activity; it thus acts as a disinhibitor of behaviour.

a personality inventory, measuring their degree of extraversion/introversion. Having done this, she picked the extreme ten per cent showing the most extraverted traits, and the extreme ten per cent showing the most introverted traits, each group being made up of nine people. These eighteen subjects were then administered a very simple test. Essentially, this consists of a metal plate, which the subject is instructed to tap with a metal stylus as fast as he can. Through a transistor switch and oscillator, the exact length of each tap, i.e. the length of time the stylus is in contact with the plate, is transferred on to a magnetic tape running through a tape recorder. This tape is then fed into a sequential event timer and recorder, whose main function is to punch out, in exact detail, the precise length of each tap and also of each gap; that is to say, the length of time the stylus is in contact with the metal plate (the tap) and the length of time the stylus is away from the plate (the gap). Tape from the output unit can then be fed directly into electronic computers for detailed analysis. It will be seen that a very simple test can thus be linked with a very complex method of data analysis. This is essential, because of the very fleeting nature of the phenomenon which we wish to observe.[25]

Figure 10 shows the results of the experiment. On the left are shown the results, for the introverts, of the first minute of tapping; on the right are shown the results for the extraverts. The vertical scale records, in each case, the length of all the gaps, which are recorded on the top row, and also the length of the taps, which are recorded on the bottom row. Let us concentrate for the moment on the top row – that is to say, the gaps. It will be seen that, for nearly all subjects very long gaps occasionally occur which stand out to unaided observation and which can be seen without any difficulty. There are two of these, for instance, for the second introverted subject, one for the third introverted subject, one for the fourth, and two for the fifth. These very long pauses may be identified as the involuntary rest pauses or blocks which we have postulated, and it is quite clear that they can be counted with relative ease. This can be done by simple visual observation, or it can be done more satisfactory by giving a precise mathematical definition of what constitutes an involuntary rest pause, and instructing the electronic computer to detect and to count them. Whichever way this is done, it was found that the introverted group had, on the average, one rest pause of this type during a one-minute performance, whereas, on the average, the extraverts had eighteen. There was no overlap whatsoever between the two groups; in other words, the introvert with the largest number of involuntary rest pauses had far fewer of them than the extravert with the smallest number of

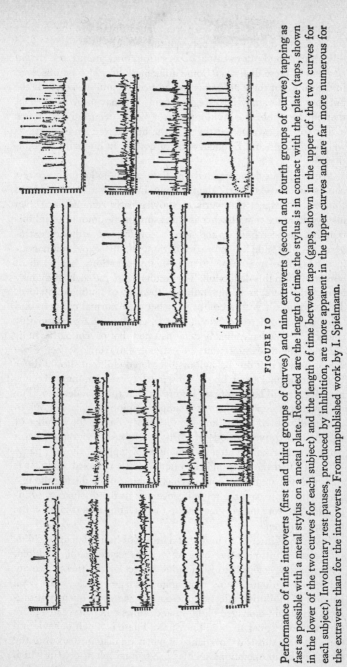

FIGURE 10

Performance of nine introverts (first and third groups of curves) and nine extraverts (second and fourth groups of curves) tapping as fast as possible with a metal stylus on a metal plate. Recorded are the length of time the stylus is in contact with the plate (taps, shown in the lower of the two curves for each subject) and the length of time between taps (gaps, shown in the upper of the two curves for each subject). Involuntary rest pauses, produced by inhibition, are more apparent in the upper curves and are far more numerous for the extraverts than for the introverts. From unpublished work by I. Spielmann.

rest pauses. It would not require very much discussion to convince the reader of the difference between the two groups, because these differences stand out to casual observation, once attention is drawn to them in these diagrams. Some differences may also be observed in the taps, but these are rather less noticeable and we may, for the purpose of this analysis, disregard them. We may notice, however, that on the whole, the involuntary rest pauses occurred very much earlier for the extraverted than for the introverted group; this, as well as their greater frequency, is, of course, in line with expectation.[25]

We have thus demonstrated that there are more involuntary rest pauses among extraverts than among introverts. We would, of course, also expect extraverts to show greater reminiscence than introverts, since reminiscence is a measure of the amount of inhibition that has been built up and since, according to our theory, extraverts should build up more inhibition. Is this expectation confirmed? There are a large number of investigations, nearly all of which confirm this deduction. The results from one such study may be included here, as an illustration of the kind of findings obtained. The study dealt with a comparison between normal children and behaviour-disordered children, that is, children of a psychopathic character.[26] We have already demonstrated that psychopathic individuals tend to exhibit traits of extreme extraversion; hence we would expect that our behaviour-disordered children should differ from the normal group by showing much greater amounts of reminiscence. It will be seen from Figure 11 that this is indeed so. The task which is depicted here is a simple tapping task, analogous to the one discussed above, and the scores are simply the number of taps delivered over periods of thirty seconds. A programmed rest pause was introduced after five minutes of tapping, the rest pause lasting for ten minutes, and then tapping was resumed again. It is clear that the amount of improvement taking place during the rest pause (that is to say, the reminiscence due to the dissipation of inhibition) is very much greater for the psychopathic than for the normal children.

It is also of interest to note that a group of brain-damaged children behaved in much the same way as the psychopathic children. This is as expected, because another aspect of the theory we are concerned with maintains that brain damage increases the total amount of inhibition affecting the cortex, and consequently it predicts that brain-damaged children and adults will behave in a more extraverted manner than will normals. There is much behavioural evidence that this is so, particularly when we take into account the results of brain operations such as pre-frontal lobotomy, in which some of the 'silent areas' immediately behind the forehead are severed from the rest of the cortex.[27] Individuals in whom this operation has been performed have often been shown to behave in an extremely extraverted fashion, whatever their personality may have been before the operation. This point is introduced here because we noted in Chapter 3 that in some cases where there was a lack of concordance between identical twins – one having committed a crime and the other not – it had been hypothesized that this might have been due to brain damage in one twin, whereas the other twin did not suffer any corresponding damage.[28] We have, therefore, another link between extraversion, brain damage, and

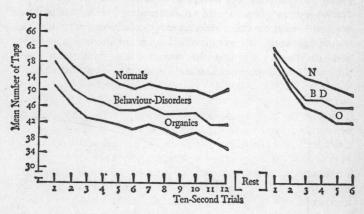

FIGURE 11

Rate of tapping of normal, behaviour-disordered and brain-damaged (organic) children. Note the differences in rate of tapping before rest, and the marked recovery after rest. This recovery (reminiscence) is significantly greater for the behaviour-disordered than for the organic children. Taken from unpublished work by J. Grassi.

criminality, a link, the nature of which we shall be dealing with a little later on.

What other types of differences can we predict to occur between extraverts and introverts? We have already mentioned that the notion of inhibition grew out of Pavlov's work with conditioning. We may accordingly predict that extraverts, who should accumulate a good deal of inhibitory potential during the process of conditioning, would be less likely to condition well and strongly than introverts, who should accumulate relatively little inhibition. The same prediction should, of course, follow from our other hypothesis, which states that introverts show greater excitatory potential than extraverts. We may inquire whether experimental facts support our theory. The most extensive work in this connexion was carried out in my laboratory by Dr C. Franks, who used eye-blink conditioning of the kind already described. He carried out two experiments, one in which he used extraverted and introverted neurotics (hysterics and dysthymics) and one in which he used extraverted and introverted normals. He found no difference between the normal and the neurotic groups; therefore, we may pool the data for the two groups. When this is done, the results of the conditioning experiment can be shown in diagrammatic form, as in Figure 12. It will be seen from Figure 12 that the introverts condition very much better than do the extraverts; indeed, at all points, the introverts show about twice as many conditioned responses as do the extraverts. We may conclude that our prediction is fully verified. We may also note that several other investigators have since studied this phenomenon and come out with similar results;

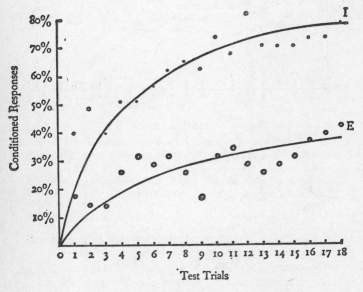

FIGURE 12

Differences in the rates of conditioning of introverted and extraverted subjects, using the eye-blink conditioning apparatus It will be seen that introverts at all stages show about twice as many conditioned responses as do extraverts The figure is reproduced with permission from the *British Journal of Psychology*, 1962, *53*, 302.

using both eye-blink conditioning and other types of conditioning, they have found that there is a distinct tendency for introverts to condition better than extraverts.[29]*

How about brain damage? We have postulated that brain-damaged people behave rather like extraverts. It would seem to follow that we should also expect them to show rather less conditioning than non-brain-damaged subjects. This was investigated in an experiment conducted by Violet Franks, who used exactly the same equipment her husband had used in the experiment already described. She studied brain-damaged and non-brain-damaged mental defective children and found the results which are depicted in Figure 13. (The fact of mental defect does not come into the results

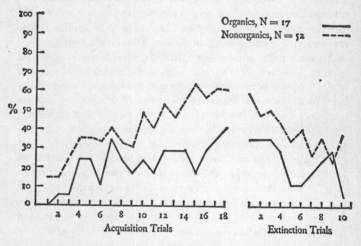

FIGURE 13

Acquisition and extinction of conditioned eye-blink responses by brain-damaged and non-brain-damaged subjects Note the poor rate of conditioning of the brain-damaged subjects (organics). From V. Franks and C. M. Franks, *Proc. London Conf. Sci. Study Ment. Def.*, 1960, May & Baker, Dagenham, 1962, 577–83.

very much, because intelligence has never been found to correlate with conditioning; mentally defective children condition just about as well as university students.) But it will be seen that the brain-damaged children condition much less well than those who are not brain damaged. Indeed, the difference between them is just about as

* One or two investigators have failed to confirm these results, but it should be noted that they used schedules of conditioning very different from those used by Franks and the other authors referred to above.

large as that found previously between extraverts and introverts. We may conclude that our general hypothesis is verified in relation to brain damage as well as in relation to extraversion and introversion.

We have spent some time demonstrating that personality is related to conditioning for a very particular reason. As we hope to show later, it is through a process of conditioning that we can hope to establish a relationship between personality and inhibition, and it is, therefore, necessary to present the data relating to conditioning in particular detail. It is perhaps appropriate to warn the reader here that, while most results have been favourable to our hypothesis linking introversion with ease of conditioning, some reports have found rather less strong relationships or none at all. This is not surprising. Conditioning is a very complex phenomenon indeed and there are many different variables which have to be studied before we can arrive at any general conclusion. Thus conditioning experiments may differ with respect to the strength of the conditioned stimulus, the strength of the unconditioned stimulus, and the length of time elapsing between the conditioned and unconditioned stimulus. The time interval between presentation of conditioned and unconditioned stimuli has been found to be very important indeed. Half a second seems to be the optimum period; when it is as long as two and a half seconds, no conditioning occurs whatsoever. There is reason to believe that the optimum period differs for extraverts and introverts; consequently, different investigators using different periods may obtain quite different results. The spacing of the trials may be important. When there is little time intervening between one trial and another, we have a condition approaching massed practice, whereas when there is a good deal of time intervening, we have a condition of spaced practice; obviously spacing of trials would affect our conclusions.

There is another complexity which we must now discuss. So far, we have been talking as if conditionability was, as it were, a general trait of personality. Is this in fact the case? Can we say that because a person conditions quickly and strongly, say on the eye-blink apparatus, that he will also condition quickly and strongly, say, with respect to his heart beat rate? Or with respect to the electrical conductivity of the skin, which we discussed previously? The answer here seems to be that, on the whole, correlations between different tests of conditionability tend to be relatively low. The reason for this is twofold. In the first place, we find that with respect to any particular kind of conditioning there are a number of what one might call peripheral factors which determine very much the degree of conditioning which can be expected. As a typical example, let us go back again to eye-blink conditioning. Here, the unconditioned stimulus is the puff of air to the cornea of the eye; this is a slightly painful stimulus which causes a reflex closure of the eyelid. Usually, exactly the same strength of puff is employed for all subjects, the assumption being that their eyes will be equally sensitive. This, however, is by no means so. In some of our work we have used industrial apprentices, for instance. Some of these individuals wear glasses because of defective eyesight and, of course, these glasses also protect their eyes from wind and rain, and other influences which might cause damage. These people, we have found, are particularly sensitive to the puff of air which is experimentally applied to their eyes and it produces very quick and very strong closure of the eyelid. On the other hand, some of these boys drive motor-bikes, at speeds up to a hundred miles an hour, often without goggles on, and the airstream which hits their eyes under these conditions is, in fact, stronger than anything we normally apply in the laboratory. To these boys, then, the particular stimulus applied in the laboratory is so weak that it sometimes does not even cause any movement of the eyelid. Therefore, in order to cancel out the effects of this factor, it becomes necessary to first of all establish a threshold, that is, the weakest strength of puff which is just barely sufficient to cause closure of the eyelid. This threshold differs from person to person, and if we want to correlate eye-blink conditioning with some other mode of conditioning, then clearly we must on some basis equate the strength of the unconditioned stimulus between people. This can only be done by establishing the threshold and then increasing the strength of the puff of air by a predetermined amount. This has not usually been done by people who have correlated different types of conditionability; to the extent that this precaution has been neglected, it is quite clear that correlations cannot be expected to be very high.

Another example may be taken from the field of conditioning involving the electrical conductivity of the skin. It has been mentioned previously that here we are dealing with a phenomenon which is mediated by sweating. Emotion produces a slight degree of sweating in the skin and this sweat, being an electrolytic agent, facilitates the flow of an electric current and thus lowers the resistance of the skin. However, people differ widely in the number of sweat glands they have in their fingers; the person who has many sweat glands will show a larger increase in conductivity than will the person who has relatively few. Again, this point is irrelevant to the crucial part of the experiment we are conducting, that is, the correlation of different methods of conditioning. But unless it is in some way controlled, quite obviously it will upset our correlations.

In other words, there are many purely technical details which interfere with the establishment of a high correlation between different types of conditioning and which must be taken into account before we can say that a particular person is, or is not, easily conditionable.

Even when we take all these factors into account, however, it is almost certain that we will find here, as we have found before, a certain degree of 'response specificity'. It will be remembered from our discussion of emotional reactivity in general, that the sympathetic nervous system does not act invariably as a whole, but that, for some people, some parts react more strongly, whereas for other people other parts react more strongly. This will inevitably affect any correlations we may find between conditionability in one modality and conditionability in another. The reason for this is as follows. It has been shown that the speed and strength of conditioning of a particular reaction is quite highly correlated with the natural vigour and strength of the particular reflex which is being conditioned. To take the example of eye-blink conditioning, we find that some people blink strongly to stimuli, whereas others blink rather weakly. Those who blink strongly are more easily conditioned than those who blink weakly. Similarly, in relation to the electrical conductivity of the skin, the so-called galvanic skin response or GSR, it is found that some people react with a very marked increase in conductivity to any emotion-producing stimulus, whereas other people react rather weakly. Now those who react strongly tend also to condition quickly and strongly with respect to the GSR, whereas those who react only weakly also condition weakly. In other words, there is a tie-up between response specificity of the autonomic system and response specificity in the field of conditioning.

Again, as in the case of the autonomic response specificity, this must not be taken too far. These responses are not completely independent of each other and relations do exist between them. We are simply drawing attention to the fact that generality is far from complete and that specificity plays an important part. This specificity may account for the fact that some reactions are conditioned more quickly in some people, other reactions in other people. In spite of all these difficulties, the evidence still suggests that conditionability as a general substrate of behaviour, is a meaningful concept, and may be retained with some advantage.

What other deductions may we make from our general proposition? One of these relates to the field of experimental investigation sometimes identified as 'vigilance'. By this term is meant the tendency or ability of a person to keep on attending to a series of weak and widely-spaced stimuli, for example, the kind of thing which might happen in war time when the radar officer of an aircraft is watching the radar screen for the telling blip which will indicate the presence of a submarine somewhere below the aircraft. He may watch the radar screen for hours without ever seeing the blip and when it comes, it may make only a weak and quite brief appearance; he has to be very alert in order to spot it and this alertness is technically known as vigilance.

Vigilance can be studied in the laboratory by means of some kind of set-up which will duplicate the essential elements of this type of experience. For instance, the subject may sit in a room which is quite empty except for a clock on the wall on which he has to fixate. On this clock is a single hand which moves around by making one slight movement every second. Very infrequently the hand makes two movements during a second and the subject is required to detect this 'signal' and to press a push-button on which his right hand is resting while he watches the clock. It is usually found that people do not miss any signals at the beginning of their vigil but after half an hour or so, their rate of response has begun to decrease considerably and they respond with many fewer signals, making a fair number of errors of omission. When extraverts and introverts are compared with respect to their performance on a test of this kind, it is nearly always found that extraverts, as expected, do much worse than do the introverts; in other words, inhibition builds up more quickly and more strongly in the extravert and inhibition prevents him from detecting the signal which constitutes the main part of his task.[30]

Other similar tasks which give similar results make use of auditory stimulation. Thus the subject may have to listen to a whole series of single digit numbers which are being read out to him on a tape recorder. Occasionally, there is a set of three odd numbers or three even numbers in succession, and whenever this occurs he has to press a button to indicate this fact. Again it is found that extraverts do very much less well than introverts. A typical example of such an experiment is given in Figure 14.

There are many other laboratory experiments which have been carried out, in order to test deductions from this general theory, and by and large it may be said that they have, on the whole, supported it quite well. We will encounter one or two of them later on in the course of this book. Here we will rather turn to another question which is of considerable importance for our line of argument. The question must be raised: are extraversion/introversion and neuroticism inherited traits of personality, or are they due to the action of the environment? Before we attempt an answer we must first of all define two terms which are quite fundamental in modern genetic research. These terms are *genotype* and *phenotype*. An indi-

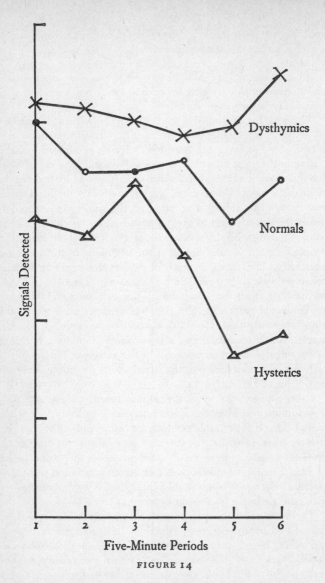

FIGURE 14

Performance on a test of vigilance as described in the text. Note the superior performance of the neurotic introvert group (dysthymics) and the inferior performance of the neurotic extravert group (hysterics) during each of the six five-minute periods. Data by G. Claridge from H. J. Eysenck (ed.), *Experiments in Personality*, Vol. II, Routledge, 1960, p. 117.

vidual's genetic constitution is usually called his genotype, whereas his actual appearance, which is the product of his genotype and the environment which has been imposed upon him, is called his phenotype. The height of a person which we measure is essentially phenotypical but it is, of course, based on a firm genetic foundation. We call it a phenotype because it is, to some extent, influenced by environmental influences, such as vitamin deficiency, too little or too much food, and so on. This differentiation is a vital one and we must apply it to our concepts of extraversion and emotionality.

Figure 15 will indicate, to some extent, the kind of picture we have in mind. Note at the bottom of the diagram our theoretical

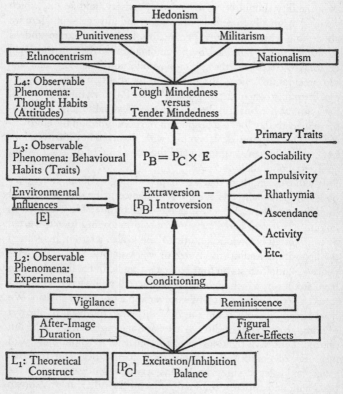

FIGURE 15

The diagram illustrates the relation between genotype (constitutional factors) and phenotype (observable behaviour). For a fuller discussion see the text. From *Nature*, 1963, *199*, 1032.

construct, the excitation-inhibition balance. This we believe to be genotypical; that is to say, entirely determined by hereditary influences and, consequently, we have in brackets appended the letters P_C, meaning by that the constitutional part of the personality. This genotypic or constitutional portion of personality can be measured with more or less success in terms of observable experimental phenomena such as conditioning, reminiscence, vigilance, and so forth. It would not be quite true to say, of course, that these phenomena are entirely dependent on heredity and are unaffected by environmental influences. What is maintained is simply that environmental influences probably affect them less than the higher order traits, to which we turn next.

At the third level, we have the behavioural habits or traits, such as sociability, impulsivity, ascendance, activity, and so on, which we used originally to define extraversion and introversion. Here we are dealing with behavioural personality, P_B in the diagram, and, as indicated, this is moulded by a combination of the constitutional personality factors – the excitation-inhibition balance – and environmental influences, abbreviated in the diagram as E. The general formula given in the diagram is $P_B = P_C \times E$; in other words, behavioural personality, the phenotypic personality which we observe in everyday life, is a product of the genotype and the environment. The diagram deals simply with extraversion/introversion, but exactly the same argument and the same kind of diagram would apply to emotionality.

It will be seen, then, that we are postulating a definite hereditary basis for personality. Is there any evidence in favour of such an hypothesis? The answer is that there is considerable evidence in favour of a strong hereditary predisposition leading to extraverted or introverted behaviour, and that there is also a strong hereditary predisposition leading to strong or weak emotionality. The evidence essentially rests on four separate strands. In the first place, we have studies in which identical and fraternal twins have been subjected to experimental tests of extraversion and of neuroticism. We have already discussed some tests of this kind, for instance, the test of body-sway suggestibility. What was done essentially, to take but one of these investigations, was to construct a whole battery of measures of emotionality, apply these to identical and fraternal twins, and calculate the correlations between identical twins on the one hand, and between fraternal twins on the other. It was shown that identical twins resembled each other far more than did fraternal twins. In fact, it was estimated that the influence of heredity was as strong in relation to emotionality as many authors had shown it to be in relation to intelligence. As a next step, the same tests were applied to groups of children suffering from neurotic disorders, who might be considered to be extremes on this dimension of emotionality or neuroticism. It was demonstrated that these children differed very significantly from normal children in respect to their standing on this trait, thus showing that the tests which had been chosen to measure the trait did in fact agree with an outside criterion and were, therefore, valid.[31]

The second kind of test consists of giving questionnaires to identical and fraternal twins, questionnaires assessing extraversion and questionnaires of emotionality. This, too, has been done a number of times and, on the whole, there is no doubt that identical twins are more alike than are fraternal twins. The influence of heredity in this case seems to be somewhat less than in the case of the objective tests, precisely what we would have expected. Going back to Figure 15, we can see that the questionnaires deal with P_B, whereas the objective tests deal more with P_C; in other words, the material dealt with by the questionnaire is everyday behaviour, which is a product of heredity and environment, with environment playing a larger part in the questionnaires than in the experimental tests, which are influenced more by the constitutional personality. Nevertheless, our theory would lead us to expect that identical twins here, too, would be more alike and, in fact, they are so.[32]

The third line of evidence is one in which parents, their children, cousins, and other relatives are studied, and deductions are made from the degree of cosanguinity to the correlation which should be observed between different family members. These studies, on the whole, also support the theory that emotionality-neuroticism and extraversion/introversion are, in fact, largely determined by heredity.[33]

The last type of study to be mentioned has been carried out only once, by Mr J. Shields of the Maudsley Hospital, and his study is important because it shows that one objection sometimes raised against twin studies is almost certainly invalid. It is sometimes argued that of course identical twins are more alike in their behaviour than are fraternal twins, because identical twins, looking more alike than fraternal twins, are also subjected to environmental influences which are more nearly alike. This is not an unreasonable argument, although the facts seem not to support it. It is often found that, on the contrary, identical twins, because they are so similar in looks and behaviour, will strive to work out separate personalities for themselves so that one will intentionally behave in a manner different from his twin; he will seek out a different environment, different friends, have different interests, read different books, and so on, just because he does not want to be an identical twin and nothing more. In other words, it is possible that being an identical twin may work in exactly the opposite direction to that hypothesized in this particular criticism. There is some evidence that our reply to this objection is, in fact, valid, but it is very difficult indeed to find conclusive evidence either for or against the objection. Of course, we could overcome the objection very simply if we could find a sufficient number of identical twins who had been brought up separately; that is to say, where one twin did not even know the other twin, and where the environmental influences brought to bear on each twin were quite distinct.

Identical twins are rare enough at best. To find identical twins who have been brought up in separation is very much more difficult. Shields was able to find forty-four pairs of identical twins who had been separated in infancy and brought up separately, and a similar number of pairs of identical twins who had been brought up together. In addition, he studied 28 pairs of fraternal twins who had been brought up together. He administered tests of intelligence, of extraversion, and of neuroticism to all these twins and his results were conclusive. He found that the identical twins who had been brought up separately were very much alike. He found correlations between them of, roughly, 0.6 for intelligence, neuroticism and extraversion. The identical twins who had been brought up together were also very much alike, but the correlations between them were, if anything, smaller than those of the twins who had been brought up separately. Now this is an extremely important finding, because it destroys at one stroke the argument that identical twins behave more similarly because environment recognizes their similarity and treats them more alike than it does fraternal twins. Exactly the opposite seems to be true. Identical twins who are brought up together seem indeed, as indicated above, to try to individualize themselves by consciously working towards a differentiation of their interests and behaviour as much as possible. When they are brought up in different environments and do not know of each other's existence, then, of course, this is not necessary and nature can, as it were, take its course. There is no new external influence which is brought to bear on the twins to counteract their natural inherited inclinations. Shields also found, of course, that fraternal twins were much less alike than identical twins, but this finding is of no particular interest here. The actual correlations he found are given in Table 2.[34]

The answer to our question about the influence of heredity is, then, a fairly definite one. We have considerable evidence that there is a strong hereditary basis for extraversion/introversion and also for emotionality or neuroticism. This hereditary influence always works

TABLE 2

Resemblance of identical twins brought up separately and brought up together, and of fraternal twins, with respect to intelligence, extraversion, and neuroticism. The figures in the body of the Table represent intra-class correlation coefficients.

	Identical twins		Fraternal twins
	Brought up separately	Brought up together	
Intelligence	0.77	0.76	0.51
Extraversion	0.61	0.42	−0.17
Neuroticism	0.53	0.38	0.11

in conjunction with environmental influences, of course, to determine actual behaviour. We cannot, in our discussion of behaviour, leave out the hereditary determination, as is unfortunately done so frequently in modern discussions. Heredity furnishes the biological foundation for behaviour and, in doing so, it exerts a strong influence as to the direction in which behaviour will develop. It does not completely predetermine the behaviour that will ultimately be shown, because it is possible, in ways which we will discuss later on, to use our knowledge of the hereditary mechanism, and of the neurological and physiological mechanisms through which it works, to influence future behaviour. It is only by realizing the importance of this underlying biological factor that we can hope to make the study of personality and of criminality a proper scientific discipline.

One more point will be discussed before closing this chapter. The reader may have noted that we have suggested a definite physiological system, the autonomic system, as underlying the behavioural trait of emotionality or neuroticism. He will also have noted that while we have suggested a relationship between extraversion and inhibition and between introversion and excitation, we have failed to suggest a definite physiological locus for this particular trait. The primary reason is that we cannot, with certainty, point to any particular part of the nervous system and say that this is the locus of inhibition and excitation. In recent years, however, there has been a growing interest in a particular structure – the so-called ascending reticular formation – which may well subserve this function. Most people are familiar with the general outline of the central nervous system. This consists of the classical long *afferent* pathways coming from the sensory surfaces to the brain, transmitting information, and the long *efferent* pathways going from the

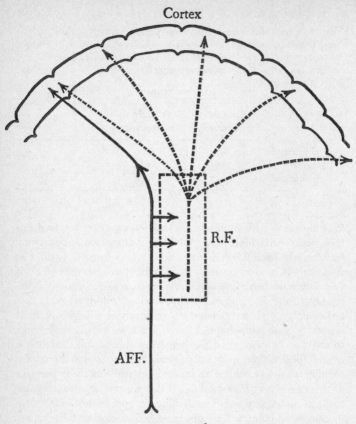

Cortex

R.F.

AFF.

FIGURE 16

The diagram shows the reticular formation (RF) and its relation to the afferent nerve fibres and the cortex. For fuller explanation see the text. From D. Gooch, in H. J. Eysenck, (ed.), *Experiments with Drugs*, Pergamon, London, 1960.

brain to the muscles and producing reactions in them. The reticular formation of the brain, which is situated at the top of the spinal cord, at the bottom of the brain itself, can be considered as a pathway for the conduction of impulses accessory to the classical long afferent and efferent pathways. Figure 16 shows, in diagrammatic form, the function of the reticular formation as an alternative pathway for impulses proceeding from the periphery to the cortex. Impulses travelling to the cortex via the classical afferent pathways also enter the reticular formation through collaterals from the afferents, giving rise to impulses which are not only directed to the primary cortical projection area of the classical afferent pathway, but may also be projected diffusely over a wide area of the cerebral cortex. There is much evidence to suggest that it is the activity of the reticular formation which determines what one might call 'cortical facilitation'; that is to say, the cortex would very soon cease to respond to information reaching it through the classical afferent pathways if it were not for diffuse bombardment from the reticular formation. Similarly, it is evident, from numerous studies, that an active inhibitory influence can be exerted by portions of the reticular formation. There would be little point in going into further detail about what is essentially a new and rapidly developing aspect of modern neurophysiology. The postulated link between the reticular formation and extraversion/introversion is still rather speculative, but there is a growing body of evidence in its favour.[35]

5 Is Conscience a Conditioned Reflex?

'I can't believe *that*!' said Alice.

'Can't you?' the Queen said in a pitying tone. 'Try again: draw a long breath, and shut your eyes.'

Alice laughed. 'There's no use trying,' she said: 'one *can't* believe impossible things.'

'I dare say you haven't had much practice,' said the Queen. 'When I was your age, I always did it for half an hour a day. Why, sometimes I've believed as many as six impossible things before breakfast.'

THROUGH THE LOOKING-GLASS

In the preceding chapter, we have shown that there exists an hereditary basis for personality, and we have accordingly distinguished between the genotypic and the phenotypic levels of personality research. We have failed, however, to demonstrate the exact causal links between the two levels, and it is clearly not sufficient to point out that introverts show certain scores on tests involving inhibition, whereas extraverts show quite different scores. This indeed is predictable from our theory and, insofar as it is found to be true, supports it. However, we would like to understand how the degree of a person's inhibitory potential or excitatory potential leads to the kinds of behaviour which we characterize as extraverted or introverted. It is the task of this chapter to deal with this problem and, in particular, to try to forge a link which will enable us to understand criminal behaviour and its relation to personality.

Let us consider Figure 17. On the baseline or abscissa are represented varying levels of sensory stimulation, from very low to very high. A low level of stimulation, for instance, would be a very soft tone; a very high level of stimulation would be a very loud tone. On the ordinate or vertical axis are shown positive or negative hedonic tone associated with these different levels of stimulation, ranging from strongly negative (feelings of displeasure or even pain, desire to escape, to end the stimulation) to strongly positive (feelings of intense pleasure, desire to prolong the stimulation or even to increase it). Between the positive and negative hedonic tones there is an *indifference level*, indicating that stimulation is neither sought nor avoided but is neutral to the subject.

The bold, curvilinear line in the centre of the diagram indicates the relationship between hedonic tone and strength of sensory stimulation, as established by a number of experimental studies. We find that extremely high levels of stimulation produce a high negative hedonic tone. This, of course, is very well known, High levels of stimulation produce pain; we need only think of the pain given by wounds or by the activities of the dentist to realize this. Very

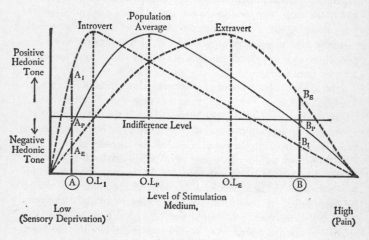

FIGURE 17

The relation between level of stimulation and hedonic tone (pleasantness-unpleasantness). Extraverts are shown to prefer high levels of stimulation, whereas introverts prefer low levels of stimulation, as compared with the general population. From H. J. Eysenck, (ed.), *Experiments with Drugs*, Pergamon, London, 1960.

loud noise or very bright lights also produce pain and, therefore, tend to be generally avoided. We also find that extremely low levels of stimulation, or what has sometimes been called *sensory deprivation*, tend also to produce high negative hedonic tone and to be bearable for only relatively short periods. In a typical experiment, all sensory input is reduced to an absolute minimum. This may be done by putting the subject into a soundproof room, cutting out all visual stimulation by making him wear dark goggles, putting cardboard containers around his hands and feet so that he cannot touch anything, in general making it impossible for him to encounter much sensory stimulation. Under these conditions, it is found that very few people are able to tolerate the sensory deprivation for any length of time; very soon they wish to get out of the room, despite the high pay offered them for serving as experimental guinea pigs and for staying in the room. If they do stay in for any length of time, they tend to develop hallucinations and to deteriorate with respect to performance on mental and other types of tests. The experience is generally described as a very disagreeable one. The greater the sensory deprivation, the more disagreeable the experience, and the less time subjects are willing to endure it. The extreme is probably reached when the subject is suspended in a bath having about the same temperature as his body; he is suspended below the surface of the water, breathing through a snorkel tube, which virtually eliminates sensation. Under these conditions, very few people are able to tolerate the lack of sensory stimulation for more than an hour or two.[35]

If an individual is exposed to continued stimulation of a particular kind, inhibition should set in, thus reducing the effective amount of stimulation received by the subject. If it is true that extraverts show greater inhibition than introverts, with the ordinary person intermediate between the two, then it follows that any given degree of stimulation would effectively be experienced by introverts as *higher* than would be experienced by the average person, while similarly it would be experienced by extraverts as *lower* than would be experienced by the average person. Objectively equal amounts of stimulation, therefore, would not be experienced as equal by extraverts and introverts; they would appear displaced to the right of the abscissa (Figure 17) by the introvert, and to the left by the extravert. Similarly, if O.L. represents the optimum or preferred level of stimulation of a given person, then $O.L._I$ would lie to the left and $O.L._E$ to the right of $O.L._P$, where the subscripts I and E refer to introvert and extravert, respectively, and P to the population average.

Again, consider two points, A and B, on the abscissa, referring to low and high levels of stimulation, respectively. If straight lines are drawn through these points parallel to the ordinate, they will cross the general curve relating levels of stimulation to hedonic tone roughly at the indifference level; in other words, for the average person, these two stimuli are equally indifferent. For the typical extravert and introvert, however, as already explained, the general curve is not representative and has to be displaced, to the left for the introvert, and to the right for the extravert. It follows, as shown in the diagram, that stimulus A will be positively hedonic for the introvert (A_I) and negatively hedonic for the extravert (A_E), while B will be negatively hedonic for the introverts (B_I) and positively hedonic for the extraverts (B_E). Similar consequences would appear to follow if we based our argument on individual differences in excitation rather than in inhibition; we are not concerned at this point with the possibility of a crucial experiment to decide between these two alternative hypotheses.[35]

Many testable deductions related to everyday behaviour follow from this hypothesis. Consider first the respective reactions of introverted and extraverted subjects to a test of pain tolerance, i.e. a test in which the subject is exposed to strong stimulation and in which the score is the length of time elapsing from the onset of the stimulation until he voluntarily withdraws, being unable to bear the pain any longer. It follows directly from Figure 17 that with *identical* objective stimulation, extraverts would experience less pain than introverts, due to the intervention of strong inhibitory potentials and would, therefore, be likely to tolerate the pain for longer periods of time. Hence the prediction follows directly from our theory that extraverts will show greater pain tolerance than introverts. Three independent investigations have shown that this correlation can be observed and that extraverts do indeed show greater pain tolerance.

Consider next the reaction of extraverts and introverts in a test of sensory deprivation, i.e. a test in which the subject, as explained before, is exposed to as complete deprivation of stimulation as can be arranged by the experimenter. His score is the length of time elapsing from the beginning of the deprivation period until he voluntarily withdraws, being unable to stand the deprivation any longer. It follows directly from Figure 17 that with objectively identical conditions of deprivation, extraverts would experience less stimulation (i.e., greater deprivation) than introverts, due to the intervention of strong inhibitory potentials, and would, therefore, be able to tolerate the deprivation for shorter periods of time. Hence the prediction follows directly from our theory that extraverts will show less tolerance for sensory deprivation than introverts. This prediction also has received considerable experimental support. It would seem to follow from these facts that any form of corporal punishment is less of a deterrent to the extravert than to the introvert, whereas isolation, in prison, solitary confinement and so forth, is much more of a deterrent to the extravert than to the introvert, because these conditions of isolation are also, by their nature, conditions of sensory deprivation. These differences in tolerance for stimulation, therefore, are important from the point of view of criminal punishment and equally important from the point of view of bringing up children.

A third prediction follows from the respective positions of the O.L.s (optimal levels of stimulation) of extraverts and introverts, on the abscissa in Figure 17. We would deduce from this difference in position the existence of a kind of *stimulus hunger* on the part of the extravert and a *stimulus avoidance* on the part of the introvert, relative to each other. We would predict that extraverts would be likely to smoke more, drink more, and eat more, particularly spicy food; have intercourse more frequently; take more risks, with the accompanying autonomic stimulation providing what has sometimes been called an 'arousal jag'; and enjoy parties and social intercourse generally because of the considerable stimulation provided. The evidence on these points is strongly confirmatory. Extraverts drink more and smoke more cigarettes; they have more illegitimate children, take more risks, and are certainly more sociable. They also make more expansive movements, thus producing greater proprioceptive stimulation, and generally behave as if they were indeed suffering from stimulus hunger. Here we seem to have a direct relationship with a certain feature of criminal conduct, particularly that of juvenile delinquents, which has frequently been remarked upon. Many of the activities of the juvenile delinquent seem to stem from boredom, from a desire for stimulation, and from an apparent willingness to take more risks. We note these points only in passing at the moment; but they do show, to some extent at least, how our hypothesis, explaining extraverted behaviour in terms of inhibition, may be used directly to predict verifiable consequences in criminal behaviour.

There are many more deductions which could be made from Figure 17 but we must now turn to a different kind of deduction which is quite crucial for the whole theory which is being presented here. To put the argument briefly, it is suggested that socialized behaviour rests essentially on a basis of conditioning which is applied during a person's childhood by his parents, teachers, and peers, and that his conduct in later years is determined very much by the quality of the conditioning received at that time, and also by the degree of conditionability which he himself shows; that is to say, the degree to which he is capable of becoming conditioned by the stimuli which are presented to him. This bare suggestion may not appeal to the reader, and we must now turn to a detailed discussion of it, because it is crucial to the future development of our general theme.

First of all, let us reconsider the general problem. We start with the observation that some people are criminals. We then ask ourselves why it is that some people apparently tend to break the law, and to go on doing so although incarcerated for a good part of their lives, and, quite generally, how it is that a small portion of society appears to set itself against the remainder. I would like to suggest that this question is put the wrong way round. What we should ask, rather, is how does it come about that so many people are, in fact, law-abiding citizens who do not go counter to the rules of our society, that so many people do not commit crimes but live peacefully without ever coming into contact with the law? The reason it is preferable to put the question in this way is very simple. By and large, experimental investigation and philosophical specula-tion have both supported a general law of behaviour which is essen-tially one of hedonism. This is often referred to in psychology as the 'empirical law of effect'. In other words, people tend to do what is pleasant to them and tend to refrain from doing what is un-pleasant. The majority of people are lacking in a great many things; they may lack food, or shelter, or warmth; they may lack a large number of objects, from motor cars to tiaras and yachts which they would like to have. At first sight, it would seem the most natural thing in the world that, when a person lacks something which he wishes to possess and when that something is available in the world around him, he should simply go and take it. What prevents him from doing so? This may seem a very simple-minded question but it is a very difficult one.

We might say that he does not behave in this manner because he knows the police would very soon apprehend him and that the effects of prison are more painful than the acquisition of the object in question would be pleasurable. But such an answer would not be very convincing, for two main reasons. In the first place, it is a well-known principle in psychology that the consequences of a given act determine the future of that act not only in terms of what may be called the quantitative aspects of the consequences, but also in terms of their temporal pattern. In other words, if an act has two consequences, one rewarding and the other punishing, which would be strictly equal if simultaneous, the influence of those consequences upon later performances of that act will vary, depend-ing upon the *order* in which they occur. If the punishing consequence comes first and the rewarding one later, the difference between the inhibiting and the reinforcing effect will be in favour of the in-hibition. But if the rewarding consequence comes first and the punishing one later, the difference will be in favour of the reinforce-ment. This formulation of the law was made by O. H. Mowrer, who comments as follows:

One can think of this problem in terms of a physical analogy. If two weights of equal mass are placed at equal distances from the fulcrum of a lever, they will, of course, exactly counter-balance each other; but if either of these objectively 'equal' weights is placed further from the fulcrum than the other, it has a mechanical advantage which enables it to tip the balance in its favour. In the functional sense, the weights are no longer 'equal', and a state of 'disbalance' results. In this physical analogy, *spatial distance* from the fulcrum provides the advantage, whereas in the psychological situation it is *temporal nearness* to the rewarding or punishing state of affairs that is the deciding factor. In this sense, the analogy is not an entirely happy one, but it will suffice to illustrate the point that in a dynamic (conflict) situation, the outcome is determined not alone by the absolute magnitude of the causal forces, but also by their relational properties.[36]

Clearly this law of integrative learning, as Mowrer calls it, would work against the effectiveness of punishment. The punishment is long-delayed and uncertain; the acquisition of the desired object is immediate; therefore, although the acquisition and the pleasure derived from it may, on the whole, be less than the pain derived from the incarceration which ultimately follows, the time element very much favours the acquisition as compared with the deterrent effects of the incarceration. On this basis alone, we would expect the result to be that the person would take the object and 'hang the consequences'! This is precisely the pattern of activity which we can observe every day in the lives of psychopaths and many juvenile delinquents, who seem completely unable to resist the temptation which is offered to them here and now, although they are intelligent enough, from the point of view of a simple intelligence test, to reason out the almost certain apprehension and incarceration which will follow the theft. 'Why', the question must be asked, 'is not everyone like this?'

The other difficulty, which arises from this rather simple-minded idea that it is the consequences of the act which deter the average person, is simply that these consequences are very far from being certain. It is almost impossible to know in what proportion of cases a crime is in fact brought home to the person concerned, and in what proportion of cases he is ultimately punished. Statistics vary from year to year, and from country to country, and from one type of crime to another, but perhaps it may be said that reasonably clever criminals will get away with their crimes much more frequently than they will be punished for them. We have already mentioned, in a previous chapter, the well-known psychopath who was finally apprehended for murder and who had, during the course of his life, committed hundreds of assaults, rapes, and other indecent acts including torture, on a variety of young girls, without ever being brought to justice. Indeed, as was noted then, these acts never came to the notice of the police. It would seem therefore, that a person may, with a fair degree of safety, indulge in a career of crime without having to fear the consequences very much. The people who are caught tend to be the stupid, the ill-taught and, frequently, the 'old lags', where rather different psychological conditions prevail which we will discuss at a later stage.

The question remains, therefore: why do most people lead relatively blameless lives, rather than indulging in a career of crime? It is well known to most people that there are simply not enough policemen in the country to discourage everyone from evil-doing if the predisposition is there; as Napoleon said, you can do everything with bayonets, except sit on them. What, then, causes the astonishing level of decent, moral, law-abiding behaviour which prevails in our society? Why is it that criminal activity, far from being universal is restricted to a small proportion of the population, probably less than ten per cent?

One answer which is very frequently given is that people refrain from careers of crime because there is in them a kind of 'inner guiding light', a 'conscience', a 'superego', which directs them to behave in a moral and law-abiding manner. Descriptively, an hypothesis of this sort is very appealing. Surely the reason that we do not steal under conditions when it is almost certain we would never be caught, must be that there is something in us which restrains us from doing so. Whether we call this something a conscience or a guiding light, or a superego, does not make very much difference. It seems clear that there is something of this sort in us which is far more powerful in controlling behaviour than the rather abstract fear of the policeman and the magistrate. However, a theory of this kind is not particularly useful, for two reasons. In the first place, we do not know what this force is or how we can measure it; and, in the second place, we do not know how it originates, or how we can produce it in other people. There is, of course, one further objection: why is it that this conscience, or inner guiding light, appears to be so strong in some people and so weak in others? What is it that determines its strength?

The answer, briefly, seems to lie in the fact that human beings appear to have two distinctive learning processes. The first of these is one with which everyone is familiar; it is related to problem-solving and, therefore, to hedonism, and it says simply that, in general, those activities which are pleasurable and which are rewarded will be learned, whereas activities which are not pleasurable and which are not rewarded will not be learned. This kind of learning might also be called rational learning. You want to learn to ride a bicycle and every correct step in the process of learning this is rewarded because you are conscious of the fact that you are coming nearer and nearer to your desired aim. Consequently, the correct movements are learned and incorrect ones fail to be learned. There is no essential difficulty in understanding this process.

The other type of learning, the process of conditioning, is rather different. It seems to work not by reinforcement but rather by contiguity. Two stimuli are associated because they occur close together in time or space, not because they are rewarded in any sense of the term. Take again the typical case of GSR conditioning in which the response is an increase in conductivity of the skin of the hand, in response to the unconditioned stimulus which may be electric shock, or some other form of unpleasant stimulation. If the shock is preceded by, say, a light which flashes in front of the subject, then very soon an association will be formed between the light and the unconditioned, autonomic reaction mediating the increase in conductivity of the skin. But nowhere is there any kind of reward or reinforcement offered. The only thing that happens is that two stimuli are placed in a relation of contiguity. Thus we may differentiate between what we call learning and what we call conditioning; in the one case we have reinforcement, in the other we have contiguity without reinforcement. This distinction is accepted as fact by many psychologists, although it is probably not quite as complete and profound as we have made it sound in our rather simplified version of this theory.*

It is interesting to note that this distinction between learning and conditioning corresponds rather well to a very profound physiological differentiation within the nervous system. We have, first of all, the central nervous system, which mediates essentially the reception of incoming impulses which transmit sensory information, and which is also concerned with outgoing impulses which activate the skeletal muscles, sometimes called the striped muscles from their striated appearance. It is this system which is essentially involved in *learning*. We also have, however, the autonomic nervous system, which is concerned with the glands and the smooth, or involuntary muscles. It is this latter system which is primarily involved in *conditioning*. On the whole, we may further say that the activity of the central nervous system tends to be voluntary; that of the autonomic nervous system, involuntary. Psychoanalysts, too,

* The view here taken is not dissimilar to that put forward by O. H. Mowrer in his book, *Learning Theory and Personality Dynamics*. There are, of course, many alternative theories and the whole matter is under much discussion by learning theorists. It is not essential for Mowrer's view to be correct in order to make use of the conditioning paradigm in the way that we have done in these pages; nevertheless I believe that something very much like Mowrer's view is a good approximation to the truth.

have recognized the existence of these two systems. Trial-and-error learning is very similar to what Freud has called the 'pleasure principle', whereas conditioning is more closely related to the 'reality principle'; in other words, as Mowrer has put it:

Living organisms acquire conditioned responses or emotions not because it is pleasant to do so but because it is *realistic*. It is certainly not pleasant to be afraid, for example, but it is often very helpful, from the standpoint of personal survival. At the same time, it is biologically useful for living organisms to be able to learn those responses which reduce their drives, regardless of whether these drives be primary (as in the case of hunger) or secondary (as in the case of fear); but it apparently is quite necessary that the neural mechanism which mediates this kind of learning be different from the mechanism whereby emotional, or 'attitudinal' learning comes about.[36]

Mowrer also likens the difference between learning and conditioning to the distinction between *teaching* and *training*.

Teaching may be defined as a process whereby one individual helps another learn to solve a problem more quickly or effectively than would be likely on the basis of that individual's own unaided, trial-and-error efforts. Here we are dealing with 'items of culture' which are individually helpful. Training, by contrast, may be thought of as involving learning whose primary objective is social rather than individual. In this connection one naturally thinks of 'items of culture' which are associated with such words as 'morality', 'character', 'social responsibility', etc. Such a distinction as the one here proposed between teaching and training is helpful in deciding the oft-debated question of as to whether 'indoctrination' is a legitimate function of education. It is also relevant to some of the issues which have arisen between progressive education and more traditional educational philosophies.[36]

The distinction between learning and conditioning is extremely important, even if we are unwilling to take it to quite the same length as does Mowrer. It will be seen that our objections to the theory that people behave morally because they fear the retribution from society, are essentially directed against the assumption that we are concerned with a process of learning. It is learning which is concerned with the temporal relation between rewarding and punishing outcomes and, as we have seen, if we assume that moral behaviour is learned, then we have no real way out of this particular difficulty. The situation would be entirely different, however, if we were to assume that moral behaviour, instead of being learned, is conditioned.

We may illustrate the way in which we consider conditioning to work in the production of a conscience by looking briefly at a very famous experiment carried out by Professor J. B. Watson, one of the originators of the behaviourist school of psychological thought shortly after the First World War. He was concerned not with criminal behaviour but rather with the genesis of neurotic disorders, particularly the unreasoning fears or phobias which are so frequently found in neurotics. His hypothesis was that these neurotic fears are essentially conditioned fear reactions and he attempted to demonstrate it in the following manner. He selected a boy eleven month of age, called Albert; little Albert was particularly fond of white rats and often played with them. Watson tried to inculcate in Albert a pathological fear of rats. He proceeded to do this by standing behind Albert with a metal bar in one hand and a hammer in the other. Whenever Albert reached out for the rats to play with them, Watson would hit the bar with the hammer. In this situation, the rat constitutes the conditioned stimulus, very much as the bell does in Pavlov's experiments with the salivating dogs; the very loud noise produced by the hammer striking the bar constitutes the unconditioned stimulus which produces a reaction of fear, withdrawal, whimpering and crying. By always associating the conditioned and the unconditioned stimulus over a given period of time, Watson argued that in due course he would produce a fear reaction to the conditioned stimulus when presented alone. This is precisely what happened. He found that after a few pairings of the two stimuli Albert would begin to cringe when the rats were introduced, would try to crawl away, cry, and show all the signs of a strong fear of these animals. This fear response persisted for a long period of time and even extended, as we would have expected it to, on the principle of stimulus generalization discussed earlier, to other furry objects, such as rabbits and a teddy bear. Thus Watson showed that, through a simple process of Pavlovian conditioning, he could produce a strong phobic reaction in little Albert.[37] Before we go on to show how Albert's phobic reaction may be extinguished, let us see for the moment how much light this experiment sheds on the possible growth of a conscience.

Consider the case of the very young child. He has to learn a great number of different things, by means of trial-and-error. As we have pointed out before, there is no real difficulty in accounting for this, because all correct responses tend to be rewarded immediately and incorrect ones, not being rewarded, will tend to drop out; gradually his performance will improve, and he will learn whatever he wishes to. But there are also many other behaviour patterns which he has to acquire, not so much because he wants to, but because society insists that he should. He has to keep clean, he has to learn to use the toilet, he has to refrain from overt aggressive and sexual impulses, and so on. The list of these socially required activities is almost endless. Clearly, learning, as defined earlier, does not come into this very much, because the child is not usually rewarded for carrying out these activities: quite the contrary. He is rewarded, in a sense, for not carrying them out, because in that case carrying them out is what he wishes to do. If somebody annoys him, he wants to punch him in the nose; if he feels like it, he wants to defecate and urinate wherever he happens to be without interrupting his game to go to the toilet. In other words, reinforcement follows immediately upon his disregard of these social mores, the patterns of behaviour which are desirable from the point of view of society. How, then, can the individual ever become socialized?

Suppose now that our little boy misbehaves. Immediately his mother will give him a smack, or stand him in the corner, or send him off to his room, or inflict one of the many punishments which have become customary with parents over the centuries. In this case, the particular asocial or antisocial activity in which he has been indulging is immediately followed by a strong, pain-producing stimulus and we have exactly the same situation as we had in the case of little Albert. The conditioned stimulus is a particular kind of activity in which the child has been indulging; the unconditioned stimulus is the slap, or whatever constitutes the punishment in this case, and the response is the pain and fear produced in the young child. By analogy with the experience of little Albert, we would expect conditioning to take place, so that from then on this particular type of activity would be followed by a conditioned fear response. After a few repetitions, this fear response should be sufficiently strong to keep the child from indulging in that type of activity again, just as little Albert was prevented from indulging in his customary play with the white rats.

There are, of course, many such activities which are punished; exactly the same situation hardly ever recurs twice. Nevertheless, we would expect a fairly general reaction of fear and autonomic 'unpleasure' to become associated with all antisocial activities, because of the process of stimulus generalization which we have referred to so many times before. In fact, stimulus generalization would be expected to be enhanced considerably by the process of 'naming', which parents usually indulge in. Every time the little child misbehaves, its misbehaviour is labelled 'bad', 'naughty', 'wicked', or whatever the term chosen by the parents might be. Through this verbal labelling the child is helped in the generalization process and finally groups all these activities together by association as being potentially dangerous, punishment-producing, and particularly as being productive of conditioned anxiety and fear responses. Thus our little child grows up, gradually acquiring a repertoire of conditioned fear responses to a wide set of different behaviour patterns, all of which have one thing in common – that they are disapproved of by parents and teachers, siblings and peers, and that they have, in the past, frequently been associated with punishment and, therefore, with the consequent autonomic upheaval.

What will happen when the child is in a situation where temptation is strong to do one of these forbidden things? The answer is, of course, that he will tend to go and do it. But as he approaches the object arousing the temptation, there should also be a strong upsurge of the conditioned emotional reaction, the fear or anxiety which has become conditioned to his approach to such an object under such circumstances. The strength of this fear-anxiety reaction should be sufficient to deter him from pursuing his antisocial activities any further. If it is indeed strong enough, then he will desist; if it is not, he will carry on, in spite of the increasing strength of the fear-anxiety response. It will be seen, therefore, that whether he does or does not behave in a socially approved manner depends essentially on the strength of the temptation and on the strength of the conditioned avoidance reaction which has been built into him, as it were, through a process of training or conditioning.

Some people doubt whether autonomic reactions of this kind can indeed be strong enough to have this effect. The empirical evidence suggests that autonomic reactions of anxiety and fear are very powerful indeed. It is well known that many neurotics suffering from anxiety, from phobic fears, and from reactive depression, all of which are conditioned responses of this type, prefer to commit suicide rather than go on living with these fears and anxieties. There is little doubt, therefore, that they are very strong deterrents and that they possess to the full the strength needed to fulfill their hypothetical function in our scheme.[37] Other critics feel that, while this may be true of some special groups of people who happen to be suffering from neurotic disorders, a normal person does not have these conditioned reactions. This also is untrue, as can be shown by experiments in the laboratory. Here let me appeal, for the sake of illustration, to a very simple game which can be bought in most British toyshops. The game is called 'Contraband' and it consists of a number of cards on which are shown pictures of cameras, jewels, watches, and other precious articles, as well as the monetary value of these articles. Every player is dealt a number of these cards and one player is appointed as the Customs Inspector. The essence of the game is that each person hands on to the next person one card, and that he has to declare the value of this card to the Customs Inspector. The Inspector can accept the declaration or, if he suspects that the declaration is under-valued, he can demand to see the card. If the card has been correctly declared, the Customs official is penalized; if it has been incorrectly declared, the player who has made the declaration is penalized. It pays the player, when handing over a valuable card, to declare something less valuable, and, of course, the Customs official must be on the alert and try to detect this.

There is clearly nothing immoral or illegal about declaring the wrong value for a card; in fact, the whole game is built on the principle that the players should try to do this. However, most people, having been brought up to regard lying, cheating and trickery as being bad, find it extremely difficult to adopt a different point of view in respect to this game. There is one card in particular, the Crown Jewels, the most valuable of all, which is almost never correctly declared because it would cost the player too much. Yet very few people indeed are able to remain calm and give the wrong declaration for the Crown Jewels. The majority blush, stammer, look away from the Customs official, and in other ways betray the autonomic upheaval caused in them by this playful lying.

Most people will know that trying to smuggle something through the Customs in earnest gives rise to even greater autonomic upheavals, and indeed, most people will be familiar, from their ordinary life experiences, with the anxiety and fear reactions occasioned by behaviour which, while not strictly illegal, is counter to the mores of the society and to the rules by which the individual has been brought up. It so happens that I was brought up in a country where the cutting of potatoes with a knife is discouraged. Even now, when I live in a country where it is quite the customary thing to do, I still feel a slight pang of guilt and anxiety whenever I cut a potato with a knife. This is the lasting effect of early conditioning!

Anecdotal accounts of this kind clearly have no scientific value. However, instead of relying on simple observation of the autonomic effect, let us substitute some electronic recording device, a polygraph, say, which records the electrical conductivity of the skin, heart rate, pulse, blood volume, breathing, and other autonomic reactions. Let us now ask a given individual a number of questions and instruct him to lie in some of his answers. Will it be possible to discriminate the lie responses from the true responses by simply looking at the pattern of autonomic reaction? The answer is that it can be done and, indeed, this is the basis of the 'lie-detector'. Though not infallible, this device tends to give the right answer, at least nine times out of ten, when used by a skilled practitioner. It tends to fail – when it does fail at all – because an individual gets away with a lie because he does not react emotionally to it, so that no particularly suspicious record is obtained of his autonomic behaviour. This is often the case with psychopaths and other individuals who, according to our hypothesis, would be precisely the ones in whom conditioning of the social responses has not yet taken place. There is a good deal of evidence of this kind to suggest that autonomic responses, conditioned according to ordinary Pavlovian conditioning, form the basis of what we would normally call our conscience. Conscience is indeed a conditioned reflex![38]

Let us continue with our analysis of the conditioning of moral and social responses. How does our account differ from one that posits a process of learning, and regards the intervention of the policeman and the magistrate and the possibility of prison or a fine as the essential feature of social behaviour? The first and most obvious difference, of course, is the difference relating to the time-interval which elapses between crime and punishment. A crime is committed; it takes a long time before the police are notified, before the culprit is detected, brought before the magistrate, sentenced, and finally sent to prison. All of this may take several months or, in some cases, even several years. But clearly the immediate gain of the crime is not outweighed by the gaol sentence which ultimately comes, possibly at the end of several years. The autonomic anxiety and fear reaction which is aroused by the crime happens immediately, however, and precedes any possible gain that the criminal might derive from his action. Time, therefore, is on the side of the angels in this case; the severity of the unpleasant reaction produced by the crime is enhanced by the immediacy of this reaction, whereas the gain may be delayed. Under these conditions, therefore, the autonomic reaction, even though it may not be terribly strong, has a powerful advantage over the ordinary legal process. Conscience can make cowards of us all!

The second difference is that the punishment of crime, in the ordinary legal sense, is a very haphazard affair. It may or may not happen and in the usual case, indeed, it does not happen. Certainly far less than half of all crimes are reported, detected, and brought home to the criminal.* The autonomic reaction, on the other hand, is not only immediate but also inevitable. Whenever an individual commits a crime, the autonomic reaction will occur. The inevitability of this occurrence makes it a far stronger threat to the criminal than haphazard processes of law.

* In London the proportion is only about 25 per cent. In Texas murder cases less than 10 per cent of the murderers are apprehended and punished; in some cities the comparable figure is less than one per cent.

A third important difference is that the punishment, in the ordinary sense, always follows the crime; the autonomic fear-anxiety reaction, however, precedes the crime. It follows upon the very conception of the crime or its preparation and may, therefore, be very influential in keeping the crime from being committed at all. Consider the youth who has been reasonably strictly brought up and who has developed very strong autonomic reactions to the thought of overt sexual relations. Imagine that one day he decides to go to a prostitute, which he has never done before in his life. The very thought produces an immediate, intensely unpleasant autonomic reaction and the closer he comes to the place where the prostitute is situated, the greater his reaction will become. It acts, therefore, as a powerful deterrent long before he has a chance to indulge in the particular immoral and antisocial activity which he is contemplating. As a deterrent, therefore, we must consider that the autonomic reaction, the conditioned conscience, of the criminal *in spe* has it all the way over the forces of law and order.

In the next chapter we will attempt to show that it is the person who fails to develop conditioned moral and social responses, due to his low conditionability and his extraversion, who tends to become the psychopath and the criminal. We will also try to show that a high degree of emotionality or neuroticism is a very important influence in this process, in the sense that it provides a higher drive for the person concerned to carry out his crimes. Before going on to this demonstration, and to a discussion of the empirical evidence available in relation to our case, however, it may be useful to discuss one particular experiment carried out in the laboratory, using rats, which serves to illustrate the kind of hypothesis with which we are dealing. In this experiment we use two strains of rats, selectively bred to be relatively very emotional and very unemotional. In highly anthropomorphic terms, the former would perhaps correspond to a neurotic type of person, the latter to a very stable kind of person.

The aim of the experiment was to teach the animals a particular rule of conduct corresponding to the rules of conduct which we try to inculcate in our children. The apparatus used consisted of a box-like compartment with a glass front; the floor consisted of a metal grille through which an electric shock could be administered. Food, in the form of pellets containing equal amounts of rat food and sucrose, could be made available in a small trough at one end of the apparatus. The hungry animals were put into the apparatus and taught to go to the food trough whenever a buzzer sounded. This buzzer lasted for two seconds and, just as it terminated, a pellet of food was dropped into the trough. Buzzer and food were presented at regular intervals, ten times per day over a period of ten days, and all rats learned to run to the trough as soon as the buzzer was sounded.

At this point in the training, the rule we mentioned above was introduced, to the effect that the rats were henceforth not to touch the food for a period of three seconds after it appeared in the trough. One might consider this as a kind of rat 'etiquette', according to which it was not 'polite' to eat until the prescribed length of time had elapsed. But the rat subjects could not, of course, be told about this rule, so conditions were established which were calculated to teach it to them. What was done was simply this. If the rat took the food within the forbidden three-second interval, it received two seconds of shock from the floor of the apparatus; in other words, the rats were 'punished' for eating within the taboo period, but were free to eat without punishment if they waited a minimum of three seconds after the food appeared. The punishment came immediately after the taboo period ended: that is to say, three seconds after the food was presented.

Animals can react in three ways to this experimental situation. First, they can take the food within the danger period and get shocked; this we may call the delinquent, or psychopathic reaction. Secondly, they can avoid the shock by not eating at all; this may be called the 'dysthymic' reaction, because it resembles the over-fearful behaviour of the anxiety neurotic, the phobic patient, or the dysthymic generally. Thirdly, the rats can wait the three seconds and then eat, thus avoiding the shock but nevertheless obtaining the food; this may be called the 'normal' or 'integrative' reaction. Psychopathic or dysthymic reactions we may call 'non-integrative'. It might at first be thought that the psychopathic rat simply has not learned that a shock is coming and that, therefore, his behaviour is due to a failure of cognitive control. However, it is quite obvious from his behaviour that this is not so. He knows perfectly well that the shock is coming; he reacts bodily in such a way as to minimize a shock, and indeed, if we may be permitted to be somewhat anthropomorphic, he often looks at the experimenter defiantly, as if to say, 'You can do your best, but I'm still going to get this food'. In some ways this reaction is very similar to that of the 'spiv' or the juvenile delinquent, who is up before the magistrate in court, who knows he is going to be punished, but who is still defying society.

Conversely, the dysthymic rat slinks away to the far corner of the box, to be as far as possible from the source of danger, and cowers there in abject fear and trembling. According to our theory, the dysthymic rat has been over-conditioned, as it were, to the fear-producing stimulus; it has over-generalized the conditioning stimulus and is now suffering from an inappropriately severe autonomic reaction. The psychopathic rat, on the other hand, has failed to form the proper conditioned response, and although it knows perfectly well (if we may be allowed to put it in this anthropomorphic way again) that the shock is coming, it nevertheless does not anticipate it with its autonomic system, as it were; consequently it braves the shock and eats in the forbidden period. The normal, or integrative, rat has conditioned sufficiently but not too much, and has, therefore, learned to behave as we have dictated.

It is interesting to note the difference between the emotional and the non-emotional animal. We find that the non-emotional animals include a far larger proportion of normal reactors, that is, animals who wait the three seconds and then eat the food. The group of emotional animals includes a far larger proportion of psychopathic and dysthymic reactors. Figures 18 and 19 show this very clearly in diagrammatic form. The first of these figures shows the results when a strong shock is used; the second figure shows the results when a weak shock is used. In both cases it is quite clear that the abnormal, non-integrative reactions grow more quickly and strongly with emotional animals, than in the non-emotional animals.

How can we explain this difference between emotional and non-emotional animals? One possible answer to this question may be put very simply, by saying that anxiety, fear, and emotion generally, is a drive. The reader may remember our earlier discussion of the general formula: performance = habit × drive. It is easy to demonstrate experimentally that anxiety or conditioned fear responses act as a drive, by demonstrating that they produce a certain amount of performance. A typical experiment runs something like this. The animal is put in a box which has two compartments separated by a door. The animal learns to open this door by manipulating a catch, enabling him to go into the other compartment and thus escape from electric shock administered in the first compartment. Having learned this trick, the animal is then presented with a flickering light which always precedes the shock. In this way we set up in the animal a conditioned fear reaction to the appearance of the flickering light. When this has been set up by pairing the two some ten or twenty times, we then present the flickering light by itself without reinforcing it with electric shock. Sure enough, the rat immediately reacts to the flickering light by opening the door and escaping into the other compartment. We now have the performance, which at first followed only the onset of the shock, coming after the conditioned anxiety response pro-

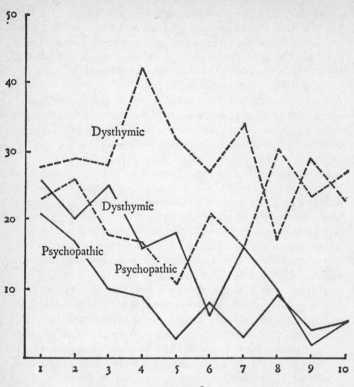

FIGURE 18

Development of dysthymic and psychopathic reactions of emotional rats (broken lines) and unemotional rats (solid lines) under *strong* shock. The ordinate shows the number of responses on ten successive days. From *Behav. Res. & Therapy*, 1963, *1*, 205.

duced by the conditioned stimulus, the flickering light. The light, therefore, has acquired drive properties, and we may say that anxiety, or fear, or emotion, acts as any other drive does.

Apply this now to the condition of the rat in our original experiment. When the buzzer sounds and the food is dropped into the tray, the animal is confronted with two powerful drives. One is the food drive, giving rise to the temptation of going and eating at once; the other is the conditioned fear drive, which would keep the animal away from the food. Which of these two drives is the stronger depends on the amount of conditioning that has taken place. If the animal has conditioned well, then the aversive drive is stronger; if he has not conditioned well, then the aversive drive

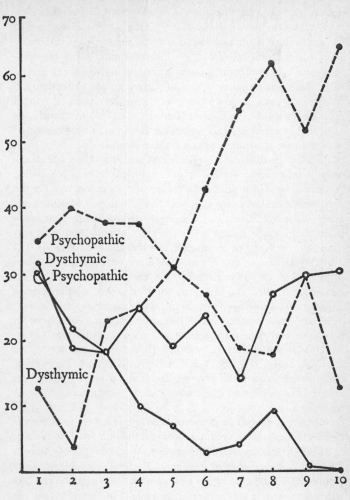

FIGURE 19

Development of dysthymic and psychopathic reactions of emotional rats (broken lines) and unemotional rats (solid lines) under *weak* shock. The ordinate shows the number of responses on ten successive days. From *Behav. Res. & Therapy*, 1963, *1*, 204.

is weaker. Thus a balance between temptation and deterrence is determined essentially by the amount of conditioning that has taken place. Both temptation and deterrent will be stronger in the emotional rat than in the non-emotional rat, because of the emotion accompanying both drives. In quite arbitrary numerical terms, let us say that temptation in psychopathic, normal, and dysthymic rats is at a strength of about 5 for the non-emotional, and 10 for the emotional animals. Let us say that the forces of deterrence are 3 for the non-emotional, psychopathic rats, 5 for the nonemotional rats, and 7 for the non-emotional dysthymic rats. And let us also assume that the forces of deterrence are, respectively, 6 for the emotional, psychopathic rats, 10 for the emotional normal rats, and 14 for the emotional dysthymic rats. In other words, we have simply doubled all the values for the emotional as compared with the non-emotional animals. It will be clear that under these conditions, the difference in points between temptation and deterrence is much larger for the emotional rats; for the psychopathic rats it will be 4 instead of 2, in favour of temptation, and for the dysthymic rats it will be 4 as opposed to 2, in favour of deterrence. Under these conditions, it is not unexpected to find that the emotional rats include a large proportion of animals succumbing to temptation or being over-deterred, and that the normal reaction is relatively lacking in this group. This demonstration and this line of reasoning are important, because they suggest that among criminals we will find a high porportion of people who are strong on emotionality or neuroticism and who, therefore, have a very labile autonomic system. We will see, later on, that this expectation is fulfilled and that, among criminals, a good proportion can be found who are effectively neurotic. In commonsense terms, we might say that strong emotions make normal integrative behaviour more difficult and make it more likely that a given person will behave in a manner which is not, over the long run, in his own best interests.[39]

We have so far talked about conscience as if it were to be identified exclusively as the agent that makes it difficult for us to indulge in forbidden, antisocial, and previously punished types of conduct. There is, however, another meaning to the term as used in ordinary conversation, and that is the tendency to show a guilty reaction when a person has overstepped the mark, as it were, and has indulged in such activities. Can we also account for the existence of guilt in terms of conditioning procedures, and how is this guilt related to the tendency to abort criminal and antisocial types of behaviour? On *a priori* grounds, we might perhaps anticipate that punishment which is administered before a given type of activity is indulged in would lead to a pronounced reluctance later on to indulge in that particular activity, whereas punishment which is administered during the activity, i.e., after it has begun would perhaps lead to later guilt feelings. There is indeed some experimental evidence to show that this may be true.

Experiments were carried out by Richard L. Solomon and some of his colleagues at Harvard University, using six-months-old puppies. Later experiments have also been carried out with young children, but we shall concentrate here on the animal experiments. These were conducted in so-called 'taboo situations', held in a training room, fairly sound-proof, and equipped with a one-way mirror. A chair was placed in a corner of the room and in front of each front leg of the chair were placed two small dishes. The experimenter sat in the chair, holding in his hand a rolled up newspaper with which he could swat the puppies on the rump. Each of the puppies was deprived of food for two days and was then brought into the experimental room. In one of the dishes had been placed boiled horse meat, which was very much liked by the puppies, whereas in the other dish was placed a much less well liked commercial dog food. The puppies usually made straight for the horse meat, but as they touched it they were swatted by the experimenter. If one gentle blow was not enough, then the puppy was swatted again and again until he finally gave up his attempts to eat the horse meat. Usually several further attempts were made, until finally the puppies turned to the commercial dog food, which they could eat without being swatted.

This training was carried on for several days, until the puppies had firmly learned the taboo on horse meat. The experimenter then turned to what was called the 'temptation testing' phase. Again the puppies were deprived of food for two days and then brought to the room, but this time with the experimenter absent. Again a choice had to be made between a dish of boiled horse meat and a few pellets of dog food. The puppies soon gobbled up the dog food, then began to react to the large dish of horse meat. In Solomon's words:

Some puppies would circle the dish over and over again. Some puppies walked around the room with their eyes towards the wall, not looking at the dish. Other puppies got down on their bellies and slowly crawled forward, barking and whining. There was a large range of variability in the emotional behaviour of the puppies in the presence of the tabooed horse meat. We measured resistance to temptation as the number of seconds or minutes which passed by before the subject ate the tabooed food.

The puppies were allowed half an hour a day in the experimental room. If they did not eat the horse meat by that time, they were brought back to their home cages, were not fed, and, a day later, were introduced again into the experimental room. This continued until the puppy finally violated the taboo and ate the horse meat, or until he had fasted so long that he had to be fed in his cage, in order to keep him alive.

There was a very great range of resistance to temptation. The shortest period of time it took a puppy to overcome his training and eat the horse meat was six minutes, and the longest period of time was sixteen days without eating, after which time the experiment had to be stopped and the puppy fed in his home cage. This great range of variability made it possible to test the influence of various experimental conditions on the growth of conscience in these puppies. For instance, it was shown that when the puppies were hand-fed throughout their early life by the experimenter, then they developed a conscience much more strongly than did other animals which had been machine-fed.

Solomon separated resistance to temptation from guilt, and he avoided, in his discussion, the use of the term 'conscience', which he suggested might be a compound of the two manifestations.

For example, in the first litter we ran, we found that when a puppy did kick over the traces and eat the horse meat, he did so with his tail wagging the whole time; and after he ate the horse meat, when the experimenter came into the room, the puppy greeted him with tail wags and with no obvious distress. On the other hand, in some preliminary work we did, we noticed that some pups showed much more emotional disturbance after they ate the horse meat than when they were approaching it. We were able to relate this to uncontrolled differences in training techniques.

Apparently when the puppies were walloped just when they *approached* the tabooed food, they built up a high resistance to temptation. However, when such puppies did kick over the traces, they showed no emotional upset following the crime. On the other hand, when the puppies were left to eat half the horse meat before being walloped, then one could still establish an avoidance of the horse meat. In the case of these puppies, however, there was much more emotional disturbance following the crime, and these, Solomon suggested, could be called guilt reactions. The presence of the experimenter was not required to elicit these reactions, although his presence seemed to intensify them when he did finally come into the room after the 'crime' had been committed. 'Therefore we believe that the conditions for the establishment of strong resistance to temptation as contrasted with the capacity to experience strong guilt reactions, is a function of both the intensity of punishment and the time during the approach and consummatory response-sequence at which the punishment is administered.'

Solomon goes on to speculate that delayed punishment is probably not very effective in producing a very high level of resistance to temptation, but might be more effective in producing emotional reactions of guilt after the commission of the crime. On the other hand, he says, it is clear that punishment introduced after the animal eats quite a bit of the horse meat does operate backward in time, and it does produce aversion and the disruption of approach responses. These approach responses, however, do not seem to be as reliably broken up by such delayed punishment.

We feel that this observation is important, since it represents two major types of socialisation techniques used by parents. In one case, the parent traps the child into the commission of the tabooed act, so that the child can be effectively punished, the hope being that this will prevent the child from performing it again. The other technique is to watch the child closely, to try to anticipate when the child intends to do something wrong and punish the child during the incipient stages. Each of these techniques, according to our observation of these puppies, leads to a very different outcome with regard to the components of 'conscience'.

Solomon thus assumed that 'conscience' has two components, one the ability to resist temptation and the other the susceptibility to guilt reactions. He further assumed that these two components are partially independent, and that by appropriate training procedures, organisms can be produced which have high resistance to temptation but low susceptibility to guilt reactions, high resistance to temptation along with high susceptibility to guilt reactions, low resistance to temptation and low susceptibility to guilt, and low resistance to temptation along with high susceptibility to guilt reactions. 'It is easy to examine these four classes of outcome and see four clinically important combinations in the neuroses, as well as the creation of a psychopath'. Solomon himself does not link up his results particularly with ease of conditioning, but he does refer to the fact that different breeds of dogs differ very much in the ease with which they acquire a 'conscience'. Thus, for instance, Shetland sheepdogs are especially sensitive to reprimand, and taboos can apparently be established with just one frightening experience and are then extremely resistant to extinction. On the other hand, he reports, Basenjis seem to be constitutional psychopaths and it is very difficult to maintain taboos in such dogs. All these findings, then, are in very good agreement with our general outline.[40]

6 Crime and Conditioning

'What sort of things do *you* remember best?' Alice ventured to ask.

'Oh, things that happened the week after next,' the Queen replied in a careless tone. 'For instance, now,' she went on, sticking a large piece of plaster on her finger as she spoke, 'there's the King's Messenger. He's in prison now, being punished: and the trial doesn't even begin till next Wednesday: and of course the crime comes last of all.'

'Suppose he never commits the crime?' said Alice.

'That would be all the better, wouldn't it?' the Queen said, as she bound the plaster round her finger with a bit of ribbon.

THROUGH THE LOOKING-GLASS

We have now propounded our theory, that it is conscience which is, in the main, instrumental in making us behave in a moral and socially acceptable manner; that this conscience is the combination and culmination of a long process of conditioning; and that failure on the part of the person to become conditioned is likely to be a prominent cause in his running a-foul of the law and of the social mores generally. We must now turn to a consideration of the evidence which may be in favour of, or counter to, this hypothesis, and we must also discuss some of the consequences which follow from it. Let us first have a good look at the evidence.

Now there are several deductions which we can make from our theory. In the first place, we would expect conditioning experiments to show that psychopaths and extraverts generally manifest less conditioning in these experimental situations than do normal people or dysthymic neurotics. Similarly, if we studied groups of criminals, we would also expect to find that they would be more difficult to condition than non-criminals. We have already noted, in a previous chapter, that extraverted people, both neurotic and normal, are indeed more difficult to condition than are introverted neurotics and normals. It will be remembered that, on the eye-blink conditioning test for instance, it was found that extraverts condition only about fifty per cent as well as introverts, and roughly similar results have been found with other types of conditioning. When we turn to psychopaths specifically, we find that, here too, there is a distinct tendency for such people to show poor conditioning.[41] Lykken, in America, and Tong, in England, have carried out extensive studies of psychopaths and have come to the conclusion that their conditioning is much less effective than that of various control groups. The work of Tong is perhaps more relevant to our hypothesis, because, in his work at Rampton (a hospital for criminal psychopaths), he was in a position to deal with psychopaths who, in addition to having this particular psychiatric label, had also in their actual life histories run a-foul of the law and had been referred to this particular prison hospital. The evidence on conditioning then, as far as it is available, tends to favour our hypothesis. It should be noted, however, that the amount of work that has been done is far from conclusive. Many more studies, involving thousands of criminals, both diagnosed as psychopaths and others, will be required before we can assert that our theory does in fact accord with reality. In particular, it will be necessary to try out a great many different types of conditioning experiments. It will be necessary to vary the parameters we mentioned before, such as the strength of the unconditioned stimulus, the length of time elapsing between the conditioned and the unconditioned stimulus, the spacing of the trials, and so forth. Furthermore, it will be necessary to distinguish between different types of criminals. As we shall see later, our theory is not intended to apply indiscriminately to all criminals, and for some criminals indeed we would predict a greater condition-ability than average. This exception to our rule will be discussed later on in this chapter; here let us simply note that while the evidence from conditioning experiments favours our theory, it is by no means sufficient to establish it firmly as a general law. It is left as a theory for which some slight support is available.

Another deduction from our theory is, of course, the more general one that people who commit crimes and other antisocial or asocial acts would, on the whole, be more extraverted than people who refrain from carrying out such acts. Here the evidence is fortunately more extensive, indeed, so extensive that we can look at only a few typical studies. Let us begin by looking at the problem of traffic accidents and violations of traffic rules. In an earlier chapter, we mentioned the fact that severe violation of the traffic laws tends to be the responsibility of people who have also run a-foul of the law in many other ways. What about less severe violations of the traffic code? There is an interesting study carried out by Bernard J. Fine of the U.S. Army Research Institute of Environmental Medicine, which was planned specifically to test this hypothesis. As subjects, he used 993 male freshmen in the general college of the University of Minnesota, who had been administered a personality questionnaire. For each of these students information was available regarding the date, type, number, and place of occurrence of traffic accidents and traffic violations. On the basis of the questionnaire responses, Fine grouped his subjects into the most extraverted, the most introverted, and an intermediate group, each constituting roughly one-third of the total group. He found that the extraverts had significantly more accidents and were also guilty of more traffic violations than were the intermediates or the introverts.[42]

Another study was reported by S. Biesheuvel and N. E. White, from the National Institute for Personnel Research in South Africa. They studied an accident group of 200 pilots in training who had been involved in flying accidents at elementary and advanced flying schools. As a control, they used 400 men who had completed both elementary and advanced training with an accident-free record. Comparison between the two groups showed significant differences, both for emotionality and also for extraversion. Those in the accident group were more emotional, more distractable, they tended to act on impulse, and were generally less cautious. Their behaviour was more variable and they were more apt to be influenced by the mood of the moment. These are all extraverted tendencies which, added to the strong emotionality of the accident-prone group, put them squarely into the psychopathic quadrant of our personality field.[43]

Consider now a rather different field altogether. Sexual promiscuity is not considered a crime, but rather a sin; nevertheless, it is obviously a case of contravening the social morality which has been preached to us from early childhood and consequently we would expect the more extraverted to be more promiscuous. One attempt to study this question was made by Sybil B. G. Eysenck, who contrasted the personalities of married and unmarried mothers. Personality questionnaires were administered to 100 mothers in the maternity wards of a large London hospital. The same questionnaire was administered to unmarried mothers in various moral welfare homes, who were seen after their confinements. The unmarried mothers were found to be both more extraverted and also to have much higher degrees of emotionality or neuroticism than did the married mothers. When compared with the general population norms too, it was found again that the unmarried mothers tended to fall into the psychopathic quadrant, i.e., were high on neuroticism and high on extraversion. Here too, then, our general hypothesis is verified.[44]

Traffic violators, people who suffer accidents, and unmarried mothers – these may seem to be a little outside the more general field of this book because, while their conduct is certainly counter to certain rules and precepts of our society, they have not committed any actual crimes. What would happen if we gave our questionnaire to actual criminals? One such study has been done by Syed, who tested a hundred women criminals in a large London prison. He found that, very much as predicted, they fell predominantly and significantly into the psychopathic quadrant, having high scores on extraversion and high scores on emotionality. Figure 6 shows the relative position of Syed's group, as well as that studied by Sybil B. G. Eysenck, in relation to various normal and neurotic groups; it will be seen that the placing of the unmarried mothers and of the criminal women is very much as could be predicted from our general theory.[45] Many other studies are available, both in America and in England, showing that criminals tend to be high on emotionality or neuroticism. Unfortunately, most of these studies have not used a questionnaire, which would enable us to get an uncontaminated measure of extraversion. However, in a number of cases, there has been used a very extensive questionnaire called the Minnesota Multiphasic Personality Inventory, which contains one scale, the so-called 'psychopathic deviant' scale, which may be relevant in this connexion. It is found, in general, that among criminal prisoners it is this psychopathic deviant scale which, more than any other contained in this inventory, discriminates this group from the normal control groups or even from neurotic groups tested in hospitals. It is also usually found that other scales measuring emotionality or neuroticism give higher scores for criminals than for normals. Here again, therefore, we find some support, at least for our general hypothesis.

Of particular interest is an unpublished study carried out by Frank Warburton, of the University of Manchester. He worked with a group of prisoners in Joliet Penitentiary in Chicago. These men were the most recalcitrant in a prison of some 2,000 inmates and had consistently had their privileges taken away from them. They can thus be described as 'second order prisoners', in the sense that if all the prisoners in the jail had been placed on an island, they would have found it necessary to provide a prison for these men. Warburton administered the Cattell Personality Scales to these men, and found that on five traits, which are grouped under the extraversion heading, four showed a highly elevated score. The fifth, dealing with social behaviour (sociability), did not properly apply to these men, since social behaviour in prison is very different from that outside. Of five traits related to neuroticism, all five showed highly elevated scales. When a combined score was derived for extraversion, and another for neuroticism, taking all scales used into account, these men were found to be very much in the psychopathic quadrant; that is to say, they had high scores on extraversion and very high scores on neuroticism. In addition, objective tests were given by Warburton, yielding results supporting the conclusions derived from the questionnaires.

Further support for this theory of the position of the criminal in the personality framework outlined above comes from a recent book by R. G. Andry, *The Short-Term Offender*. His study was mainly concerned with the personality correlates of recidivism in prisoners serving sentences not exceeding six months, and his main conclusions were that recidivists were characterized by emotional disturbances (neuroticism), and by tough-minded, extrapunitive (extraverted?) behaviour, as well as by immaturity. On the basis of psychological arguments not unlike those to be presented, Andry makes certain suggestions for differential treatment of criminals of these various personality types; they will be only briefly quoted here, as a more detailed discussion will be given later in this book. Andry's first suggestion is that 'among neurotic offenders it is unlikely that recidivism will be reduced by conventional prison treatment but, in fact, may well be increased'; he considers it 'likely that it [recidivism] will be reduced by treatment involving regular psychotherapy (and/or behaviour therapy and chemotherapy)'. His third suggestion is that 'rigid discipline and some degree of punitive treatment over a fairly long period has more chance of modifying the antisocial attitudes of extrapunitive offenders than has any known form of therapy alone (although a combination of both seems indicated)'. We shall see in a later chapter that there exists some experimental evidence to lend at least limited support to these suggestions.

As typical of many studies, we may perhaps discuss, in greater detail, a recent book by T. C. N. Gibbens, of the Maudsley Hospital in London, in which he studied 200 Borstal boys, that is, juvenile delinquents who had committed crimes of some seriousness, who were roughly sixteen to twenty-one years of age, and who had been sentenced to attend the special punitive, corrective institutions commonly referred to as 'Borstals' in England. In addition to intensive psychiatric investigation, Gibbens also administered the Minnesota Multiphasic Personality Inventory and compared the responses of the Borstal boys with those of a control group. As had been expected, it was the psychopathic deviant scale which gave the best discrimination between the groups.

Gibbens also administered an objective test which had previously been shown to be correlated with extraversion, the Porteus Mazes Test. Originally this had been introduced as a test of intelligence;

it consists of a printed maze pattern through which the subject has to find his way, tracing his path with a pencil from start to finish, the score being simply the length of time it takes him for his relative success or failure. Now in this test, the subject has to obey certain rules, he must not lift his pencil from the paper, he must not cross lines printed on the sheet, and he must not cut corners. In terms of our theory, it had been predicted that the extraverted person would be more likely to contravene these rules because of his failure of socialization, due to inadequate conditioning. And, in one or two studies, it had indeed been found that extraverts tended to give higher deviant scores in this test, when it is scored simply for the number of contraventions of the instructions. A special score, the Q score, was introduced by Porteus as being independent of intelligence and as measuring this particular tendency which, incidentally, has also been found to be strong in people who had been subjected to lobotomy, the brain operation which, as we have pointed out earlier, has the effect of making people more extraverted.[46]

Apart from the study by Gibbens which has been discussed, there have been five different investigations studying the scores of delinquents and comparing them with those of non-delinquents. All these studies have been done by Americans, and the findings have been that, on the average, delinquents have a score of about fifty of these contraventions, whereas normals have a score of only about twenty. A similar comparison was made by Gibbens, who found, for delinquents, a score of thirty-five, and for non-delinquents, a score of fourteen. Both, in other words, were much lower than the corresponding American norms, which, itself, may be of interest, in view of the much greater rate of crime in America as compared to England. The important thing to note, however, is that in both the American and the English studies, the delinquents have a much higher score than do the non-delinquents. In other words, we find that in relation to this test, delinquents, as compared with non-delinquents, behave very much as do extraverts when compared with introverts.

Gibbens continued his studies with an assessment of body build. Before we are ready to understand the meaning and significance of this, we will have to digress briefly. When we take even the most casual look at people, one of the first things to impress us is the enormous variability in their bodily configuration or physique. It has been assumed ever since Hippocrates, the famous physician who lived in 430 B.C., that the different types of body build which people show have related both to their temperament and personality, and also to their tendency to develop different diseases. Hippocrates was particularly impressed by the differences between the long, lean type of body build and the short, stocky one; he called the former the habitus phthisicus, or tubercular type, and the other the habitus apoplecticus, or apoplectic type, suggesting that the long, lean person was more prone to tuberculosis and the stocky one to apoplexy and heart disease. Many writers since have followed his lead and we have a large number of different types named in a variety of different ways. The thick-set habitus apoplecticus has been named, among other things, the abdominal type, the digestive type, the nutritive, the phlegmatic, the vital, the hyperplastic, the food type, the connective type, the lateral type; and the habitus phthisicus has been called the cephalic type, the mental type, the cerebral-asthenic type, the sensation type, the linear type, and the asthenic type. Perhaps the most widely accepted typology was that suggested by the German psychiatrist, Kretschmer, shortly after the First World War, who labelled the thick-set type the *pyknic* and the lean, linear type the *leptosome*. He also introduced a third type roughly intermediate between the other two, which he called the *athletic* type. He proceeded to link up this bodily typology with psychiatry, by postulating that psychotics of pyknic body build tended to suffer from manic-depressive insanity, whereas psychotics of leptosomatic body build tended to suffer from schizophrenia. There is indeed some such relation but it is not strong enough to be of any very great use for diagnosis.[47]

More recently, Kretschmer's system was taken over by the American anthropologist and psychologist, W. H. Sheldon, who applied it more widely and particularly related body build to normal personality. He postulated, like Kretschmer, the existence of three main body types, which he called *endomorph*, for the thick-set, pyknic type; *mesomorph*, for the athletic type; and *ectomorph*, for the equivalent of Kretschmer's leptosome. He further postulated that there were three relatively independent factors of bodily growth, and that each person could be rated according to the strength of each of these components on a seven-point scale. Each person is accordingly given a number consisting of three digits which indicates the strength of the three components. Thus, 117 would be a person characterized by an almost complete lack in endomorphy and mesomorphy and a complete dominance of the ectomorphy component. All other combinations are similarly derived in terms of three numbers and it will be seen that there are 343 theoretical possibilities of deriving different somatotypes from these three components. Sheldon reports, however, that only 76 have been encountered by him in actual practice. Sheldon tends to favour photography rather than direct measurement. He lines up his nude subjects, takes photographs of them in a standard position, and then these photographs are rated for the relative contribution of the three components.

Sheldon believes that these components have a different embryological origin. There are three germ layers in the embryo; the ectoderm, endoderm, and mesoderm. Sheldon believes that it is the exaggerated functioning of one of these layers which produces the three types. Taking Kretschmer's pyknic type, for instance, Sheldon maintains that in him the digestive tract, especially the gut, held a more or less predominant position in the organic economy.

In these people, the most manifest external characteristic is a conspicious laying-on of fat, which is an indication of predominance of the absorptive function – the function of the gut – over the energy-expending functions. The functional elements of the digestive system are derived embryologically almost entirely from the endoderm, the innermost of the three original embryonic layers. We can quite naturally, therefore, refer to the extremes of type one as exhibiting a condition of *endomorphy*.

In a similar way, bones, muscles, connective tissue, and the heart and blood vessels were seen by him to predominate overwhelmingly in the variants of type two, which corresponds to Kretschmer's athletics. This type is, therefore, called the mesomorph, as these functions are derived predominantly from the mesoderm, the second embryonic layer. As regards the third type, Kretschmer's leptosome, 'the principal derivatives from the embryonic ectodermal layer are the skin itself, hair and nails, sense organs, and the nervous system, including the brain. Relative to total bodily mass, all these organs are conspicuous in the bodily economy of the extreme variants of type three. Hence we have named them ectomorphs, or persons exhibiting ectomorphy.'

To correspond to these bodily types, Sheldon also posits the existence of three different types of temperament, which he calls viscerotonia, which is supposed to go with the body type of endomorphy; somatotonia, which is supposed to go with the body type of mesomorphy; and cerebrotonia, which is supposed to go with the body type of ectomorphy. A brief description of these three temperaments is as follows.

The viscerotonic is relaxed in posture and movement; he loves physical comfort and eating, has slow reactions, loves polite ceremony and is sociable. He is amiable, greedy for affection and approval, tolerant and complacent, sleeps deeply, is relaxed and extraverted. The somatotonic is assertive, loves physical adventure, is energetic and likes exercise, loves domination and power, likes to take risks and chances, is physically courageous and aggressive and psychologically callous. He is rather ruthless, unrestrained, indifferent to pain, generally noisy and also extraverted. The cerebrotonic loves privacy, is mentally over-intensive, rather restrained, tends to be apprehensive, is rather self-conscious, and dislikes social intercourse. He is hyper-sensitive to pain, sleeps rather poorly, is introverted, and needs solitude when troubled. We may sum up Sheldon's system by saying that the cerebrotonic is the typical introvert, as we have described him before, whereas both the viscerotonic and the somatotonic are extraverts. They differ in that the two types stress different aspects of extraversion. The viscerotonic stresses the *sociability* side, the somatotonic stresses rather the *impulsive* side of extraversion.[48]

Sheldon reports quite high correlations between personality ratings and somatotype ratings of body build, both made by him. Indeed these are so high as to be quite improbable, and it has been pointed out that a person holding a definite theory about the relationship between body build and temperament, rating the same persons with respect to both body build and temperament, is almost bound to find that his ratings are contaminated by his knowledge. Thus the figures reported by Sheldon may mean little more than that he was consistent in applying his theory. Other people have duplicated his work and the general consensus of opinion is that the correlations are in the expected direction, but they are relatively low: at most, about o.3. This indeed is in very good agreement with previous studies by English workers, which have shown, by and large, similar correlations between introversion and the leptosomatic type of body build, and extraversion and the pyknic type of body build. What Sheldon has added essentially is a division of the pyknic or thick-set type of body build into two sub-types: the mesomorphs, whose body build incorporates a great deal of muscle, and the ectomorphs, whose body build incorporates a great deal of fat. As regards personality correlates, his main contribution has been to suggest that the pyknic with the considerable degree of muscle will tend to be impulsive, the pyknic with a good deal of fat, rather sociable.

Body build is determined by hereditary factors to a considerable degree, and its correlation with temperament has sometimes been suggested as proof of the hereditary determination of personality as well. This is not necessarily true. We might simply be dealing with a reaction on the part of the individual concerned to the limitations imposed on him by his body build. As has sometimes been said, the fat boy cannot fight and he cannot run away, so he might just as well be friendly and sociable if he wants to get on in life. In other words, on this hypothesis, we would not say that temperament is inherited as body build is, but rather that the behaviour of the person is determined by the body build which he has inherited, in a rather indirect way. Similarly, we would expect the mesomorphic type of boy to be more adventurous, simply because his strong musculature enables him to do things, to be aggressive, and to indulge in various activities which the fat or the lean boy are unable to do because they lack the appropriate muscular equipment. Heredity would thus play some part in the determination of behaviour, but it would be, as it were, at second remove.

How does all this apply to our problem of criminality and personality? We have already noted that Lombroso studied morphological anomalies in criminals and proposed the doctrine that the criminal, as found in prison, was an atavistic anomaly presenting morbid physical stigmata. We have also noticed that this doctrine is now completely discredited. (It may be noted incidentally that it was less obviously absurd in Lombroso's time than it is now. When he was investigating the nature of criminality there were no mental defective institutions and many mental defectives were in fact in prison, guilty of minor offences of various kinds. At least a certain proportion of mental defectives suffer from quite specific disorders, such as mongolism, which indeed alter their appearance and make them look rather startlingly unlike ordinary people. It is presumably due to the presence of people of this type that Lombroso proposed his doctrine.)

In modern times, the famous American anthropologist, Hooton, studied 17,000 prison and reformatory inmates and measured their body configuration. He found quite significant differences in various body measurements between persons convicted of different types of crime. He found, for instance, that the criminals with pyknic body build (extraverts?) headed the list of crimes for rape, sex offences and assault, but were lowest in murder, whereas the leptosomatic criminals (introverts?) had the highest incidence of murder and robbery but the lowest incidence of crimes such as burglary, assault, rape, and other sex offences. This is interesting, because rape, sex offences, and assault are precisely the impulsive type of crime which we would expect to find in extraverted people who, as we have seen, tend to be of the pyknic type of body build. However, not too much should be made of Hooton's figures, because many different racial strains, in almost pure culture, are found in America, and it is quite possible that different nationalities such as the Italians and the Swedes, for instance, differ both with respect to body build and with respect to the lawbreaking habits which they have acquired in the course of their lives. We cannot, therefore, make any very confident deductions from Hooton's figures.

However, a very well-known pair of American criminologists, Sheldon and Eleanor Glueck, of the Harvard Law School, conducted an enquiry which gave some very important and interesting results. They compared a group of 500 delinquent boys aged eleven to eighteen years with 500 non-delinquent controls who had been matched for age, intelligence, racial origin, and residence in under-privileged neighbourhoods. Comparing anthropometric measurements and somatotype distribution along the lines that Sheldon had pioneered, they found that there was little difference in general body size, but that the delinquent group was considerably more mesomorphic and less ectomorphic than the non-delinquent group.[50]

Sheldon himself, with some of his colleagues, carried out a study in which 200 delinquent youths, somatotyped according to his system, were compared with 4,000 college students. It was found that this sample of delinquents differed very much from the college somatotype distribution, having a distinct massing in the endo-morphic-mesomorphic sector, as compared with the ectomorphic. The students, on the other hand, tended to be ectomorphic rather than either endomorphic or mesomorphic. In terms of our system of temperaments, these findings show the criminals to have body types typical of extraverts, whereas the students had body types typical of introverts.[51]

In England, Epps and Parnell studied a group of 177 young women between the ages of sixteen and twenty-one who were undergoing Borstal training. They compared the body configuration of these young women with 123 university women aged eighteen to twenty-one. They found that delinquents were heavier in body build, were more muscular and fat; in temperament they showed a predominance of somatotonia and viscerotonia. Here also we find a distinct tendency for the criminals to be extraverted compared with the students, who are introverted. [52] It may be added that the Gluecks, in addition to carrying out their studies of body build, also carried out surveys of the main personality traits of their delinquents, and found that their temperaments were, 'Restlessly energetic, impulsive, extraverted, aggressive, destructive'. They also found them to be highly emotional.

We may now continue our discussion of Gibbens' studies. He also somatotyped fifty-eight of his lads, and the resulting distribution of body types is shown in Figure 20. This kind of semi-triangular scheme is customary for presenting data of Sheldon's body types. The numbers inside the diagram refer to various combinations of the three components, and help to identify the particular point in the diagram. It will be seen that nearly all the Borstal lads studied by Gibbens lie in the top, left-hand corner, with very

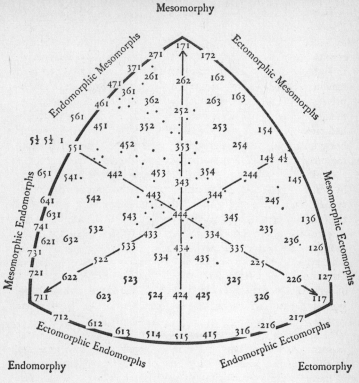

Borstal Lads, 1953.

N = 58

FIGURE 20

Body-build of fifty-eight juvenile delinquents detained in Borstal institutions. Note the preponderance of endomorphic meso-morphs, i.e., thick-set, brawny lads of an athletic stature, and the almost complete absence of ectomorphs, i.e., the slight, lean, 'beanpole' type. From T. C. N. Gibbens, *Psychiatric Studies of Borstal Lads*, Oxford University Press, New York, 1963.

few exceptions; in other words, they are very nearly all endomorphic mesomorphs. For comparison, we may look at 283 Oxford under-graduates, also presented in Gibbens' book. These are shown in Figure 21 and it will be seen that here the endomorphs are, if anything, under-represented and that there is a great number of ectomorphs, a group of people almost entirely missing from the Borstal group. All these figures, both from America and from

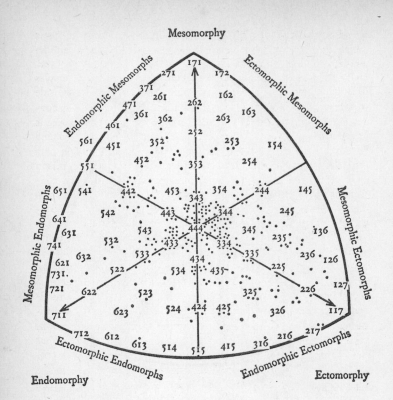

Oxford Undergraduates, 1948–50
N = 283

FIGURE 21

Body-build of 283 Oxford undergraduates. Note the fairly even distribution of body types with perhaps a slight preponderance in the lower right-hand corner, signifying lean and slight body-build. From J. M. Tanner, in G. A. Harrison, J. M. Tanner, J. S. Weiner, and N. Barnicut, *An Introduction to Human Biology*, Clarendon Press, New York, 1963.

England, are in agreement then that criminals, on the whole, tend to be athletic in body build, that is stocky and muscular rather than fat, and that they tend to show a temperamental tendency towards extraversion, particularly towards impulsiveness. These data, therefore, seem to support our general hypothesis.

Are there any contradictory data which might lead us to doubt the validity of our theory? We may perhaps begin by noting that questionnaire studies employing sociability items, that is, items which are usually diagnostic of extraversion, have not, on the whole, produced good differentiation between criminals and normals. Whether this is indeed an argument against our theory is difficult to say. As we pointed out before, it is the impulsive side of extraversion rather than the sociability side which we may consider to be associated with criminal behaviour. However, there is an even more powerful reason for imagining that this unpredicted failure is little more than an artifact. Consider the position of a criminal, particularly a long-term criminal who has been in prison for perhaps ten or twenty years. Imagine his reaction when confronted with questions like the following. 'Would you be very unhappy if you were prevented from making numerous social contacts?' 'Is it difficult to "lose yourself," even at a lively party?' 'Do you like to mix socially with people?' 'Do you like to have many social engagements?' 'Do you generally prefer to take the lead in group activities?' 'Are you inclined to be shy in the presence of the opposite sex?' 'Are you inclined to keep quiet when out in a social group?' 'Can you usually let yourself go and have a hilariously gay time at a party?' If a prisoner, after twenty years incarceration, comes out with a low score of sociability on questions such as these, this is not an altogether unforeseen result, and we need not consider it particularly inimical to our theory.

The same argument, of course, might apply in reverse to the observation which has often been referred to, that prisoners tend to score very high on tests of emotionality or neuroticism. It might be said, not without reason, that scores on questions of this type are high simply because the person answering the questionnaire is in prison; in other words, that it is his incarceration which produces the emotionality rather than the emotionality producing his criminal behaviour, in whole or part. This is not an unreasonable objection, but, on the whole, it may not be entirely correct. It has not been found, for instance, that the scores on emotionality tests rise as a function of the length of time a person has spent in prison. A person imprisoned for ten years does not score any higher than a person who has been in prison only a few days. Of course, it could be that the fact of imprisonment itself rather than the length of the sentence, or the length of time spent in prison, determines the emotional reaction; but again it is doubtful whether this is a very good argument. We have found that even in cases where the violation of the rules of society has been less severe, and where the person has not gone to prison – as in the case of traffic violators or unmarried mothers – there is a considerable degree of emotionality which, quite obviously, could not have been due to their being incarcerated. Again, it might be said that possibly the emotionality in the unmarried mothers is produced by the precarious situation in which they find themselves. This cannot be true of the traffic violators, because there the 'crime' is too slight and the punishment too unimportant to influence responses on a questionnaire of the type used.

Nevertheless, it must be admitted that this is a point which requires much further study. In particular, it would be useful if predictive studies could be carried out with questionnaires; in other words, it would be desirable to study large numbers of subjects in a population where the rate of delinquency is known to be high. If these studies were carried out before individuals committed their crimes and were sent to prison, we could then follow them up and see whether a high score on emotionality on the original testing was correlated with a later tendency to commit crimes and be sent to prison. In the absence of any study of this kind, we can only conclude that this question had best be left open.

We must now turn to a rather different kind of objection which rests on a purely theoretical basis. We have argued that conscience is a conditioned response and we have also argued that extraverted people, because they condition poorly, will, on the whole, tend to have weaker consciences than introverts, who condition extremely well. This argument, however, makes an unwarranted assumption; it assumes that all people, extraverts and introverts alike, will be subjected to an identical system of conditioning or indoctrination. Now this is patently untrue, and we must next take up the question of determining what conclusions would follow from a more complicated and realistic state of affairs, where different degrees of conditioning are administered to different people. The argument we are now presenting may be put in experimental terms. If extraverts and introverts are conditioned on the eye-blink conditioning apparatus, and if both groups are given, say, twenty training trials, then we can demonstrate that introverts will condition about twice as well as extraverts; in other words, we will find that about 60 per cent of the introverted group will have formed strong conditioned responses but only 30 per cent of the extraverted group. But let us assume that instead of giving everybody the same number of conditioning trials, we give some people only two conditioning trials, others fifty, others a hundred, and others none at all. Under those conditions it would obviously be foolish to look for any very high correlation between introversion and conditioning; any such correlation would be over-shadowed by the incidental fact of whether the individual had had many or few conditioning trials. The final rate of conditioning would depend entirely on the number of trials he had in fact had. Now when we look at society as it is at present, we see that on the whole, it is this latter condition which obtains, rather than the hypothetical one of equal conditioning for all. We know, for instance, that in middle-class families there tends to be a much greater stress on moral and social behaviour, and firmer control over aggressive and sexual modes of conduct, whereas in some working-class families, far from frowning upon aggressive conduct and applying conditioning methods to suppress it, there is rather a tendency to encourage it and to take pride in the prowess of the growing boy. We also know that there are considerable differences in the childrearing practices of different nations. There is, for instance, considerably more stress on social conditioning in England than there is in the United States, where there has been a very marked tendency toward what might be called parental abdication of responsibility; that is, there has been a tendency for American parents to take some of the psychoanalytic and Freudian precepts of *laissez-faire* policy too literally. It is this, rather than any hypothetical differences in conditionability between Americans and English people, which may be responsible for the difference in crime rates in the two countries.

If we assume that there are indeed individual differences in the amount of conditioning which is given to the growing child, then we cannot expect a perfect correlation between extraversion and conditionability on the one hand, and criminality on the other. We would have to take into account the degree of conditioning which has in fact taken place; our general rule would only apply if we could, in some way, equate individuals with respect to their upbringing. We might also note, in this connexion, another important feature which is implicit in much of what was said earlier. It will be remembered from our discussion of generality and specificity that emotional reactions, whether conditioned or unconditioned, tend to be relatively specific. Now it would also seem to follow from our hypothesis that conditioning itself will be relatively specific, depending on precisely what is included in the range of conditioned stimuli by the parents. Thus a boy may be brought up in an Irish family where there is a very severe process of conditioning in relation to sexual morality, but where there is a complete absence of conditioning with respect to aggressive, fighting behaviour. The child might then grow up to be a very 'moral' member of society as far as sexual behaviour is concerned, but he might be involved in many fights and might even go to prison for his aggressive behaviour. There would be lacking, in his case, a congruence or concordance between one aspect of moral, law-abiding behaviour and another. This incongruity need not be interpreted as fatal to our general theory (rather it seems to follow from it), provided that we can demonstrate a deficiency in the conditioning schedule applied to this particular child with respect to aggression and a high amount of conditioning applied in the sexual sphere. In analysing individual cases and also in making predictions for group behaviour, it is extremely important to bear in mind this point. Specificity of responses is not universal but it does limit the generality of our theories and of our empirical findings, whether we are dealing with human or sub-human organisms.

We can extend the argument presented above a little further. We have so far postulated that human reactions will differ according to whether a particular type of reaction has been conditioned or not, and by conditioning in this sense we have always implied that the individual will be conditioned in what we call the 'right' direction; that is, towards moral and social behaviour. This hypothesis unfortunately is not true of a small proportion of society. Consider the child whose mother is a prostitute and whose father is a thief. It is unlikely that the conditioning schedule which they will bring to bear on him will encourage him to behave in a socially acceptable manner. They probably will not label certain kinds of conduct as bad which society would prefer to have suppressed: on the contrary, they might even tend to encourage these. In other words, we may now be dealing with a situation quite different from that which we have envisaged so far. In our discussion hitherto we have assumed that a socialization process (conditioning in the 'right' direction) was imposed on the child and we observed individual differences among children with respect to their ability to benefit from this socialization process. We must now consider those people who have had imposed on them an 'antisocialization process', to coin a term, and consider the consequences in terms of their ability to 'benefit' from this process. Clearly the exact opposite of what we have posited heretofore will take place. Now it will be the introverted child, the child who conditions well, who will condition to the precepts emerging from this 'Fagin's kitchen'. Instead of becoming conditioned to be a good and law-abiding citizen, we now have our introvert being conditioned to be a 'good' law-breaking thief or prostitute. In line with our theory we should predict that now it would be the introvert who would become the less law-abiding citizen, whereas the extravert, by virtue of not conditioning so well, would have a better chance to escape from this fate.[53] The number of cases where this may have happened fortunately is probably quite small. It may be true that there is no honour among thieves; nevertheless, antisocial behaviour tends to be very disruptive, even in the smallest community such as the family, and a certain amount of training will be administered even under those conditions. Thus a mother or a father may have no objection to lying and stealing themselves; but they will tend to object to having their children lie to them or steal from them; they will, therefore, tend to administer punishment, if only intermittently, for antisocial activities, as long as these are directed against them. However, it must be borne in mind that the quality of the child's upbringing, the degree of conditioning, and the kind of conditioning which he receives, will be very important in his future development, and the degree to which we have concentrated on his own free activity, his own degree of conditionability, is too one-sided to make any prediction possible. It would follow from what has been said that factors militating against a consistent scheme of conditioning in the home and at school would work against the development of a socially responsible adult. There are many findings in the research literature to show that this is indeed so. The Gluecks, in their large-scale studies, showed, for instance, that there was a significant relationship between criminal behaviour and the incidence of unwholesome aspects of home life, notably in respect to such factors as family cohesiveness, affectional relations of parents and children, supervision, and discipline. There would be little point in cataloguing these findings or discussing them at any length; they are fairly obvious from a commonsense point of view and they are in good agreement with our general theory. What I would like to emphasize in this connexion is rather that these factors of unsatisfactory upbringing, although undoubtedly important, are perhaps less so than one might have thought at first. Thus, for instance, D. J. West, who carried out a study of habitual prisoners on behalf of the Institute of Criminology at the University of Cambridge, found that:

Most of the prisoners came of hard-working, respectable parents. Only four per cent had a parent with a record of criminal convictions, although seventeen per cent had either a parent or brother with a record. The total number of known brothers or half-brothers of the hundred prisoners amounted to 183, of whom twenty-three were known to have had convictions. The great majority of these brothers were not merely noncriminal but actually in satisfactory employment and behaving as responsible fathers of families and generally useful citizens. This contrast was frequently remarked upon by the prisoners, whom time and time again described themselves as the only black sheep in the family.[54]

This study, which is typical of many, shows two things. In the first place, it shows that most habitual prisoners come from families where a reasonable system of conditioning is in force; and secondly, it shows that the great majority of the offspring of these families (almost ninety per cent) turn out to be good, decent, solid citizens who do not commit crimes of any kind. In these circumstances, we clearly cannot have recourse to differences in conditioning to account for the fact that a few are criminals and the majority are not; we must turn to individual differences in ability to condition to explain these otherwise inexplicable data.

However that may be, we must still explain one important fact which would seem to present some difficulty for our general theory. How is it possible that there are so many habitual prisoners: old lags, offenders who have been in and out of prison for many years, who have apparently never become conditioned, in spite of all these terrifying and painful experiences? Unless we postulate that we are dealing with persons who cannot be conditioned at all, it would seem that this accumulation of conditioning experiences should have been sufficient to finally inculcate in them an appreciation of the moral values. Is not the fact that this has not taken place a strong counter-argument to the general theory which we have put forward? There are two answers to this. The first is a very simple and straightforward one. Conditioning is a process which occurs only under certain highly specialized conditions. We have already noted, in connexion with the eye-blink conditioning experiment, that conditions are optimal when the interval between the conditioned stimulus, the tone, and the unconditioned stimulus, the puff of air to the eye, is about 500 msec. (one-half second), and that when it is as long as two and one-half seconds, no conditioning takes place at all. In other words, for conditioning, the interval between conditioned and unconditioned stimuli is all-important. When we consider crime, however, and the punishment which society metes out to the criminal, we have seen that the interval may be very long indeed. It may be weeks, months, or even years, and under these conditions we do not expect conditioning to take place. This conclusion may have to be modified to some extent. Human beings, unlike rats, have what Pavlov called a second signalling system, that of speech, superimposed on the primary signalling system, namely that of conditioning. There is unfortunately very little work in this field, but it is conceivable that, at the time of sentencing the prisoner and while the prisoner is serving his sentence, the conditioned stimulus, which should have been the actual commission of the crime itself, may be substituted for by some kind of ideational representation, either verbally or sub-vocally. In other words, it is possible to assume that when the prisoner is being sentenced, he may, at that time, reiterate ideationally the circumstances of the crime, by thinking about it either in words or in images. It is possible that the connexion between these images and the actual commission of the crime is sufficiently strong to potentiate a certain amount of conditioning. It is unfortunate that nothing, in practice, is known about the feasibility of this ideational mediation process in connexion with social punishment of this kind, but it may be surmised that, at best, the conditioning that takes place would be much weaker than it would be if the proper conditioned stimulus had been applied.

Our second argument in accounting for the existence of the recidivist 'old lag' is too complex to be presented here; its importance is such that it will be reserved for a separate chapter.

7 Punishment or Cure?

Alice looked round her in great surprise. 'Why, I do believe we've been under this tree all the time! Everything's just as it was!'

'Of course it is,' said the Queen; 'what would you have it?'

'Well, in *our* country,' said Alice, still panting a little, 'you'd generally get to somewhere else – if you ran very fast for a long time, as we've been doing.'

'A slow sort of country!' said the Queen. 'Now, *here*, you see, it takes all the running *you* can do, to keep in the same place. If you want to get somewhere else, you must run at least twice as fast as that!'

THROUGH THE LOOKING-GLASS

If one man digs ten holes in one hour, how many holes will ten men dig in ten hours? The answer, of course, may be anything between none at all and a thousand. One of the ten may be a non-union man and the others may go on strike; in that case, no holes will be dug at all. Or the employer, now that he is employing ten men instead of one, may pay them at piece-work instead of hourly rates and they may dig far more holes than they did before. Then, of course, the union might step in and decide that they are working too diligently and demand that henceforth they will work at half that rate of digging.

Arithmetic is a wonderful thing, but it does not necessarily apply to psychological problems. Take, for example, the famous case of the munitions emergency. During the First World War, when England was caught unprepared and badly in need of munitions, workers were exhorted to work fifty, sixty, or even seventy hours a week, in order to produce more. The argument underlying this was a typically logical one: if a person produces four thousand cartridges in forty hours, he will produce fifty thousand in fifty hours, and sixty thousand in sixty hours. Some of the people concerned may have realized that this formula had practical limits, but they continued to insist that people work longer and longer hours, until psychologists eventually showed working longer hours actually produced fewer rather than more cartridges. In other words, a person working forty hours produced more cartridges than a person working seventy hours. One would think that the point should have been well taken: quite the contrary. At the beginning of the Second World War, England was again caught unprepared and again the same emergency arose. Undeterred by previous experience, the politicians insisted that the workers should go on working fifty, sixty, even seventy hours a week. And again it was found, exactly as before, that increasing the number of hours worked did not increase either the relative or the absolute number of cartridges they produced.

Much the same thing has happened with respect to punishment. It seems reasonable to assume that because you punish a person for committing a crime, therefore he will be deterred from repeating it, and other people will be deterred from even trying it. Most people would find no fault with this argument. Indeed, some people might wish to extend it to say that the more severely you punish a person, the more he will be deterred from repeating the act, and also the more other people will be deterred from undertaking it. Statistics have been published in many countries showing that there is very little basis for this hypothesis. The number of murders which are committed in a country seems to be quite unrelated to whether capital punishment has been abolished or reintroduced, for example; the number remains much the same regardless of this difference. You may flog people for certain types of offences, but rather than deter them, it seems to have the opposite effect. Although the punishment is severe, the rate of recidivism is, if anything, greater than it would have been without the flogging.

Another common fallacy is also instructive. Suppose that certain criminals are released on parole, and suppose that they are responsible to a given officer, who supervises their activities and to whom they must report periodically. You would imagine that the larger the case load of that officer, the less successful the paroles would be, on the whole. In a rigorous experiment done in California, parolees were allocated at random to officers having case loads of fifteen, thirty, sixty, and ninety men. Certain offenders, selected on a random basis, were released three months early. A two-year follow-up was undertaken which failed to reveal any difference in outcome, due either to time of release or to size of the case load.

It has proved surprisingly difficult to demonstrate that any form of treatment or punishment has any measurable effect on people. Psychotherapy or psychoanalysis is the most commonly cited case in point. For many years, psychoanalysts have claimed that psychotherapy of the type suggested by Freud 'cured' psychoneurotic disorders. It has been found that about two out of three severe neurotics tend to get better after several years of such treatment.

However, investigations in which control groups of comparable neurotics were not treated by any form of psychotherapy have shown that these neurotics also improved considerably or were cured completely after some two years, to the extent of about two out of three. When the rates of recovery were compared between psychoanalytic treatment and spontaneous remission, it was found that there was no significant difference; in other words, whether a person did or did not receive psychoanalytic treatment made no difference in his recovery.[55]

Much the same has been found whenever different types of sentence have been compared. Whether you let a person go with a warning, put him on probation, or send him to prison for a short or a long period of time, may affect his future conduct, but the available statistics do not seem to encourage any belief that one method is superior to another. There is one exception to this general rule, which we shall come back to later on. For the moment, let us simply note that many commonsense expectations in this field are being discredited, and that we will have to rely on a more empirical approach if we want to set up fruitful hypotheses.

Before proceeding, let us first consider the concept of emotion. We have dealt with emotionality rather briefly in the preceding chapters, but have concentrated more on extraversion/introversion and the associated concept of conditionability. However, we have noted that emotion can act as a drive, and we have also noted our general formula: performance = habit × drive. We would, by this formula, expect people who were strongly emotional to show better performance, on the assumption that motivated people perform better than people who are not motivated, and that emotion constitutes a drive, or a motivating factor. However, this way of looking at things is too oversimplified. For one thing, it assumes that the habits which we are putting into our formula are the correct ones; this, of course, is not necessarily true. We may possess the wrong habits; if we then worked under a high degree of motivation or emotion, the motivation would potentiate the wrong habits and would, therefore, make it more difficult for us to rid ourselves of them and to acquire the correct ones. In these circumstances, then, we would expect exactly the opposite to our previous expectation. We would expect that under strong emotion people would be more resistant to deterrence from pursuing the wrong course of action, and would find it more difficult to learn the correct course of action.

These facts give rise to a well-known psychological law, the so-called Yerkes-Dodson law (also known in its modern form as the 'inverted-U hypothesis'). This law has two parts. The first part says that the relationship between motivation or drive and performance is *curvilinear*, with an optimum somewhere near the middle of the range. This means that as motivation increases so does performance, but that once the optimum has been passed, any increase in motivation will produce a decrement in performance. The second part of the law maintains that the optimum for any given task depends on the complexity of the task; the more complex and difficult a task, the lower the optimum motivation, whereas the simpler and more straightforward the task, the higher the optimum motivation, for that particular task. Figure 22 shows, in diagrammatic form, the consequences of this law, which has been well-documented experimentally.[56]

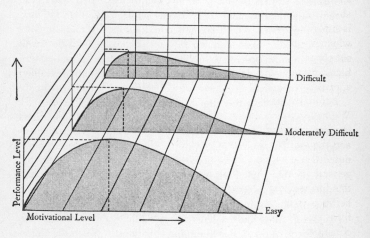

FIGURE 22

The diagram illustrates how performance is influenced by both motivation and task difficulty. According to the Yerkes-Dodson Law, best performance is achieved under conditions of intermediate amounts of motivation or drive. The more difficult the task, the lower, the optimum drive. Reproduced by permission from *Scientific American*.

We have already noted that prisoners and criminals generally tend to have a rather high level of emotionality. It would seem to follow that this emotionality would potentiate the antisocial habits which they have developed, to such an extent that they would find it far more difficult than normal, non-emotional people to supplant these with a proper set of habits. Punishment, presumably by greatly increasing the degree of emotion present, would, therefore, have a negative rather than a positive effect; it would lead to still greater rigidity in the reactions of the prisoner, rather than leading to any kind of change. This general conclusion seems particularly apposite in view of the fact that little effort is made by society to inculcate proper social or moral habits in the prisoner. Punishment is supposed to be sufficient for this purpose, making formal training or reconditioning unnecessary. Under these circumstances, it is perhaps not surprising that punishment does not have the effect which society so confidently expects of it.

We may perhaps draw a comparison between the case of the prisoner in the dock and an experimental demonstration frequently made in the laboratory of stereotyped or fixated behaviour. Among the earliest studies of this was an experiment carried out by an American animal psychologist, G. V. Hamilton, in 1916. He used an apparatus from which animals could escape by choosing the correct exit door from a choice of four. The correct exit door was varied in random order and, under these conditions, his rats showed various kinds of adaptive or non-adaptive behaviour, including repetitive or stereotyped reactions. These may be defined as instances of persistent re-entrance of an alley during a given trial, when as many as ten successive punishments therein failed to direct the subjects' activities, away from that alley, and towards the untried alleys. This stereotyping was particularly likely to occur when the rats became very emotional. A similar experiment was later carried out by J. B. Patrick, who used human subjects. He also found a marked increase in stereotyped behaviour.[57]

More important in this connexion, however, has been the work of N. R. F. Maier, at the University of Michigan, in Ann Arbor. He made use of the Lashley jumping apparatus in which the animal is placed on a stand and has to jump to one of two windows. These windows are covered by cards having different symbols painted on them. One of these cards, when struck by the animal, falls over and allows him to go through; the other one remains fixed and, if he jumps to it, he bumps his nose and falls into a net at the bottom of the stand. The problem presented to the rat may be soluble, in which case he is required either to jump always to the left or to the right (position response), or to jump at a particular card (symbol response), whether it appears on the left or right side. However, at times the rats may be presented with an insoluble problem, in which case the cards are presented in a random sequence so that no response can be learned which will always be rewarded and which escapes punishment. Presented with an insoluble problem, the rats very soon show a stereotyped reaction; that is, they always jump to the same card or to the same side. Once such a fixation has been developed, it has been found, it is extremely difficult to get the animal to abandon it. Even when the problem is made soluble and even when the correct window is left open, the rat will still repeat his fixated response and jump to the other side.

Maier stresses the fact that behaviour of this type arises under conditions where the animals are severely frustrated and, accordingly, he labels this 'frustration-instigated behaviour', in contrast to 'motivation-instigated behaviour', which is the more normal type of conduct of animals and human beings. Frustration produces a considerable increase in emotion and, therefore, would tend, as we have shown previously, to make a reversal of behaviour very much more difficult. Maier summarizes the properties of frustration-instigated behaviour as follows:

(1) Frustration-instigated behaviour is characterized by a stereotyped, fixed, compulsive reaction, whereas motivation-instigated behaviour is characterized by plasticity and variability.

(2) Reward has no effect on frustration-instigated behaviour and punishment is either ineffective or it may even intensify the behaviour by increasing the degree of frustration.

(3) The degree of frustration can be relieved by the expression of the fixation response, whether or not it is adaptive, whereas responses expressed by a motivated individual are satisfying only when the responses are adaptive.

(4) Frustration-instigated behaviour tends to be non-constructive in nature and involves a more primitive form of conduct and a regression to earlier modes of adaptation, whereas motivation-instigated behaviour tends to be constructive in nature, and to involve selective adaptation and learning.

Maier goes on to apply this distinction to a discussion of various common abnormalities of behaviour. For instance, he distinguishes two types of stealing. Stealing may be motivation-instigated as, for instance, in the case of a boy who has a very strong desire to own a watch because every other boy in his neighbourhood has one. In his case, the most effective method of treatment would be actually to give him a watch or help him to save money to buy one. However, the stealing may be frustration-instigated, as in the case of a boy who steals to get attention from his parents, who show an obvious preference for his younger sister. In this case, Maier would advocate as treatment, not the provision of the watch, but the provision of attention, i.e., of the removal of the frustration the boy feels because he is neglected.

Maier considers two types of destructive behaviour. It may be due to failure on the part of the parents to provide appropriate opportunities for the child. For instance, he may take a watch apart and try to put it back together, not because he is destructive but because he wants to carry out some experiments in watch construction. Treatment here would obviously consist of providing appropriate materials with which the child can experiment freely. On the other hand, destructive behaviour may be symptomatic of frustration and a desire to hurt the parents. In this case, the treatment would be different.

Maier also distinguishes between two types of criminal behaviour. One type, such as theft, fraud, kidnapping, or tax evasion, he considers to be motivated behaviour which is a function of the subject's relative evaluation of possible consequences of success and failure. On the other hand, there are certain types of crimes, especially sex crimes and murder, which, according to him, bear the marks of frustration-instigated behaviour and which seem impervious to the influence of the most severe punishments, whether anticipated or actually experienced.

It follows from this discussion of Maier's theories that the effects of reward and punishment depend entirely on whether the behaviour to which they are applied is frustration-instigated or motivation-instigated. In the latter case, punishment may itself constitute a frustrating situation, in which case it will either increase the strength of any frustration-instigated behaviour already present, or transform the motivated state into a frustrated one. As he puts it: 'Punishment can only serve as a negative incentive when the organism is in a motivated state and when its intensity is not great enough to excite the frustration process and cause it completely to dominate over the motivation process'.[57]

We need only note here that Maier's conclusions are in good agreement with those of other experimental psychologists as far as the effects of punishment are concerned. These effects always tend to be extremely variable and unpredictable. Punishment may produce the desired end, that is, the elimination of a certain type of conduct, but on the other hand, it may have exactly the opposite effect, stamping in the undesirable conduct even more strongly than before and making it a stereotyped pattern. Sometimes punishment may have no effect at all, one way or the other, and it is not even possible to say that strong and weak punishments differ in their effects in any predictable way. It is not surprising, therefore, that empirical studies of the effects of punishment on criminals have led to more confusion, so that no positive statements of any kind can be made. It is suggested that the old lag, the recidivist with many crimes behind him, and no prospect of any change in his pattern of behaviour, very closely resembles the frustrated rat with its stereotyped behaviour pattern, self-punishing and maladaptive as it may be. By repeatedly sending him to prison and punishing him for each criminal episode, society merely stamps in this type of conduct and does nothing to convert him into a useful, law-abiding citizen. Perhaps a different approach is required to achieve this aim.

What are the social purposes of punishment? There are essentially three purposes. Perhaps the first, in order of time, is simply vengeance. The criminal has offended society; he must be punished and made to feel on his own body the evil effects of what he has done, the principle of 'an eye for an eye and a tooth for a tooth'. Few people nowadays would endorse punishment simply from the point of view of vengeance; at least in our society, the rational tendency would be to accept the biblical exhortation, 'Vengeance is mine, saith the Lord'. However, at a less rational, more personal level, vengeance probably contributes a share to the motives behind punishment.

A second purpose of punishment is protection of the law-abiding public. What better method of protecting the public from the ravages of a criminal than by locking him up, thus making it impossible for him to commit crimes, at least while he is incarcerated? The sentence of preventive detention, for instance, places maximum emphasis on the protection of the public from the dangerous criminal in insisting on his removal from society for an indefinite period, without regard for rehabilitation. The indeterminate sentence, so popular in America, is similarly based largely on public protection, although it possibly lays greater stress on rehabilitation.

The third aim is that of deterrence, both as far as the criminal himself is concerned, and as far as others are concerned. Punishment, it is assumed, should deter the criminal from further crimes, and his punishment should deter others from following in his footsteps. As we have seen before, it is doubtful whether punishment acts as a very effective deterrent; certainly there is little evidence to show that the methods currently in use are very effective. Nevertheless, at least in theory, a good deal of the rationale behind punishment is based on this notion. These have been the aims and these have been the methods of penal philosophy for the last two thousand years. Perhaps it would not be too impertinent to say that very little improvement has taken place during this time. Our methods are still as primitive and as unsuccessful as they were in the days of Socrates or in the days of the Roman Empire. What has gone wrong?[58]

Samuel Butler, the English novelist, in his book *Erewhon*, posed the problem in a paradoxical form. In this country of Erewhon, he wrote, people who were suffering from diseases were sent to prison and treated harshly, whereas those who committed crimes were sent to the doctor and given medicines to cure them of their disease; in other words, he posited an exact reversal of the kind of thing that goes on in our society. Is there any reason to take this suggestion seriously and adopt a curative, rather than a deterrent point of view, in relation to our criminals? At first sight the prospects are not particularly good. Let us have a look at a famous enquiry which was carried out in Boston just before the beginning of the Second World War. This is the Cambridge-Somerville Youth Study. The experiment has been summed up as follows, by Teuber and Powers, two of the people who worked on it.

For approximately eight years, from 1937 to 1945, this large-scale treatment effort was directed at the prevention of delinquency by guidance, counselling, and therapy, in a group of over 600 underprivileged boys. . . . By setting up a control group and by keeping unusually detailed records the study made provision for quantitative measurement of the effects of therapy and for systematic attempts at an objective description of the therapeutic relationships.

The first step in the programme consisted of the selection of subjects from among under-privileged boys aged six to ten, whose names had been obtained from welfare workers as 'being likely to become delinquent'. A list of names of 650 boys was obtained, and these were individually matched on variables such as age, intelligence quotient, school grade, delinquency rating, and ethnic and socio-economic background. The decision as to which boy in each pair should be assigned to the treatment group (T) and which to the untreated control group (C) was made by the toss of a coin. In this way, two equivalent groups of 325 boys were obtained, whose chances of delinquency, as far as could be determined, were nearly equal.

As soon as a boy had been selected as a member of the treatment group, he was assigned to one of the counsellors employed by the study, and treatment was begun. Both adherents of the psychoanalytic school, and followers of Carl Rogers' non-directive approach participated in the treatment programme. 'Regardless of the individual counsellor's predilection, all treatment consisted of individual, face-to-face contacts. These individual relationships between counsellors and boys thus served as the independent variable; they represented "treatment". . . . They were restricted to the treatment group and consistently withheld from the control group'.

The follow-up extended from the end of the treatment period in 1945, when treatment had lasted between two and eight years in individual cases, to 1948, when the outcome was evaluated. The outcome was as follows. The total number of court appearances from the beginning of treatment had been recorded and it was found that ninety-six T boys and ninety-two C boys were involved: the number of offences being 264 for the T group and 218 for the C group. A similar picture is given by the number of appearances before the Court Prevention Bureau. Here we find that forty-nine T boys and forty-nine C boys appeared on one occasion; and sixty-five T boys and fifty-two C boys two or three times. Teuber and Powers comment as follows:

Such an outcome of the delinquency prevention programme of the study appears to be not only negative but paradoxical. Instead of confirming the expectation that the treatment group would be less delinquent than the matched control group, there is a slight difference in favour of the control group. This apparent advantage of the control group may be offset, however, by other factors which more detailed statistics seem to reveal. There is a slightly greater incidence of serious recidivism ... in the control group and the rating of all offences according to 'seriousness' likewise shows a slight advantage of the treatment cases over the controls; there is a tendency on the part of the controls to commit a proportionately greater number of the more serious offences. None of these trends, however, are as yet significant. Unless further developments change the picture ... the direct comparison between T and C groups fails to show that the major hypothesis can be sustained; treatment did not ... reduce the incidence of delinquency in the treatment group.

It is not surprising that the authors, in contrasting this negative outcome of the control investigation with the enthusiastic belief of the counsellors, concluded that, 'Quantitative indices ... are better than professions of faith bolstered by the therapist's prestige and the skilful use of the illustrative case'.

The reactions of the therapists themselves are of some interest. In a detailed study of the therapist-boy relationship, it was found that a number of therapists completely misinterpreted the attitudes and feelings of the boys towards them and that it was precisely these therapists who, 'considered their counselling relations as a highly effective tool in producing changes in their charges'. The attitudes of the therapists themselves are worthy of comment:

To some of the counsellors the whole control group idea ... seemed slightly blasphemous. ... They insisted that the relationships established had their value in themselves, irrespective of their possible effects on the boys' behaviour, and they were not perturbed when seemingly negative results of the delinquency-prevention programme became known. Other counsellors reacted differently; they felt that research was superfluous, since all the necessary rules of conduct in therapy were already known. When they were informed of the outcome of the study, they reacted in a characteristic fashion: those who were analytically trained and oriented asserted that the results would have been positive, had analytic principles been applied by all staff members, consistently, throughout the course of the treatment period. Congruously, those counsellors who were followers of Carl Rogers's non-directive approach averred that the systematic use of non-directive methods would have produced more definite success.

We may deduce from this and from other studies that have been carried out, in which psychotherapy has been used with criminals or potential criminals, that there is little reason to believe these methods of treatment can effect any cure or amelioration, or can serve in a preventive manner. This is not surprising; as we have seen before, even in relation to neurosis, as they were originally developed, these methods fail to have any demonstrable effect.[59]

Must we conclude that there is no way we can change the behaviour of people, either for the better or for the worse? Fortunately, the outlook is not as bad as it may seem from looking at such studies as the Cambridge-Somerville Youth Study mentioned above. Recent work on behaviour therapy with neurotics has shown that considerable improvement can be effected in a relatively short time, and perhaps this work can be extended to the treatment of criminals. To introduce this new type of investigation, let us return to our discussion of little Albert and his conditioned phobia of white rats.

The reader will recall our discussion of the autonomic system and its two branches, the sympathetic and the parasympathetic. What we have done was condition a sympathetic response in little Albert to the conditioned stimulus, the sight, the feel and the smell of rats. What can we do to eliminate this conditioned sympathetic response? One answer was given by Watson in an original paper, which has since been developed into a method of treating neurotic disorders in human beings, both children and adults, by Professor J. Wolpe, originally from South Africa, now living in the United States. He calls this the method of 'reciprocal inhibition', and its principle is based on the fact that the two parts of the autonomic nervous system, the sympathetic and the parasympathetic, are mutually antagonistic in their action. For example, when the sympathetic system accelerates the heart beat rate, the parasympathetic slows it down. Watson and Wolpe argue that a conditioned sympathetic response to a given stimulus, can be eliminated by conditioning a parasympathetic response to the same stimulus. The parasympathetic response, being antagonistic to the sympathetic one, will inhibit it reciprocally and, in that way, will cancel it out, leaving the individual very much as he was before the original conditioning took place. How can this be done?

In the case of Albert, we might do something like this. We know that the sympathetic system inhibits digestion and that digestion is aided by the activity of the parasympathetic system. We might try giving little Albert some chocolate to produce a parasympathetic response. But since he is so afraid of the rats when they are right in front of him that he will simply refuse to take the chocolate, we must introduce an important variation into the experiment, the so-called distance gradient. This is demonstrated in Figure 23.

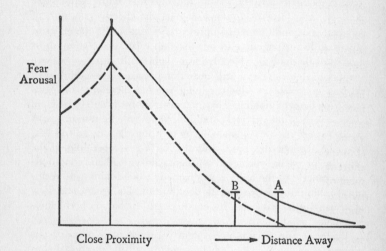

FIGURE 23

The diagram illustrates the fact that the nearer a feared object is, the greater the amount of fear produced. The solid curve indicates the amount of fear experienced by a phobic subject at the beginning of the experiment; *A* indicates the degree of relaxation and reassurance induced by the experimenter. The broken line indicates the lessening of fear produced by this conditioning process, enabling it to be repeated at position *B*.

What is signified by this phrase is that the strength of fear experienced when we encounter a particular object which we fear is roughly proportional to the distance of that object from us: the nearer the object, the greater the fear. In the diagram we have plotted the amount of fear experienced on the vertical axis and the distance of the object from us on the horizontal axis. It is possible to measure the amount of fear experienced by taking polygraph recordings of the activity of the autonomic system, demonstrating that the closer Albert is to the rats, the greater the sympathetic arousal in him.

The amount of sympathetic arousal in our subject can be minimized by simply putting the rats at the far end of the room, as far away from little Albert as possible; under these conditions, although hesitant, he will consent to take the chocolate. With the conditioned stimulus present, and the unconditioned stimulus, the chocolate, producing digestive (parasympathetic) activity, parasympathetic conditioning to the presence of the rats can take place. The parasympathetic activity, being incompatible with sympathetic activity, will decrease, to some degree, the effective strength of sympathetic conditioning still present. Schematically, the effect of this is to lower the curve in our diagram relating the strength of fear to distance of the object from the subject. In other words, we can now bring the rats a little nearer and repeat the experiment of feeding chocolate to Albert, adding another increment of parasympathetic conditioning. This increment subtracts still more from the strength of the original conditioned sympathetic response, and again lowers the curve, enabling us to bring the rats still nearer. We can continue this process until, after a few repetitions of the experiment, we have achieved sufficient parasympathetic conditioning to cancel out the original sympathetic conditioning, and reciprocal inhibition has reached an equilibrium. The infant will now play happily with the rats, his conditioned fear having been eliminated.[60]

Under certain circumstances it may be necessary to carry this process even further, into what we might call the ideational continuum. As as example, take the case of a middle-aged woman who was suffering from a cat phobia. She was so fearful of cats that she would not even leave her room, lest she encounter a cat in the street. The same type of de-conditioning was attempted with her, but her fear was so great that she would not tolerate even the smallest cat in the same room with her, at any distance. Consequently the parasympathetic conditioning had to begin by making use of ideational representation of cats, that is, stimuli such as the letters C A T written on a card, or the experience of talking about cats, or pictures of cats. Only after these stimuli had been presented, and a parasympathetic response produced, was it possible to introduce a live cat into the room at a maximum distance, and gradually bring it nearer. In her case, too, after a very short time, this parasympathetic conditioning had completely supplanted the original sympathetic conditioning, which had taken place when, as a small girl, she saw her father drown a kitten. The patient was completely cured and even became the proud possessor of a large tabby.

Wolpe and others have applied these principles to random samples of neurotics suffering from a variety of disorders, from anxiety states and reactive depressions to hysterical and obsessive compulsive symptoms. They have shown that, under these conditions, a success rate of over ninety per cent can be achieved in relatively few sessions; in the majority of cases, twenty to thirty sessions are required for a cure. Wolpe has also shown that the cure, once achieved, is permanent; neither does a symptom return, nor is there any other symptom likely to take its place. [61] These results have been confirmed by several other workers. There have also been several clinical experiments, in which patients have been matched for the particular neurotic disorder of which they were complaining, and then assigned by the toss of a coin to either behaviour therapy or psychotherapy. Their progress was then noted, and it was demonstrated, at a high level of statistical significance, that those who received behaviour therapy recovered more quickly and more thoroughly than did those receiving psychotherapy. It is possible, therefore, to achieve a degree of success well beyond the rate of spontaneous remission in relation to the amelioration of neurotic disorders. We may take this as support for the possibility of treating criminal and delinquent disorders in a similar manner.[62]

When we turn to these types of disorders, however, we must reverse the application of the principle of reciprocal inhibition. This reversal can be clearly demonstrated in certain neurotic disorders which border on the criminal and occasionally overstep the mark. The neurotic disorders we have been talking about so far are essentially ones which disturb the individual who is suffering from them. A person who experiences strong anxiety, strong depressive tendencies, or obsessive-compulsive reactions, is very upset and worried by these experiences and may seek help desperately. But we also find frequent cases where the opposite is true, where what has been conditioned, through some quirk of fate, is a parasympathetic response; that is to say, a reaction which, on the whole, gives him pleasure, and which he would be reluctant to abandon. Examples of this, for instance, are homosexuality, or attachment to a member of the same sex and the derivation of pleasure from such an attachment; fetishism, or the substitution of some normally neutral object for the normal sexual object, or at least the addition of such an object to the normal sex outlet; and transvestism, or the derivation of sexual pleasure from dressing up in clothing appropriate to the opposite sex. In these cases what is required is the conditioning of a sympathetic response to stimuli which, in the normal run of things, produce conditioned parasympathetic responses in our subjects. The unconditioned stimuli are, respectively, members of the same sex, of the opposite sex, or the objects of fetishes, whatever they may be. There are many ways of accomplishing this conditioning, but the two most frequently used are either electric shock used in connexion with objects of this type, or an injection with apomorphine, a drug which produces sickness and vomiting after a short period of time.

Let me cite one example to illustrate this type of treatment. The patient, a married man aged thirty-three, after he had attacked a perambulator, was referred from the out-patient department of a mental hospital, with the suggestion that prefrontal lobotomy should be performed on him. This was the twelfth such attack known to the police, and they took a very serious view of his recent action of following a woman with a perambulator and smearing it with oil. In the past he had slashed two empty prams on a railway station before setting them on fire and completely destroying them. On five other occasions he had cut or scratched prams over a period of months, when he was the subject of police investigations. He had spent some time in a mental hospital before being transferred to the neurosis unit, but left and pursued his furious vendetta against prams. When the patient was finally taken to court, he said that he had had impulses to damage prams and handbags since about the age of ten, and that, although the police knew of only twelve perambulator incidents, the number of times he had so indulged was actually much greater. He had sometimes made several attacks in one day but he estimated the average at about two or three a week, fairly consistently. With handbags, he was usually quite content if he could scratch them with his thumb nail and, as this could be done unobtrusively, this particular fetish had only once led him into trouble with the police. He had received many hours of analytic treatment and had been enabled to trace his abnormality back to two incidents in his childhood. The first occurred when he had been taken to a park to sail his boat and had been impressed by the feminine consternation manifested when he struck the keel of his yacht against a passing perambulator. On the second occasion, he became sexually aroused in the presence of his sister's handbag. He had been led to see the significance of these events and to understand that perambulators and handbags were, for him 'symbolic sexual containers'; but this insight had had no effect on his behaviour.

Dr. N. J. Raymond, of the Department of Psychiatry at St.

George's Hospital, London, who carried out the treatment, describes it in the following way:

It was explained to the patient that the aim of treatment was to alter his attitude to handbags and perambulators by teaching him to associate them with an unpleasant sensation instead of with a pleasurable, erotic sensation. Although he was frankly sceptical about the treatment, he said he was willing to try anything, for his despair had been deepened by recent sexual arousals when handbags appeared in the ward on visiting day, and by illustrated advertisements in newspapers.

A collection of handbags, perambulators, and coloured illustrations was obtained and these were shown to the patient after he had received an injection of apomorphine and just before nausea was produced. The treatment was given two-hourly day and night, no food was allowed, and at night amphetamine was used to keep him awake. At the end of the first week treatment was temporarily suspended, and the patient was allowed to go home to attend to his affairs. He returned after eight days to continue the treatment, and he reported jubilantly that he had, for the first time, been able to have intercourse with his wife without the use of the old fantasies. His wife said that she had noticed a change in his attitude to her, but was unable to define it. Treatment was recommenced and was continued as before, save that emetine hydrochloride was used whenever the emetic effect of apomorphine became less pronounced than its sedative effects.

Five days after the treatment had re-commenced he said that the mere sight of the objects made him sick; he was now confined to bed and the prams and handbags were continually with him, the treatments being given at irregular intervals. On the evening of the ninth day he rang his bell and was found to be sobbing uncontrollably. He kept repeating, 'Take them away,' and appeared to be impervious to anything that was said to him. The sobbing continued unabated until the objects were removed with ceremony and he was given a glass of milk and a sedative. The following day he handed over a number of photographic negatives of perambulators, saying that he had carried them about for years but would need them no longer. He left hospital but continued to attend as an out-patient. After a further six months, it was decided empirically to re-admit him for a 'boosting' course of treatment. He agreed to this, although he did not consider it at all necessary. Nineteen months after he had first had aversion therapy he still appeared to be doing well. The patient reports that he no longer requires the old fantasies to enable him to have sexual intercourse, nor does he masturbate with these fantasies. The wife reports that she is no longer constantly worrying about him and about the possibility of police action against him. Their sexual relations have 'greatly improved'. The probation officer reports that the patient has made 'very noticeable progress' and that 'his general attitude to life, his conversation, and his appearance have all shown a marked improvement'. As regards his work, he has been promoted to a more responsible job and he has not been in any trouble with the police.[63]

In citing this particular example of the application of behaviour therapy, to a case where a patient had come into conflict with the law, it is not suggested that this particular method could be applied directly to the solution of problems of criminality. The case was cited merely to indicate the way in which modern learning theory, and the general views about personality dynamics outlined in this book, can be applied to the solution of a particular problem. Other problems, of course, require other methods and no one would argue for a moment that the success of this particular method of treatment, which has been duplicated with many similar cases as well as with transvestites, homosexuals and others, can necessarily be expected with the typical kinds of criminals and delinquents we have in our prisons. What it demonstrates, however, is that by a suitable experimental conditioning regime we can decondition a very powerful impulse to perform a certain act, in this particular case, an aggressive and illegal one; and that, therefore, the theory on which the treatment is based holds considerable promise, even in regard to other types of criminal conduct, to which it has not yet been applied.

Criminals and delinquents pose two problems, of which the elimination of certain conditioned responses is only one. The other, and possibly more urgent one, is the creation of new conditioned responses of a more desirable, socially acceptable nature. Is there anything in the literature to suggest that learning theory could help us in doing this? It may be instructive to look at one particular symptom which has been treated very effectively by behaviour therapy. The symptom in question is that of enuresis or bed-wetting, which is so very frequent in children and which has always been extremely difficult to deal with by orthodox medical treatment or by psychotherapy. Essentially, what seems to happen in the case of the child suffering from enuresis is that a conditioned reflex has not been established between the conditional stimulus, the enlargement of the bladder beyond a certain point, and the beginning of urination, on the one hand, and waking up, stopping the urination, and going to the toilet, on the other. Failure to build up such a conditioned response we would expect to be more pronounced in extraverts and in people who, in general, condition poorly. Many investigators have found that juvenile delinquents and criminals generally tend to show a much higher incidence of enuresis than do normal people. This is, of course, precisely what we would have predicted in terms of our theory.

What can we do to produce the missing conditioned response? The answer to this problem was first given by O. H. Mowrer of the University of Illinois, who made use of the 'bell and blanket' method. In this method, the patient is made to sleep on a blanket which has on it a number of electrical contacts. These are linked to a battery and a bell. Whenever the subject begins to urinate in his sleep the urine, which is electrolytic, makes a contact between the electric wires in the blanket, and the bell begins to ring. This immediately produces reflexive cessation of urination and wakes up the patient, who then goes to the toilet. Gradually the conditioned response of waking up and going to the toilet is built up and, usually after a short time, the patient is cured of his enuresis. There is ample statistical and experimental evidence to show that this system is extremely successful in producing this particular conditioned response and that it also tends to eliminate all the fears and anxieties which have built up in the patient and his family because of his failure to keep dry at night.[64]

Again, it is not suggested that this method can be applied directly to the kind of problems presented by the criminal. It is cited here merely to indicate that, with sufficient ingenuity, it is possible to make deductions from learning theory, which may lead to a solution of these problems. What may be the most appropriate method for the treatment of criminals remains to be discovered.

Before making suggestions in this connexion, I would like to stress one point in particular which has usually been overlooked in many discussions of the treatment of criminals, and which is equally applicable to the upbringing of children. Throughout the centuries, there has been a swinging of the pendulum in opinions about the upbringing of children, between those who swear by the old saying, 'Spare the rod and spoil the child,' and those who accept the principles of *laissez-faire*, of letting children grow up more or less as they will. The arguments presented by the 'Spare the rod and spoil the child' school are that the child has to be trained in the social mores of his society, and that this cannot be done without some infliction of pain. The argument of the *laissez-faire* school, on the other hand, tends to be that the infliction of pain on children is unjustified and is likely to lead to neurotic disorders later in life. At the moment, the pendulum seems to have swung a long way towards the *laissez-faire* school, although there are indications that this may have gone too far and that the pendulum is about to swing back in the other direction. Can psychology say anything useful in relation to this particular conflict?

The main contribution which psychology can make in this connexion is a very simple one. According to learning theory, we would say that both sides are right in what they positively assert, and that both sides are wrong, in leaving certain points unsaid. Certainly, sternness and discipline in some degree are required if the child is to grow up into a moral, law-abiding citizen. The failure on the part of so many parents to provide such a background is undoubtedly responsible, in part, for the present outbreak of juvenile delinquency and the growth of crime throughout the Western world. The *laissez-faire* school is quite right in postulating that too severe discipline may often lead to neurotic disorders of one kind or another. Clearly, the path to follow is through a middle ground, to treat children with a sufficient degree of severity to achieve the conditioning required by society, but not to treat them so severely that they fall prey to neurotic disorders.

Although this answer may seem quite obvious, unfortunately it is not at all easy to put it into practice. The reason for the difficulty is that we tend to talk about an abstraction, that is, children in general, when what we have to deal with is a particular child at a particular moment. As we have seen, children are by no means all alike; some are introverted, some are extraverted, some condition poorly, some condition quickly. The severity of discipline required by an introverted child is very much less than the severity of discipline required by an extraverted child. Treat them both alike, and you might find that your extraverted child (because he conditions so poorly) ends up as a delinquent, whereas your introverted child (because he conditions so well) ends as a neurotic! What is required, of course, is to suit the type of upbringing to the type of child. Unfortunately, very few parents know whether their children will condition well or poorly; consequently they proceed largely by trial and error, supplemented by some knowledge of popular ideas of psychology and psychoanalysis. We cannot expect that the upbringing which the child gets in the usual case is the kind of upbringing that will be best suited to make him a normal, non-neurotic, law-abiding individual. A great deal of experimental work is needed before we will be able to give positive answers and guidance to parents who come with a request for help. Unfortunately, child guidance clinics are currently of little value in this connexion. The evidence is fairly conclusive that even when children are referred to them with neurotic disorders of one kind or another, child guidance clinics do very little, if any, better than chance. In other words, here also spontaneous remission claims as many successes as does the most successful child guidance clinic with all its psychiatrists and clinical psychologists. The reason for this is the acceptance on the part of so many workers in this field of unproven theories and methods which have not been empirically validated. Until there is considerable change toward a more scientific approach to these issues, it is unlikely that parents will receive much help with their problems from those who are expected to be best able to aid them by virtue of their training and experience.

What has been said here of children applies equally to adult criminals. Those who are extraverted, who condition poorly, obviously require a good deal of firmness in their treatment; however, those who are introverted, who condition well, and who turn to crime largely as a result of conditioning in an unfavourable environment, might be permanently damaged by excessive severity. The attempts of society to treat both types alike probably means sitting between two stools and getting the worst of both worlds. The likelihood of this is indicated by an experiment carried out by D. Grant of the U.S. Navy. Members of the Navy, who offended against discipline in various ways, were intensively interviewed and were then classified in two groups which Grant labelled as 'socially mature' and 'socially immature', but which we will call introverted and extraverted because the description given of these groups suggests that this was the criterion for differentiating between them. Each offender was then assigned one of three treatments, two of which (T_1 and T_2) were intensive 'living group therapy', whereas the third (S) was the more common type of training which you would find in a naval correctional establishment. A follow-up was carried out, to assess the success of the different types of treatment. The interesting point of the Grant study was that there were no differences in the percentages of successes of the three treatments when considered overall; however, when the treatments were broken down by type of offender, clear differences emerged. The results of this study are shown in Table 3. The ordinary, correctional type of treatment did not differentiate in any way between socially mature and socially immature types of offender, the percentage of successes being almost identical for both. The intensive casework methods, however, showed a very marked differentiation; with T_1, the socially mature were treated successfully in seventy per cent of the cases, the socially immature in only forty-one per

TABLE 3

Percentage successes in allocating socially mature and immature offenders to therapeutic type of treatment (T_1 and T_2) or to punitive type of treatment (S).

Personality type of offender	Treatment		
	T_1	T_2	S
	per cent	per cent	per cent
Socially mature	70	72	61
Socially immature	41	55	60
All	59	65	61

cent of the cases. Similarly, for T_2, the socially mature were treated successfully in seventy-two per cent of the cases, the socially immature only in fifty-five per cent of the cases.[65]

This study should be interpreted with caution. It is not clear whether the socially mature are identical with or even similar to the introverted type of person we have been talking about, or the socially immature similar to the extravert. It is not known precisely what factors within the T_1 and T_2 treatments resulted in their being effective for some and not for others. We cannot even be certain that the differences found were actually due to the treatment rather than to some other factor which might have been left uncontrolled. Nevertheless, this study suggests the *kind* of investigation which will have to be carried out before we can make any positive recommendations about the social applications of modern learning theory. Intensive, large-scale experimental work along these lines is desperately needed, in order to put the treatment of criminals on a scientific basis.

8 The Task of Society

'If I'd been the whiting,' said Alice, whose thoughts were still running on the song, 'I'd have said to the porpoise, "Keep back, please: we don't want *you* with us!"'

'They were obliged to have him with them,' the Mock Turtle said: 'no wise fish would go anywhere without a porpoise.'

'Wouldn't it really?' said Alice in a tone of great surprise.

'Of course not,' said the Mock Turtle: 'Why, if a fish came to *me*, and told me he was going on a journey, I should say "With what porpoise?"'

'Don't you mean "purpose"?' said Alice.

ALICE'S ADVENTURES IN WONDERLAND

In our chapter on the work of Lange and others who established the strong hereditary components of criminality, it was pointed out that therapeutic nihilism – in other words, the belief that when a given propensity is inherited, nothing can be done about it – is not necessarily implied by emphasizing genetic factors among the causes of crime. The typical anxiety neurotic is born with a central nervous system which makes it very easy for him to form conditioned responses, and he is born with an autonomic nervous system* which is over-reactive. These innate tendencies make him extremely prone to develop those conditioned autonomic responses we call neurotic symptoms. Nevertheless, knowing the facts enables us to treat him successfully along the lines laid down in the preceding chapter; behaviour therapy is most successful in deconditioning him, once traumatic events in his everyday life have produced the original conditioning. There is no therapeutic nihilism involved in following the facts wherever they may lead.

Exactly the same thing applies in the field of crime and delin-

---

* The term 'autonomic system' is used here, as elsewhere in this book, as a kind of shorthand notation to include certain other structures, such as the hypothalamus, whose activities in turn affect those of the autonomic system. A detailed discussion of the very complex anatomical and physiological details seems out of place in a book of this kind; the reader may like to consult E. Gellhorn's *Physiological Foundations of Neurology and Psychiatry*.

quency. Here also, the fact that we are dealing with people who have inherited a central nervous system which conditions only rather poorly, as well as an autonomic nervous system which tends to over-react, does not mean that nothing can be done. Obviously, we must first know the facts; we must next elaborate theories which might give us answers to the problems raised; and we must then carry out experiments which will tell us whether our theories are valid. To illustrate these points, let me give an example of the kind of deduction which may be made, which has been tried and found to work.

We start out with the problem that some people are very easy to condition, others very difficult, and that those who are difficult to condition will not, on the whole, develop moral responses as early, as quickly, and as strongly as those who condition easily. There are two distinct things we can try to do to deal with this highly extraverted, highly emotional group. One thing we might do is submit them to a much more rigorous and efficient system of conditioning than the normal person or the typical introvert. This, of course, would have to be done during childhood and it would require a good method of diagnosing this particular disability quite early in life. In practice, this should not be too difficult; experimental psychologists have worked out methods of conditioning which can be administered to children. Much research would be required to see which of the various methods used would be most efficacious, and which would be the cheapest to install in schools and elsewhere; but in principle it should be possible to test every child in the country with respect to his conditionability, just as it is possible to test every child with respect to his intelligence. It would be more expensive and more difficult, but if it were judged to be worthwhile it could be done. Once this particular aspect of the child's nature was known, we could then pick out those who, by virtue of their poor conditionability, are predestined to become criminals and delinquents, and recommend to their parents a kind of up-bringing which would minimize that possibility. This would be one way of dealing with the problem.

The other approach is more biologically oriented and depends ultimately on the notion that there must be ways of influencing the central nervous system directly, to alter the position of a person on the extraversion/introversion continuum. We already know of one way to do this; brain injury, and, in particular, the operation known as lobotomy, are known to produce marked shifts of a given individual on this continuum. Unfortunately, from our point of view, the shift is in the wrong direction; the person becomes more extraverted and less conditionable rather than more introverted and more conditionable. Brain operations, therefore, apart from every other consideration, are out of the question, simply because they would work against rather than toward a greater degree of socialization of the individual concerned. Fortunately there is another way open to us, and that is the use of drugs.

Research has shown that there are two kinds of drugs which are relevant to our discussion of extraversion/introversion. First of all, there are the stimulant drugs, such as caffeine and amphetamine; these drugs, when administered to a given person, will increase his excitatory potential, decrease his inhibitory potential, and generally make him more introverted. At the other end of the scale are the depressant drugs, such as alcohol and barbiturates; hypnotic drugs, sedatives and tranquillisers also belong in this group. These drugs have effects opposite to those of the stimulants; they increase inhibition, decrease excitation, and, therefore, lead to more extraverted behaviour as well as to a lessening in conditionability.* Figure 24 shows the course of an eye-blink conditioning experiment with three groups of normal people who have received, respectively, a dose of a stimulant, a dose of a depressant, and a placebo, which is an inert, dummy tablet. It is readily seen that the group which received the stimulant conditions much better than the placebo group, whereas the group which received the depressant conditions much worse than does the placebo group. In other words, it is possible, at least for brief periods, to shift a person's position on the extraversion/introversion continuum. Can we apply this finding in our treatment of delinquency?

Several experiments have been conducted, largely with behaviour-disordered children and juvenile delinquents. The treatment consisted of medication with one of the stimulant drugs, usually amphetamine, and observations were made of the behaviour of the children and juveniles concerned. There were no particular attempts to alter their moral and ethnical behaviour and no attempts at psychotherapy. The success of the treatment, which was usually continued over a period of weeks, was quite astonishing. It has been reported by many different investigators that under these circumstances there was a considerable, almost immediate improvement in the behaviour of the patients concerned. They became much more amenable to discipline and much more socialized in their pattern of activities; often they ceased to show behaviour

* The statement that alcohol increases inhibition may seem misleading since most students of physiology think of alcohol as causing an *abolition* of those processes of inhibition which are produced by the cortex and exert a restraining influence over the lower centres. The inhibitory function of the alcohol is on the cortex itself, thus disinhibiting the lower centres.

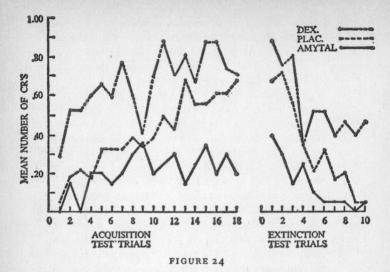

FIGURE 24

The acquisition and extinction of conditioned eye-blink responses by normal subjects administered a stimulant drug (dexedrine) or a depressant drug (amytal). The third group was administered a dummy tablet (placebo). It will be noticed that the stimulant drug aids conditioning, whereas the depressant drug depresses it. By permission from C. M. Franks and D. S. Trouton, *Journal of Comparative and Physiological Psychology*, 1958, *51*, 221.

problems. Usually the improvement ceased when the drug treatment itself was stopped, but sometimes the improvement in behaviour continued well beyond this point and seemed to become and enduring feature of the individual.

One typical study was carried out by two American psychiatrists, Cutts and Jasper, who investigated twelve behaviour problem children. When given a stimulant drug known as benzedrine, half of these children showed marked improvements in behaviour. When the children were given phenobarbital their behaviour became definitely worse in nine out of twelve cases. A similar study has been described by Donald B. Lindsley and Charles E. Henry, who studied thirteen behaviour problem children with a mean age of ten and a half years, of average intelligence. They write:

Behaviour disturbances were of sufficient degree of intensity to render the children distinct problems in management at home, at school or in the community, and to make their admission to the hospital for treatment advisable. The behaviour of each child was characterized by a number of undesirable traits such as negativism, hyperactivity, impulsiveness, destructiveness, aggressiveness, distractibility, seclusiveness, sex play, stealing, lying and a variety of other characteristics. These varied in combination, number, and degree for each child.

The behaviour of the children was rated in the ward, on the playground, and in the schoolroom, with particular reference to the problem behaviour for which they were referred. After establishing a baseline, during an initial control period when no drugs were given, the children were administered benzedrine over a period of a week; during this time they were again rated. During the following week, each subject received phenobarbital, which is a depressant drug that would be expected to exacerbate their symptoms. Finally, after an interval of two weeks, the children were again rated under conditions of no drugs, this constituting the terminal control.

The authors state that, 'Under the influence of benzedrine marked improvement of behaviour was noted by all observers. Phenobarbital resulted in an exacerbation of symptoms. ... Behaviour scores on the sixth week of the study during the final control period ... were reduced considerably below the level of the initial score'. The results are shown in Figure 25. The authors also took electroencephalographic recordings and they state:

During the preliminary preparations an unique opportunity for observation of each subject was afforded under conditions which required co-operation. During the period of benzedrine medication, sociability, co-operation, attention, and alertness all seemed to be improved. Phenobarbital generally resulted in quite opposite reactions and attitudes. Under its influence practically all subjects were glum, irritable, uncommunicative, and annoyed by requests for co-operation.

It is also stated that, 'Under benzedrine medication all subjects show better than ten per cent improvement in their behaviour scores over those of the initial control periods; nine subjects show better than fifty per cent improvement'. In view of the short periods of medication, these results seem remarkable.[66]

In another study, Bradley and Bowen studied the effects of amphetamine on one hundred behaviour problem children. Of these, they found that fifty-four became more 'subdued'. By this term they mean,

... that in some conspicuous way a child became less active than before. ... Many children began to walk and move quietly in contrast to previous running and rushing about. A number spoke in a normal or lower tone of voice instead of shouting raucously. Some of these same children, instead of quarrelling and arguing boisterously, began to avoid expressing differences of opinion or conducted their discussions in tones which were not offensive. In certain instances, children appeared subdued because they began to spend their leisure time playing quietly or

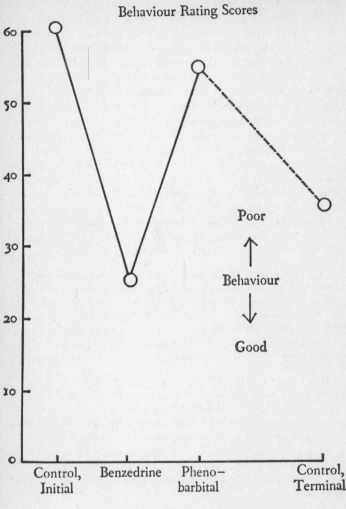

Behaviour Rating Scores

FIGURE 25

The data plotted show the effects of the administration of a stimulant drug (benzedrine) and a depressant drug (phenobarbital) on the observed scores of thirteen behaviour-problem children. The depressant drug exacerbates their antisocial behaviour; the stimulant drug improves it considerably. Redrawn from D. D. Lindsley and C. E. Henry, *Psychosomatic Medicine*, 1942, *4*, 140.

reading, whereas formerly they had wandered aimlessly about, antagonizing and annoying others. The general impression given by all the children who became definitely subdued was that they were effectively exerting more conscious control over their activities and the expression of their emotions. In general, they were conducting themselves with increased consideration and regard for the feelings of those about them.

As an example, Bradley and Bowen cite the case of John, a ten-year-old boy who was admitted to the hospital because of hyperactivity, destructive behaviour, poor school progress and failure to mingle satisfactorily with other children. It appears that he teased his companions incessantly, quarrelled with them, pushed them, and took their toys. This overactivity had been noted since early childhood, but the social problems arising from it became exaggerated when he entered school. Although he was under psychotherapeutic treatment for fifteen months, he was over-active, irritable, noisy, and disturbing in the ward, in the playground, and in the classroom, where he had made little progress. He demanded a great deal of attention in school, worked acceptably only when given individual instruction, and was unreliable when the teacher left the room. He was restless and distractible in all activities. At mealtimes, he stuffed food in his mouth, laughed and talked noisily, and constantly teased the other children. He gave no evidence of profiting from suggestion or training. When amphetamine was started:

There was immediately a definite change in his behaviour. On the ward, John was much quieter and none of his usual hyperactivity was noted. He was prompt for meals and school, and became pleasant and congenial with children and adults. He co-operated well in all matters of routine; no longer restless, but applied himself to daily tasks. In the class room he accomplished a great deal every day and showed excellent initiative. During leisure periods he was frequently busy with school work which he had requested be given him to do in his free time. He also occupied himself with reading and became interested in jig-saw puzzles. Several times John remarked spontaneously that he was glad he was receiving 'the pills', because they made him 'do better in school and ward work'. . . . Following discharge from the hospital John received amphetamine sulphate periodically. At times it produced dramatic improvement in his behaviour in school and at home. At other times, when unfavourable environmental conditions existed, little effect was observed.[67]*

* It should be noted that some children became stimulated by the drug rather than showing more subdued behaviour. 'Such children became more alert, accomplished their daily tasks with more initiative and dispatch, became more aggressive in competitive activity, and showed an increased interest in what was going on about them. As a result of these changes, they gave the impres-

Perhaps we can explain these findings along the following lines. The individual, although subjected during a long period of time to the conditioning processes of society, fails to condition because of certain defects in his central nervous system. With the use of the drug, the properties of his central nervous system are modified to make him more receptive to conditioning and, for the period of drug administration, he is effectively in the position of an introvert. He conditions, if anything, better than the average person and during this period, a large number of socially desirable conditioned responses are formed. Thus his conduct improves markedly and we now have a secondary process of conditioning taking place. Whereas previously he behaved in such a way that punishment rather than rewards came his way, he now behaves in a socially approved manner and he is praised and rewarded for these activities, thus strengthening the links which are being forged within his central nervous system. When the drug is withdrawn, the established conditioned responses do not extinguish. Conditioned habits, once acquired, remain unless they are deliberately extinguished. His improved conduct, therefore, remains, although we would not expect him to form additional conditioned responses with the same ease as he did when under drug treatment.

Many of the altered behaviour patterns shown by psychopaths and behaviour problem children appear immediately, and cannot be accounted for in terms of conditioning. They are likely to be due to a shift towards introversion, in terms of greater excitatory potential and lessened inhibitory potential. If the reader will glance back to Figure 17, and the discussion given there of the different reactions of introverts and extraverts, he will be able to see how a stimulant, an 'introverting drug', could have an immediate effect of the kind observed. It is also of some interest in this connexion that many observers have found psychopaths much more tolerant of stimulant drugs than are introverts, or normal people; this is the counterpart of the well substantiated observation that introverts are more tolerant of depressant drugs, i.e. of drugs which make them more extraverted. If we think of extraversion/introversion as a continuum on which each person has a fixed place, and if we think of stimulant and depressant drugs as capable of shifting a person's position in the introverted or extraverted direction, then

sion of being more self-sufficient and mature. They also appeared happier and more contented.' This paradoxical effect appeared mostly in children who were pathologically shy, withdrawn, and under-active in the first place. Too little is known about these children and the particular effects observed to make it possible to state to what extent their reactions to the drugs contradict the general theory which we have formulated above.

the extravert has farther to go in the introverted direction (is more tolerant of stimulant drugs), while the introvert has farther to go in the extraverted direction (is more tolerant of depressant drugs).[68]

The reader will have noted that we listed alcohol among the depressant drugs; most people are well aware that alcohol may lead to extraverted behaviour, and indeed, this aspect of its action has become almost proverbial. It may sound a little odd to say that alcohol leads to cortical inhibition, when in fact it leads to behaviour which is obviously uninhibited; but we have already drawn attention to the ambiguous nature of the term 'inhibition'. Cortical inhibition refers to the action of the drug on the higher neural centres. These centres have as part of their function the inhibition of the lower centres and of instinctive activity. The drug which inhibits these inhibiting centres, therefore, leads to a disinhibition of conduct, to what most of us would call uninhibited conduct. There is no real difficulty about this point.

We suggest that there is a close relationship between alcohol and criminal conduct, as well as between alcohol and traffic violations, road accidents, and so forth. We have postulated that all these behaviours are related to extraversion. We now point out that a depressant drug, which according to our theory should shift behaviour in the direction of greater extraversion, does indeed have the effect of increasing the commission of crimes and immoralities and the rate at which traffic violations and accidents occur. The results, therefore, fit in extremely well with our general theory.

I know of no attempts to apply these particular deductions from modern learning theory to the treatment of criminals in prison.[69] To do so would require the introduction of quite a novel principle into prison life. We would have to try deliberately to produce desirable social reactions, and put the prisoner through a process of positive conditioning. Haphazard attempts are occasionally made, but most of these attempts take little account of modern learning theory and the knowledge gained through animal and human experimentation in the psychological laboratory. In principle, however, there is no reason why these bits of information, these general laws, should not be applied in the prison situation, and there is no reason why these methods should not be coupled with a type of drug treatment analogous to that described above, in relation to behaviour disorders. Until such experimental work is done, however, it is impossible to say precisely just how useful these methods might be.

Two objections are sometimes made to proposals of this kind. The first of these involves the manipulation of a fundamental right of citizens in a democracy, the advisability of which may be questioned. We live in a country and under a government where the rule of law is absolute. Each one of us is equal to every other before the law, and while this equality is perhaps not always respected, nevertheless, in principle, the judge is impartial and metes out justice without regard to race, status, colour, or creed. The introduction of experimental methods into this field requires that criminals be allocated to different types of treatment, or different types of punishment according to some principle of allocation which is independent of the judiciary. If we wanted to compare the effects of a system such as that described above, with, say, the typical way in which criminals are dealt with nowadays, we would have to match criminals with respect to a large number of different characteristics – age, sex, and social background, intelligence, type of crime committed, and so on. We would then have to allocate randomly one of each pair to the behaviour therapy treatment, the other to the traditional type of prison sentence. Clearly, this would be an interference with the ordinary processes of law, which might not be tolerated by large numbers of people. We have here a conflict between two desirable ends; one is the traditional impartiality of the law towards the criminal, and the general principle that all men are equal before the law; the other is the wish to rehabilitate criminals and make them better citizens, which requires that we do experiments of this kind.

This conflict is one which also commonly plagues the medical profession. Suppose that we have a rather poor method of treating a particular disease and that a new drug is introduced which, allegedly, is much superior to the orthodox treatment. The only way of testing the new drug is to take a group of patients suffering from the disorder, allocate them at random to two groups, and treat one of these groups by means of the new drug and the other group by means of the old and inefficient treatment. The patients are then studied to determine whether the recovery rate of the control group, treated by means of the old treatment, is inferior to that of the experimental group, treated by means of the new drug. This procedure is also commonly condemned because, so people say, patients are being treated as guinea pigs. There is clearly a conflict here between two desirable alternatives. We would like to feel that all patients are given equal opportunity to receive the best possible treatment. The problem arises because it is simply not known which is the best treatment, and without such experimentation we will never know. Ethical questions rarely have clear-cut answers, and certainly the psychologist, as a scientist, is in no better position to suggest an answer to this particular problem than anyone else.

This is a decision which the citizens of a free country have to make for themselves.

The other objection is less difficult to deal with. Many people react to my proposed method of treatment of fetishism and neurosis discussed in the last chapter, by exclaiming in horror, 'Surely this is nothing but brain-washing?' There are two answers to this objection and to the implied argument that brain-washing, as such, is undesirable. In the first place, it is difficult to assign any meaning to the objection. Nobody knows what brain-washing is; it is a term applied to methods used, usually by our enemies and people we do not like, to inculcate opinions of which we disapprove into other people. The methods which are used are usually poorly understood; the Russians or the Chinese are accused of brain-washing their prisoners, but precisely what the term denotes is usually left undefined. Is this brain-washing in any sense different from, say, the methods used by the Inquisition in mediaeval Spain to change the opinions of infidels and atheists towards the Catholic religion? Is brain-washing identical with torture, or does it have other implications? It is difficult to evaluate the method when the term for it is so ill-defined and used in so many different ways by different people. 'Brain-washing' is simply an emotional term denoting nothing specific but connoting disapproval; as such, it has little scientific value. This, then, is one answer.

A second possible answer to this objection is that, if these methods are considered to be brain-washing, then society is already using methods of brain-washing on a large scale. After all, we try to inculcate respect for authority and for property in the criminals in our prisons, and we try to do this by means of a system of punishment, incarceration, and so on, which, in principle, is no different from the 'brain-washing' suggested above. The only difference between the established methods and the method suggested here is that the established methods are known to be inefficient and ineffective. If what is suggested here is wrong, then what is being done by society is at least equally wrong, and has not even the advantage of being successful.

This argument can, in fact, be extended in a way that might surprise a good number of people. To introduce this extension, let us assume for the moment, that an implacable enemy of our society set out to corrupt our morals and to increase the amount of juvenile delinquency and adult crime in the country. How would he set about it? He would start by noticing that his task was essentially similar to that of the behaviour therapist who is faced with a patient who has a phobia for cats. The patient has acquired this phobia through a process of sympathetic conditioning; in a similar way, the citizens of a country acquire a 'phobia' for criminal activity through a process of sympathetic conditioning. We have shown how, to eliminate the cat phobia, we simply use the principle of reciprocal inhibition. In other words, we require the patient to encounter the fear-producing object, the cat, under conditions where the impact of the fear-producing stimulus is lessened by removal along the distance gradient and, if necessary by using ideational representations of the object; and where this confrontation is accompanied by reassurance, relaxation, and parasympathetic stimulation generally.

Now our hypothetical enemy can just as easily apply this principle to the corruption of our citizens. He will try to invent a device which will reach the great majority of citizens in their own homes, a setting which might be assumed conducive to considerable parasympathetic stimulation. Perhaps they have just eaten and are resting in their easy chairs, with the family together and in a state of peace and relaxation. Into this background he will introduce, by some diabolical means, such as a modern electronic device, pictures of crimes and criminal activity, of violence, of sexual immorality and so forth, which, not being real, do not produce so much sympathetic arousal that the individual ceases to watch. Let us call this diabolical invention, used by our declared enemy, television, and let us observe what is happening. The individual has been strongly conditioned against violence and against sexual immorality, so much so, that if he encountered this in everyday life, the strong sympathetic stimulation would produce a very unpleasant reaction, and he would either go away from the situation or actively interfere in order to stop the violence. However, the violence, let us say, introduced here, like the picture of the cat shown to the woman suffering from the cat phobia, is in symbolic, representational form only; therefore, the arousal of the sympathetic system is much less. Furthermore, this stimulation is counteracted by the parasympathetic stimulation he is receiving in his own home. Under those conditions, the result should be, as in the case of reciprocal inhibition of neurotic responses, a weakening of the conditioned sympathetic response to immoral and antisocial behaviour. Continue this over a long period of time and you have the ideal method for the elimination of socially desirable responses, moral integrity, and ethical behaviour.

What I am suggesting is simply that processes of conditioning, of indoctrination, and of 'brain-washing' if you like, are going on all the time in our society; indeed, they are quite inescapable, because any kind of activity which strongly arouses one's autonomic system will also produce, under most circumstances, a decrement, or an increment, in conditioning. No amount of theoretical objection or moral indignation will alter the facts of the case. To object to the beneficial employment of conditioning, therefore, while continuing to tolerate the detrimental use of conditioning, as in the case of certain television programmes, certain films, certain types of advertising, and so on, seems to me to be a wilful refusal to face the facts. It would be nice if human beings were rational beings, whose conduct was determined by the use of intelligence and guided by wisdom. However, the experimental evidence is now pretty conclusive that this picture of *homo sapiens* is unfortunately entirely false. Our conduct is guided much more by certain biological impulses which we share with the lower animals, and to disregard and neglect these facts is probably the most important reason for the sad state in which our society finds itself today. Man is the most savage and deadly animal which has ever lived in this world, yet we fail to recognize the danger.

Another argument, related to the preceding one and often raised in discussions of the causes of criminality, concerns responsibility. Legally, of course, the notion of free will, responsibility, intent, and so on, plays a large part in the assessment of culpability – as, for instance, in the McNaughton Rules, which still govern a good deal of our thinking about murder and the possibility of extenuating circumstances such as insanity. The deduction which may be made from our general theory is relatively uncompromising. We would regard behaviour from a completely deterministic point of view; that is to say, the individual's behaviour is determined completely by his heredity and by the environmental influences which have been brought to bear upon him. Therefore, to attribute to different individuals, greater or lesser degrees of responsibility seems, from this point of view, a rather meaningless procedure. I may illustrate what I have in mind by postulating a series of hypothetical cases. First of all, let us assume that we have an individual – call him Smith – endowed with a normal central nervous system, and brought up along conventional lines, who has never shown any tendency toward law-breaking behaviour. Suppose he suffers a severe brain injury, through no fault of his own, and as a consequence of this, loses the ability to acquire conditioned responses easily and also extinguishes a good many of those he has already acquired. By virtue of this and also the increased amount of cortical inhibition produced by his injury, he now undertakes an antisocial career involving stealing, rape, and possibly murder. Would we consider him responsible in any meaningful sense of the term? Would we not say that we are dealing with a person who is ill, who has suffered severe damage to his nervous system, and who cannot be held responsible for the consequences of this damage, clearly beyond his power to remedy?

Let us now turn to Mr Brown. He also has been born with a normal central nervous system and he also has been given a good average upbringing, leading to normal behaviour patterns throughout the major part of his life. He is a salesman by profession and most of his work is done in France, where he has, in fact, made his residence. He has acquired, in the course of life, the French habit of drinking a good deal of wine with his meals, which eventually produces a marked effect on his brain. This effect is very similar to that of brain damage, producing an extinction of existing conditioned responses, great difficulty in acquiring new conditioned responses, and a considerable degree of cortical inhibition. As a consequence of these events, he now begins to lead a relatively amoral life. He leaves his wife, he defrauds the company which employs him, and in other ways deviates from the moral precepts by which he was brought up. To what degree can he be considered responsible for these events?

Next take Mr Jones, who, through no fault of his own, is born with a central nervous system which easily produces cortical inhibition, which is extremely difficult to condition and which easily produces extinction of conditioned responses. In other words, he is born with the kind of central nervous system which Smith acquires through his brain damage, and Brown through his wine-drinking. To what extent can we regard him as responsible for the things he does, the crimes he commits, and the anti-social activities in which he indulges? Is he any more responsible for his heredity than is Smith for the brain damage which he suffered quite innocently? The end result of the two factors is exactly the same, a central nervous system which is impervious to the socialization process.

Consider Harriet, a girl born with a normal central nervous system, who happens to be the daughter of a prostitute and a pimp. From early life she is brought up in an atmosphere where immorality is considered the norm and where socialized behaviour is frowned upon as being unusual, stuck-up, and odd. In due course she is trained by her parents in the arts of the prostitute and is initiated into this life at a very early age. She is given no other training and has no facility for making a living in any other way. Should she be blamed for living a life of sin, if not of crime? Here, clearly, we have a case where heredity may be quite normal, but where environment influences of an unusual kind determine her deviant behaviour.

These are extreme cases and the reader may feel that it is unfair to discuss the question of responsibility in terms of such clear-cut and somewhat unusual people. However, they will serve to illustrate the point. In every person's life it is his heredity and the environmental influences which have been brought to bear upon him that determine his conduct. He is not responsible for the one nor for the other. In what sense, then, can we say that a person is responsible for the actions which he undertakes? Religion indeed preaches that freedom of the will and personal responsibility have been given to us by God, but religion does not explain precisely how this freedom of will manifests itself in actual conduct or how it interacts with the forces of heredity and environment. The only answer you are likely to get from the Church on these matters is the old one of *credo quia impossibile* which is not a very helpful one. It simply appeals to the miraculous and refuses to explain. Neither, of course, does the Church act upon its precepts. The Church has never been in favour of letting individuals live their own lives, of leaving their conduct to this freedom of will which it extols. Instead, it has always taken great care to put strong environmental pressure upon people to act in accord with its dictates. This tendency reached its highest point during the Middle Ages, when the Church claimed powers exceeding even those of kings and governments, and when the Inquisition took upon itself to see that the freedom of will and individual personal responsibility should be allowed only if they were in line with the Church's teaching. In other words, the Church behaved very much like Henry Ford when he said that people could have his tin lizzie in any colour, as long as it was black!

I do not wish to belabour this point. Essentially what the deterministic psychologist says is that human conduct is always determined by specifiable causes. What the opponent maintains amounts to saying that behaviour is, at least to some extent, random, that it is not caused in any sense by motive, prior teaching or learning, or in any other way. This is not always clearly recognized, but it follows directly from the facts. Let us consider the case of a particular individual, James, who has a choice of either absconding with £100,000 or staying on at a low-level and uninteresting job. To say that he has a freedom of will to decide between these alternatives means nothing if we are saying simply that there are certain motives, drives, and learned behaviour patterns pulling in one direction, while others pull in another, and that the stronger set of motives, behaviour patterns and so on will win. If this is what we mean, then we are dealing with a completely deterministic event. If we are saying that there is a genuine freedom involved in this, then we are saying that the individual may act without regard to his motives, and the learning and conditioning that has gone on throughout his life, and that the decision is completely undetermined, or random. It is impossible, of course, for science to prove a negative, for example, to show that such randomness never occurs. Some people have found support, in Heisenberg's principle of indeterminacy in physics, for a belief that random events of this kind may happen in the central nervous system and that, to that extent conduct is not determined but is free. This possibility cannot logically be excluded; but I doubt if it would give much genuine support to the believers in free will. What they mean by free will is usually something entirely different from such random activity or 'white noise' in the central nervous system.

I do not wish to be dogmatic on this point, particularly as it is not vital to our discussion. There is no doubt that, to some extent at least, human conduct is conditioned, and therefore determined, by the forces that we have been discussing. It is not necessary to claim that it is *entirely* so determined. Further experimentation will narrow down the area of disagreement and show us precisely to what extent we can predict human conduct on the basis of knowledge of heredity and previous conditioning. It certainly would not follow, as some people have argued, that the complete denial of freedom of will leaves us in a state of therapeutic nihilism; quite the contrary. Because we know that conduct is determined, we are enabled to study scientifically the mechanisms by which it is determined, and thus develop appropriate ways of changing it.

Before closing, let me discuss briefly a few points which might otherwise cause the reader to be more critical of the theory developed here than it deserves. In the first place, let me restate my conviction that it *is* a *theory*. What I have put forward is the outcome of considerable theoretical and experimental work, but it is not contended that this is even remotely sufficient to elevate the suggestions made to the status of scientific laws. Theories in science, particularly in the early stages of science, can best be evaluated in terms of two criteria: how well do they succeed in integrating known facts? and, do they suggest new and hitherto untried experiments? It must be left to the reader to say whether, in these terms, the theory is worthwhile; absolute truth is not one of the attributes claimed for this particular hypothesis, nor is it likely to attend any scientific theory.

In the second place, let me disavow any claim to having discovered the secret of criminal conduct. Criminal behaviour is without doubt determined by a very large and heterogeneous array of social and psychological factors; any claim to have discovered a single cause underlying this complexity is certain to offend scientific credibility. All that can be said is that the innate predisposition to form weak and fleeting conditioned responses is a powerful cause of antisocial conduct in a great number of people; it is not the only such factor, nor does it suffice by itself to produce such behaviour. But it is not therefore unimportant simply because it is not all-important; an explanation of part of a phenomenon is not to be despised because it does not deal with the total phenomenon.

In the third place, let me anticipate an objection which is almost certain to have formed in the mind of the reader. Is all this not vastly over-simplified? Can such a small base really support such a huge superstructure? Is not life very much more complicated than we seem willing to admit? The answer to such objections must, of course, be in the affirmative; life is complex, and our theory is greatly over-simplified. But to make such an objection is to mis-understand the nature and purpose of scientific theories. Life in all its fullness is too complex to be understood or controlled; we have to single out certain important aspects which are relevant to the phenomena in which we are interested, in the hope that this will enable us to formulate theories regarding these limited fields, and to gain even limited understanding and control. We may then become more ambitious and extend our search, attempting to cover larger areas, to increase our understanding, to integrate our knowl-edge with that derived from other fields, and thus slowly seek to reduce the area of our ignorance. Science is not built in one day, and its first, fumbling efforts inevitably invite the criticism of over-simplification. Have we neglected certain important factors? Have we made assumptions which are only partially true? Have we used approximations rather than exact figures? Have we begged many important questions? Certainly. This is inevitable in the early stages of scientific development; to demand perfection from the first only ensures that the first step will never be taken. Even New-ton was severely criticized for his lack of mathematical rigour in the development of the calculus, and it was not until Cauchy made good these deficiencies 150 years later, in his *Cours d'Analyse*, that universal acceptance ensued. The appropriate question in scientific theories is not whether they cover all possible facts – they never do – but whether they aid understanding, help in the experimental control of phenomena, and lead to better theories. In spite of its over-simplifications, this is the aim of the theory presented here.

A programme of technological development is implied in the theory developed here. I have not tried to spell out the practical steps which would follow from acceptance of the theory, except in-cidentally; I have been concerned with a search for truth, rather than with writing a cookbook for penal reform. Nevertheless, one or two points may need emphasis. Like any other technology, a technology involving what is sometimes evasively called 'human engineering' is ethically neutral. It can be used for good, bad, or indifferent purposes. I have mentioned the difficulties which arise if our only reaction to conditioning methods is to murmur, 'Brain-washing!' The term is nearly always used to convey, not so much a description of the method used, as an abhorrence of the doctrine involved. In a word, I preach, you indoctrinate, he brain-washes! If I am right in thinking that social values are always inculcated in human beings through a process of conditioning, then we shall be able to reserve our indignation for the proper target, which is the wrong choice of values, rather than the choice of an inefficient instrument for their transmission.

The reader will have noted the implications in the use of the terms 'right' and 'wrong' in connexion with the term 'values'. This is not a book on values, and I cannot devote much space to a discussion of what is known to be one of the thorniest of problems. I would say that *the criterion for the goodness or badness of values lies not in their antecedents, but in their consequences.* In other words, values are not to be considered good because they derive from the religious or ethical teachings of a particular person or group, or because they are hallowed by tradition; values are good because they are conducive to human contentment and happiness. The question of the goodness or badness of values thus becomes a scientific question, and one where psychologists, anthropologists, and sociologists should have a genuine contribution to make.

Much is already known in relation to this question, but nothing is perhaps more firmly established than the fact that everyone has his own private road to salvation. Every person differs from every other person, both with respect to heredity and with respect to environment, and it follows that one person's values will not necessarily be those of another. Laws, rules, and ordinances inevitably set limits to the rights of human individuality, and are therefore bad; their only excuse is that they prevent even worse excesses. Rules should therefore be limited to the absolute minimum required to guarantee the survival of society, but within those limits it is probably most humane to conduct the necessary conditioning process with the greatest possible efficiency, rather than haphazardly and inefficiently, as at present. Similarly, the rehabilitation of those who have erred should be carried out by efficient, rather than by currently fashionable methods – methods which enforce the maximum of suffering for a minimum of correction and deterrence. That any improvement in the efficiency of conditioning right beliefs and values brings with it the dangers that wrong beliefs and values will also be conditioned with greater efficiency is, of course, true; it is debatable whether this danger should dissuade us from pursuing research in this field, particularly when it is clear that such restraint on our part would by no means be paralleled by similar restraint on the part of others whose value-systems might, on the whole, be considered inferior to ours. Facile optimism should certainly not be encouraged in this respect, but neither should equally facile defeatism.

The conclusion that different criminals need different treatment, in order to change their value-systems and their patterns of conditioning in a direction more in line with social needs, implies radical changes in our attitude to legal matters. The implication has already been discussed that the punishment should fit the criminal, not the crime; this in turn implies the need for a large-scale diagnostic service to determine such factors as the conditionability of the criminal, his emotional reactivity, and his previous reinforcement schedule. It also follows that research facilities would have to be built into the legal system, so that sentencing would become part of an empirical attempt to improve the rate of success in rehabilitating criminals. All this will undoubtedly antagonize many people, to whom the criminal is a wilfully wicked person who needs to be punished, rather than a poorly conditioned person, who needs to learn the appropriate social responses. The attitude taken here should appeal to religious people, on the principle that revenge belongs to the Lord; to humanists, on the principle that revenge inflicts suffering for no useful purpose, and possibly even strengthens the attitudes it is meant to destroy; and to practical people everywhere, on the principle that if crime is to be fought, then it should be fought efficiently, rather than inefficiently. The research needed, and the other changes proposed, would cost money, but this is surely a case where even a small investment is likely to bring rich dividends. Most industries consider that it is reasonable to invest from 1 to 5 per cent of profits in research devoted to improving methods of production; Great Britain, where the total cost of crime is estimated to be in the region of £500,000,000 per annum, spends less than one ten-thousandth (.01 per cent) of this amount on any form of research in this field. The comparable figure in the United States is better, coming up to .1 per cent, but even that is ridiculously low considering the seriousness of the situation. Psychologists are often expected to solve all the problems of society, but even when these are at least partially soluble, an enormous research effort is required, which calls for financing on the same scale as the production of such socially useful devices as the nuclear fission bomb. Somehow, this support never seems to be forthcoming for research in matters not leading to the killing and maiming of vast numbers of fellow citizens, though there may be good psychological reasons for this curious state of affairs. Perhaps the process of conditioning by which we acquire our value system is in need of improvement.

This general need for research in penology, education, psychiatry, politics, and indeed all disciplines which deal with the control of human behaviour, is perhaps best seen in the perspective of the non-scientific attitude we still have in this field, and have had in the recent history of physics and astronomy. Only 200 years ago, the philosopher Hegel announced categorically that no planet other than the seven already known would ever be found, on the basis that seven was in some way a mystic and sacred number; he was unfortunate in his timing of this pronouncement, because it only barely anticipated the discovery of planet number eight! We now laugh at his discomfiture, but he was taken very seriously in his own time, and our own dealings with human beings are not based on any firmer ground than Hegel's prediction was in his time. Of all the problems for investigation, that relating to the constructive use of pain is perhaps the most neglected, and the one most overgrown with myths, sentiments, and savage creeds.

The need for the most careful experimental investigation, under controlled conditions, of the effectiveness of any type of treatment can perhaps be illustrated best by the well-known study carried out by Mannheim and Wilkins in England. They were concerned with the relative success of two types of Borstal institutions called, respectively, 'open' and 'closed'. The open Borstal seemed to be about twice as effective as the closed one; about one in three of the offenders dealt with in open institutions committed further crimes within three years from release, whereas about two out of every three of those trained in closed institutions became recidivists.[70] This suggests that open Borstals were better than closed; but let us point out that every Borstal lad is first sent to a reception centre where he is observed and then allocated to the training institution considered most suitable for him. This allocation will work in favour of sending the better type of boy to the open and the worse kind of boy to the closed institution. It is possible to draw up statistical tables for any given boy on the basis of his previous conduct and education, which will indicate the likelihood of his recidivism; it is then possible to give each boy – whether he goes to an open or to a closed Borstal – a point score which indicates the relative likelihood of his becoming a success or failure. We can then, by statistical treatment of the data, hold constant the differences in allocation and see whether there remains any difference in success rate. After making allowances for the type of boy sent to the two institutions, the overall difference between the open and the closed Borstal dropped from 22 per cent to 8 per cent. Even this slight difference is not necessarily due to the influence of the open institution. It might be, for instance, that when a 'bad risk' went to an open Borstal, one of the important curative factors was the high proportion of 'good risks' to be found there. It might be possible, therefore, that the explanation of the higher success rate of the open Borstal may be due partly to the composition of the group of lads there, rather than being due to the method of treatment adopted. In addition, it may be noted that later studies, carried out along similar lines, have failed to find any difference between the two institutions when the appropriate corrections have been made.

To summarize, let me illustrate the position as I see it, by taking an actual example. Many children, and not a few adults, suffer from *enuresis nocturna*; they wet their beds every night, or at least a large proportion of nights. This habit, as we have seen, is related to criminality; many more criminals than non-criminals are enuretic. We may regard this as a kind of miniature model of criminal activity: it is antisocial, in the sense that society strongly impresses on the child that he or she should remain continent, and that, in spite of this teaching, the child continues with his disapproved conduct. What do parents do when this happens? Many, if not most, regard their children as being deliberately wicked, and beat the ever-lasting daylights out of them. This relieves parental feelings, but has the unfortunate effect of increasing the anxiety level of the child, thus strengthening even more firmly the habit they wish to eliminate. The result, of course, is even greater parental disapproval, more bed-wetting, and so on, in an ever-widening vicious circle.

Some parents, following the siren voices of psychoanalysts, send their children for psychotherapy, on the supposition that they are mentally or emotionally 'ill' in some poorly defined way. As this hypothesis is in fact untrue, psychotherapy produces no effect on the enuresis, and the child goes on wetting his bed. The evidence showing this type of treatment to be ineffective is now very strong indeed. All that can be said in its favour is that at least it is likely to inhibit the parents from chastising the child, thus giving spontaneous remission a good chance to do its work.

The scientific approach advocated here, as we have pointed out before, is quite different from both these methods. The failure of the child to form the required conditioned reaction (waking up and going to the toilet) to the conditioned stimulus (distension of the bladder and beginning of urination) is regarded as neither wicked nor evidence of some deep-seated personality disturbance; it is regarded simply as evidence of poor conditionability. Putting the child through a simple process of conditioning, the bell-and-blanket method, works quickly and well. In the vast majority of cases it leads to a considerable improvement in the emotional state of the child, who was naturally anxious and depressed by his troubles, and alleviates the cause of much parental disapproval. It does not lead, as was feared at one time, to the eruption of some other, possibly worse, neurotic symptoms. While certain interesting theoretical problems connected with enuresis and its treatment are still unsolved, we may say that for all practical purposes we know the causes, and we know the cure.

This method uses pain constructively; it uses the absolute minimum of painful stimulation – a loud bell waking up the child during the night – and it does so in accordance with a rational hypothesis about the precise effects of this stimulation. Parents who beat their children use pain destructively; they use a maximum of pain and effect the exact reverse of their actual goal. It will be only too clear to the reader that society, at present, is behaving very much in the manner of the parent in our story; it is the aim and purpose of this book to suggest a more scientific approach that would be more effective than the blind lashing out that is currently so popular. The bell-and-blanket method may sound terribly mechanical; are we not treating the child as if he were a machine? Soviet Russia has indeed denounced such methods as being 'mechanistic', which is a deviation from true Marxist practice only one whit better than 'idealism'; but surely such words are irrelevant in this context. If the child behaves like a physical system with a fault in the transducer, and if eliminating this fault restores the system to working order, it is difficult to see why this procedure should be condemned, while the ineffective thrashing of the child (comparable to simply kicking the physical system in exasperation) should be regarded as in some way morally, ethically, or philosophically superior. To some degree, the human being is indeed a machine; it is the task of science to find out the precise extent to which this is true. Whether human beings are nothing *but* machines is a philosophical question, not admitting of an answer at the moment, and not relevant to our problem. The established facts are our only safe guide in coming to a decision on the important question of how to treat our criminals.

9 Some Questions Answered

'Come, we shall have some fun now!' thought Alice. 'I'm glad they've begun asking riddles – I believe I can guess that,' she added aloud.

'Do you mean that you think you can find out the answer to it?' said the March Hare.

'Exactly so,' said Alice.

'Then you should say what you mean,' the March Hare went on.

'I do,' Alice hastily replied 'at least – at least I mean what I say – that's the same thing, you know.'

'Not the same thing a bit!' said the Hatter. 'Why, you might just as well say that "I see what I eat" is the same thing as "I eat what I see"!'

ALICE'S ADVENTURES IN WONDERLAND

The theory of criminal behaviour here presented has aroused a good deal of interest, and has given rise to many questions which could not have been answered adequately in so short a volume. In addition, much research has been conducted into this field since the original publication of this book, and partly at least in response to the hypotheses there put forward. It seems useful to take up some of these questions, even though only briefly, and try to answer them in this last chapter. The first, and possibly the most important, relates to the actual distribution of personality scores in prison populations; our theory demands that prisoners should have higher extraversion and neuroticism scores than normal control groups, and a proper test of this prediction is of course of the greatest urgency. A few selected investigations have already been cited (Figure 6), but it may be asked if these are representative; many other investigations have been carried out on the personality of prisoners, and it is possible that these may not bear out the impression given in that figure. In answer to this question, Table 4 is given below; this summarizes over a dozen retrospective studies (i.e. studies in which the personality of criminals already convicted is being studied), and while not exhaustive does include all those published investigations which allow some reasonable assessment of the two personality variables in which we are interested.

In many cases measures of personality have been used which do not allow of any direct scoring in terms of extraversion and neuroticism. To give some indication of the general trend of results, certain signs have been given in the last two columns, i.e. under E and N; these signify whether the results are equivocal (=), support on the whole the hypothesis, but rather weakly (+), support the hypothesis significantly (++), or support the hypothesis very strongly (+++). Another sign is also used (?) to indicate that the data do not seem relevant to the personality trait in question. It had been planned to use minus signs to indicate disproof of the hypothesis, but these proved unnecessary. It is clear of course that these evaluations are to some extent subjective; other judges might have been more or less severe or lenient. Certain comments are appropriate to all these investigations; these will be considered below.[71]

TABLE 4

	Adolescents	E	N
1. Gibbens, T. C. N. 1963	107 male delinquents	+	?
2. Glueck, S., Glueck, E. 1950	500 male delinquents	++	?
3. Little, A. 1963	290 male delinquents	=	++
4. Peterson, D. R. 1959, 1961	116 male delinquents	+	+
5. Pierson, G. R., Kelly, R. F. 1963	970 male delinquents	++	?
6. Price, J. R. 1968	100 female delinquents	+++	+++
	Adults		
1. Bartholomew, A. A. 1957	48 male and 24 female offenders (British)	=	++
2. Bartholomew, A. A. 1957	100 male offenders (British)	=	++
3. Bartholomew, A. A. 1963	150 male offenders, 159 female offenders (Australian)	+	++
4. Field, J. G. 1960	369 male offenders (British)	+	++
5. Fitch, J. H. 1962	700 male offenders (British)	=	++
6. Syed, I. 1964	100 female offenders (British)	+	++
7. Warburton, F. W. 1965	38 psychopathic criminals (American)	++	+++

It will be seen that the results are favourable, rather than unfavourable; there is a reasonable number of plus signs in both the

E and the N column, rather more in the latter than in the former. This outcome might be considered mild support for the theory. There is however one criticism which must be made of all these studies, namely that the control groups with which the criminals have been compared are not properly chosen to present a true comparison. Criminals are of a certain age and sex, come from a certain social class, and have a certain level of intelligence and education. Only if the control group has been specially chosen so as to be comparable with the criminal group can the respective personality trait scores be properly compared. Standardization groups (the usual control groups) must be presumed to differ from the criminal groups in one or more of these variables, and consequently any differences observed might be due to these other variables, rather than to criminality. This is perhaps unlikely, but in future work it is hoped that such considerations will be borne in mind.

On the other hand, there are reasons to believe that the published figures underestimate the degree of extraversion of the prisoners. In the first place, many of the questions making up the inventory are not very applicable to a person incarcerated for many years in prison; asking him whether he likes going to parties, or would be unhappy without frequent social discourse, may seem like mockery to him, and is likely to elicit more introverted answers than would be the case outside prison. In the second place, while E and N are independent over the general population, the evidence suggests strongly that in neurotic and other high N groups this independence breaks down, and correlations of up to .4 and above have been reported. Now there is almost universal agreement in the studies quoted that criminals have quite high N scores; consequently their E scores, when compared with a normal standardization sample, would be somewhat lower, and might be considerably lower. In other words, a proper sample for investigating the E component in the personality of criminals would have to be selected in such a way that its members had identical mean N scores as the criminal sample. In the absence of such a sample it may be surmised that the published figures underestimate the relative extraversion of the criminals studied, possibly to quite a significant amount. It is interesting that in spite of this complication none of the published studies has in fact shown a reversal of the predicted effect; none of the criminal samples in Table 4 has actually turned out to be introverted.

This brings us to a second question. Given that incarcerated criminals show certain personality traits of extraversion and neuroticism, does it follow that these are causal in the development of the criminal personality, and have actually preceded the incarceration?

It seems possible that personality may change in response to the traumatic events of being tried, convicted and imprisoned; these events might make a person more emotional and indeed neurotic, thus accounting for the high N scores of prisoners. (It seems rather more difficult to account for the high E scores of prisoners in this manner.) While psychologically not impossible or even implausible, this hypothesis is contra-indicated by the results of certain prospective studies in which children or adolescents were studied and then followed up over a period of time; those who then became criminal were found to have been previous to the commission of the crime, or the imprisonment, both extraverted and high on N. Hathaway and Monarchesi reported one such study in 1953 and in 1957[72], and Michael[73] another in 1957, both dealing with American school children. Perhaps the most impressive, however, is an investigation recently published by Sir Cyril Burt; appearing in 1965, this article reported the follow-up of children originally studied some thirty-five years previously. Seven hundred and sixty-three children, of whom 15 per cent and 18 per cent respectively later became habitual offenders or neurotics were rated by their teachers for emotionality/neuroticism and for extraversion/introversion. Of those who became habitual offenders, 63 per cent had been rated as high on emotionality; 54 per cent had been rated as high on extraversion, but only 3 per cent on introversion. Of those who became neurotics, 59 per cent had been rated as high on emotionality; 44 per cent had been rated as high on introversion, but only 1 per cent on extraversion.[74] Thus we see that even the probably rather unreliable ratings made by teachers of their pupils at school can predict with rather surprising accuracy the later adult behaviour of these children. Taken together with other predictive studies mentioned this seems rather conclusively to indicate the close relationship between E and N, on the one hand, and criminality, on the other. It may further be noted that the arguments put forward in connexion with the retrospective studies, i.e. that the control groups are not properly comparable, do not obtain in this case; we start with one fairly homogeneous group of children going to the same schools, and coming from the same neighbourhood, and we follow them through life and group them at the end of the follow-up according to whether they have or have not become habitual offenders – a quite objective criterion, although of course a fallible one in that some criminals may have been undetected at the time of writing.

These figures raise another question. It has been stated several times that criminals are not a homogeneous group, and that it would be idle to try and find any universal traits characterizing such a heterogeneous universe of people. It is then sensible to compare more or less random groups of criminals with normal samples? Surely the theory should specify more in detail which groups of criminals would be expected to show high E and N scores, and which might be expected to deviate from this pattern. Such an objection is very much in line with the spirit of this book, and with the hypotheses put forward. There is little in common between such 'criminals' as Lady Macbeth, Kohlhase (the hero of Kleist's famous story who turns on society when he is unjustly penalized by corrupt authority), and the Arkansas teacher who violated the fundamentalist laws of his state by teaching evolution – to say nothing of hunger-striking suffragettes, Ghandi imprisoned by the British Raj, and Hitler held captive after the beer-cellar *Putsch*. The only reason for quoting such studies as those in Table 4 is that most investigators have not heeded this important point, and their data are almost the only ones available.

Theoretically, one would perhaps say that there are certain quite large groups of criminals which are quite likely to be introverted rather than extraverted. For instance, there is a large group of people characterized by inadequate personality, rather dull and helpless, who drift into crime not because they are in any sense antisocial, but because they simply cannot cope with the complexities of modern life. They are often solitary figures, without friends and family, and their 'crimes' often consist of smashing a shop-window and then waiting to be arrested, thus earning for themselves a bed, warmth, and some food, preferring prison and its modest comforts to the harsh actuality of sleeping rough (and hungry) through a typical English winter's night. At the other end of this continuum we have the actively antisocial, psychopathic criminal who almost glories in his criminal activities and seems bereft of conscience or guilt feelings; such men often indulge in gratuitous violence, lying and deceit. It is with this latter (and much more dangerous) group that our theories are concerned, and the admixture of the former in any unselected sample, such as those studied by most investigators, clearly makes it much more difficult to give our theory a proper chance. Little has in fact been done to sort out internal differences, i.e. differences in personality between different types of prisoners; this must be one of the most important research areas for the future.

Pierson and Kelly, in their 1963 study, in which they tested 970 American male delinquents, comment on the heterogeneity of their sample; they specify the inclusion of a tough-hostile and a schizoid-withdrawn group.[75] It is the former with whom our theory deals; the inclusion of the latter would make comparisons with normal control groups rather pointless. Similarly Marcus, who studied 797 British male offenders, suggests the existence of an active-aggressive and a passive-inadequate group of offenders.[76] Fields has actually shown an association between passive-inadequate behaviour and introversion, and 'emotional indifference', characteristic of the active-aggressive type of convict, and extraversion.[77] It seems likely that future work, concentrating on differences within the prison population along these lines, will throw much light on the adequacy of our hypothesis.

Related to the question just discussed is another one. The picture of the aggressive, ruthless, hostile, insensitive psychopath painted above accords ill with the customary description of the normal extravert who is sociable, talkative, and given to overt displays of emotion; is it not possible that there is another personality factor, additional to those we have been discussing so far, which must be added to the amalgam to make the picture convincing? The answer to this question is probably Yes; there is indeed a third factor which the writer has been studying for many years, and which has recently become susceptible to questionnaire measurement. This factor is called psychoticism; just as there is a continuum from normal to neurotic, along which predisposition to neurotic breakdown (neuroticism) can be measured, so there appears to exist a continuum from normal to psychotic, along which predisposition to psychotic breakdown (psychoticism) can be measured. When we consider the questions answers to which define this empirically derived factor, we find that the person high on P is characterized by the following traits: (1) solitary; not caring for other people, (2) troublesome; not fitting in, (3) cruel; inhumane, (4) lack of feeling; insensitive, (5) sensation-seeking; avid for strong stimuli, (6) hostile to others; aggressive, (7) liking for odd unusual things, (8) disregard for danger; foolhardy, (9) likes making fools of other people; upsetting them.

This factor was derived from studies of normal people, both adults and children; yet the description derived from the pattern of traits observed seems very close to that of certain types of prisoners. Do prisoners actually score high on P inventories? The answer is given in Figure 26; the data are derived from over 1,000 normal male subjects, 179 adult male prisoners, and 56 neurotics, almost equally divided between the sexes. It will be seen that the prisoners have scores almost identical on both N and P with actual psychotic patients, of whom there were 156 males and 154 females, all certified. This does not mean of course that the prisoners were psychotic, in the clinical sense; the inventory does not deal with psychiatric symptoms, but rather with the underlying character

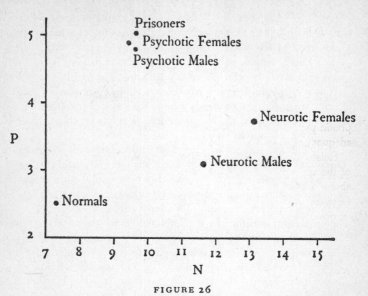

FIGURE 26

Scores on the neuroticism and psychoticism scales of the
Eysenck Personality Inventory of prisoners, normal, neurotic,
and psychotic subjects.

structure. These (hitherto unpublished) data suggest strongly that
further work on this new dimension may throw much needed light
on the personality of prisoners.

A theoretical question relating to our theory of conscience has
puzzled many readers. In everyday terminology we attribute two
rather separate consequences to our possession of a 'conscience'
when confronted with temptation. The first, and the one almost
exclusively stressed in the body of this book, is *resistance to temptation*; conscience enables us to overcome the illicit promise of
reward by throwing into the balance the immediate punishment of
conditioned fear/pain responses. But we often give way to temptation, all the same, and then conscience shows itself by giving rise
to *guilt feelings*; can these too be explained in terms of a conditioning
paradigm, and if so, how does their genesis differ from that of
resistance to temptation? The theoretical answer would seem to
be related to the delay in punishment during the original conditioning situation(s). If punishment (negative reinforcement) follows
immediately upon approach to the forbidden goal, and prior to
consummation of the forbidden act, then what is conditioned is
fear of approach to the goal; in other words, we acquire resistance
to temptation. But if for one reason or another punishment is

delayed until the goal has been reached, and the consummatory act has begun, then the conditioned fear/pain attaches itself to the after-effects of the consummatory act, and appear subjectively as *guilt*. Thus, as emphasized throughout this book, timing is of the essence; the whole principle of conditioning emphasizes the importance of this timing, and whether we achieve our goal of preventing antisocial acts, or merely achieve the genesis of guilt feelings after the execution of the antisocial acts, depends on this delicate question of appropriate timing.

Aronfeld and Reber, working with children[78], and Solomon, Turner and Lessac, working with dogs, have lent powerful support to this interpretation[79]. We have already discussed at some length Solomon's earlier experiments (pp. 127–29); hence we may perhaps continue with a brief account of his most recent work. Using the same paradigm as before, he slapped the dogs who approached the forbidden food either (1) before they could start eating (0 seconds delay), or (2) 5 seconds after beginning to eat (5 seconds delay), or (3) 15 seconds after beginning to eat (15 seconds delay). All three groups learned the avoidance response in roughly similar numbers of conditioning sessions; however, important differences emerged when they were left alone in the room with the two food dishes. The 0 seconds delay group ate the 20 grams of dry chow pellets and then withdrew to the walls of the room far away from the horsemeat. 'It was only after several days of starvation that these subjects moved close to the horsemeat dish. When they finally broke the taboo, their mood appeared to change abruptly . . . they wagged their tails while eating the meat, ate voraciously without pausing, and after finishing the meat did not appear to be apprehensive.' In other words, these dogs feared to approach the forbidden goal, but once the deed was done had no guilt feelings.

The dogs in the groups where punishment had been delayed 'behaved *as though the experimenter were still there*. After eating the few dry chow pellets, they put their forepaws on the experimenter's empty chair, or hid behind the chair, and wagged their tails when they looked at the chair. When they finally broke the taboo and ate the horsemeat, they ate in brief intervals and ran away between bites. They appeared to be frightened during and after finishing the meat.' These guilt feelings even generalized during training to the dry pellets, which they were permitted to eat; by contrast, the 0 seconds delay dogs during training exhibited fearfulness 'only during the approach to food and not during the eating itself'. It may seem fanciful and anthropomorphic to attribute 'guilt' to non-human experimental subjects, such as dogs, but if we judge purely in behavioural terms then the behaviour of the dogs whose punishment was delayed, in its furtiveness, slinking away after brief nibbles at the forbidden food, and general air of doing the wrong thing and being afraid of punishment by some power not present to the senses, reminds one strikingly of human beings acting under some strong guilt feelings.

Furthermore, of course, work with children already mentioned supports the main animal findings. We may thus conclude that there is some evidence to support our hypothesis regarding the importance of timing in producing either the *avoidance* or the *guilt* reaction. The relevance of this finding to the upbringing of children needs no emphasis; after all, we want them to *avoid* the forbidden act, rather than *feel guilty* after committing it! The former achievement is a useful one, the latter may satisfy our ethical sense of retribution, but is socially pretty useless. It may also be noted that here we have hit upon a mechanism which explains the fact that introverts are not always found to indulge in socially acceptable behaviour; it seems possible that in these cases parents and teachers have failed to apply negative reinforcement (punishment) without undue delay, so that these children have grown up, not avoiding temptation, but feeling guilty over succumbing! This hypothesis may repay further study.

Many other questions will no doubt suggest themselves to the reader; to most of them there is probably no answer at the moment. The purpose of theories, such as those here presented, is not so much to lay down the law, as to summarize existing knowledge (pitifully small though our store of such knowledge really is!) and to suggest promising ways of advancing such knowledge. Another useful function of theory is integration with existing knowledge in other fields; *ad hoc* theories have abounded in criminology, but have not advanced our knowledge very much. Theories like the present, closely tied to lawful consistencies in other fields, such as conditioning and personality, may 'explain' and help to 'understand' criminal behaviour in a way that *ad hoc* theories cannot do. However, when all is said and done, there remains still a gigantic gap between the frightening complexity of real-life criminality, and the simplified experimental laboratory studies of the psychologist. This gap must be bridged if ever we are to gain control over crime in all its manifestations.

Epilogue

What in this book may be considered new? The principle of association as applied to the training of children and adolescents in 'doing right' is certainly of venerable antiquity; Plato emphasized it in the rules he laid down for his 'guardians', and many later writers have taken their cue from him. Most explicit, perhaps, has been David Hartley, who summarized, in 1749, his *Observations on Man, His Fame, His Duty, and His Expectations* as follows:

There are many immediate good Consequences, which attend Virtue, as many ill ones do upon Vice, and that during our whole Progress through Life. Sensuality and Intemperance subject Men to Diseases and Pain, to Shame, Deformity, Filthiness, Terrors, and Anxieties; whereas Temperance is attended with Ease of Body, Freedom of Spirits, the Capacity of being pleased with the Objects of Pleasure, the good Opinion of others, the Perfection of the Senses, and of the Faculties bodily and mental, long Life Plenty, Etc. . . . Now these Pleasures and Pains, by often recurring in various Combinations, and by being variously transferred upon each other, from the great Affinity between the several Virtues, and their Rewards, with each other; also between the several Vices, and their Punishments, with each other; will at last beget in us a general, mixed, pleasing Idea and Consciousness, when we reflect upon our own virtuous Affections or Actions; a Sense of Guilt, and an Anxiety, when we reflect on the contrary; and also raise in us the Love and Esteem of Virtue, and the Hatred of Vice in others.

The Moral Sense or Judgment here spoken of, is sometimes considered as an Instinct, sometimes as Determinations of the Mind, grounded on the eternal Reasons and Relations of Things. Those who maintain either of these Opinions may, perhaps, explain them so as to be consistent with the fore-going Analysis of the Moral Sense from Association. But if by Instinct be meant a Disposition communicated to the Brain, and in consequence of this, to the Mind, or to the Mind alone, so as to be quite independent of Association; and by a moral Instinct, such as Disposition producing in us moral Judgments concerning Affections and Actions; it will be necessary, in order to support the Opinion of a moral Instinct, to produce Instances, where moral Judgments arise in us independently of prior Associations determining thereto.

In like manner, if by founding the Morality of Actions, and our Judgment concerning this Morality, on the eternal Reasons and Relations of Things, be meant, that the Reasons drawn from the Relations of Things, by which the Morality or Immorality of certain Actions is commonly proved, and which, with the relations, are called Eternal, from their appearing the same, or nearly the same, to the Mind at all Times, would determine the Mind to form the corresponding moral Judgment independently of prior Associations, this ought also to be proved by the Allegation of proper Instances. To me it appears, that the Instances are, as far as we can judge of them, of an opposite Nature, and favour the Deduction of all our moral Judgments, Approbations, and Disapprobations, from Association alone. However, some Associations are formed so early, repeated so often, riveted so strong, and have so close a Connexion with the common Nature of Man, and the Events of Life which happen to all, as, in a popular way of speaking, to claim the Appellation of original and natural Dispositions; and to appear like Instincts, when compared with Dispositions evidently factitious; also like Axioms, and intuitive Propositions, eternally true according to the usual Phrase, when compared with moral Reasonings of a compound Kind. But I have endeavoured to shew in these Papers, that all Reasoning, as well as Affection, is the mere Result of Association.

The main contributions of modern psychology to this general theory are these. In the first place, psychology has left behind simple, unaided observation, and has made use of the priceless opportunities afforded for exact and quantitative study of human behaviour by the psychological laboratory. Psychology is no longer a subsidiary of philosophy, it relies no longer on commonsense reflections upon life, or on arm-chair theorizing; by becoming experimental it has made the first faltering steps towards becoming scientific.

In the second place, psychology has derived from laboratory studies a number of generalizations and theories, of varying complexity; these in turn may now be applied to everyday events, in the hope not only of understanding human behaviour, but also of changing it. Admittedly these theories are much less powerful than those of physics, or astronomy, or chemistry, and they command less universal agreement; nevertheless they cannot be dismissed out of hand as useless and premature. Consider how quickly the older and more mature sciences outgrew their earlier theories, and how, almost unnoticed, they changed the face of the world. Psychology has set out on the same road, and sooner or later society will have to take heed of its views.

In the third place, we now have some knowledge of the importance of individual differences in the application of our general laws and theories; as the physicist would not use gold and quick-silver interchangeably, so also would the psychologist refuse to treat alike the introverted and extraverted, or the stable and the neurotic. The need to suit the treatment to the individual characteristics of the patient is now commonplace in psychology; here too, society cannot remain ignorant of modern advances and shelter behind mediaeval theology and pre-Christian morality.

In the fourth place, we now have available statistical techniques and methods of experimental design which enable us to take our theories out of the laboratory and test them in the crucible of everyday life situations. The easy criticism that what happens in the laboratory is irrelevant to everyday life becomes harder to sustain when on all sides the evidence is growing that there is in reality no such division; the laws of science are not bounded by the walls of the University ivory tower! Sooner or later, society will have to replace its happy-go-lucky, unreasoning ways of dealing with offenders by rational, scientific methods, firmly founded on painstaking observation and empirically-based theory; three thousand years of failure to solve the problem of crime would suggest even to the most conservative that the old ways might not be the best!

In summary, modern psychology holds out to society an altogether different approach to criminality, an approach geared only to practical ends, such as the elimination of antisocial conduct, and not cluttered with irrelevant, philosophical, retributory and ethico-religious beliefs. It firmly holds to the distinction between private sin and public crime, leaving the former to morality and theology, and concerning itself only with the latter. We have now reached the point where we can hope to combat crime effectively; shall we have the courage and the wisdom to give up our ancient hates and fears, and grasp the opportunity?

References

1. For a review of this controversy, see H. J. Eysenck, *The Structure of Human Personality*, Methuen, London; Macmillan, New York; 1960.
2. I. P. Pavlov, *Conditioned Reflexes*, Oxford University Press, New York, 1927.
3. E. L. Thorndike, *Educational Psychology*, Columbia University Teachers' College, New York, 1903.
4. The books by H. Hartshorne and M. A. May were published in New York by Macmillan. For a recent discussion, see R. V. Burton, 'The Generality of Honesty Reconsidered', *Psychol. Rev.*, 1963, *70*, 481–99.
5. G. W. Allport, *Personality*, Constable, London, 1937.
6. See the article by John Parry, 'Criminal Traits in the Road Offender', *The Observer Weekend Review*, 5 May 1963.
7. T. Willett, *Criminal on the Road*, Tavistock Publications, London, 1964.
8. W. A. Tillman and G. E. Hobbs, 'The Accident-Prone Automobile Driver', *Amer. J. Psychiat.*, 1949, *106*, 321–31.
9. P. E. Vernon, *The Assessment of Psychological Qualities by Verbal Methods*, H.M.S.O., London, 1938.
10. R. R. Sears, 'Experimental Studies on Projection: I', *J. soc. Psychol.*, 1936, *7*, 151–65.
11. H. J. Eysenck, *The Scientific Study of Personality*, Praeger, New York, 1952.
12. S. B. G. Eysenck and H. J. Eysenck, 'The Validity of Questionnaire and Rating Assessments of Extraversion and Neuroticism and their Factorial Stability', *Brit. J. Psychol.*, 1963, *54*, 51–62.
13. H. J. Eysenck, *Dimensions of Personality*, Praeger, New York, 1947.
14. C. G. Jung, *Psychological Types*, Harcourt, New York, 1933. A good summary of Jung's views will be found in C. S. Hall and G. Lindzey, *Theories of Personality*, Wiley, New York, 1957.
15. H. J. Eysenck, *The Structure of Human Personality*, op. cit.
16. H. J. Eysenck (ed.), *Handbook of Abnormal Psychology*, Pitman, London, 1960; Basic Books, New York, 1961.
17. C. G. Jung, op. cit.; H. J. Eysenck, *The Structure of Human Personality*, op. cit.
18. H. G. Gough, 'A Sociological Theory of Psychopathy', *Amer. J. Sociol.*, 1948, *53*, 359–66.
19. Most of the studies summarized here have used the Maudsley Personality Inventory or the Eysenck Personality Inventory (Educational and Industrial Testing Service, San Diego, 1962, 1963). The original data and full references may be found in the Manuals accompanying these inventories. Although their conclusions have not yet been published, several studies have been done using these inventories, including one carried out by F. Warburton, in collaboration with R. B. Cattell, on Chicago criminals; he kindly made his results available for inclusion here. Additional data were

obtained from A. A. Bartholomew, 'Some Comparative Australian Data for the Maudsley Personality Inventory', *Austral. J. Psychol.*, 1963, *15*, 46–51; and 'Extraversion-Introversion and Neuroticism in First Offenders and Recidivists', *Brit. J. Delinq.*, 1959, *10*, 120–29. Standard scores were used to reduce to a common basis the results of studies using different measuring instruments. The problem of predicting delinquent behaviour on the basis of questionnaire responses has been tackled by S. R. Hathaway and E. D. Manarchesi, *Analysing and Predicting Delinquency with the M.M.P.I.*, G. Cumberledge, London, 1963.

20. For references and discussion, see J. Shields and G. Slater, 'Heredity and Psychological Abnormality', in H. J. Eysenck (ed.), *Handbook of Abnormal Psychology*, op. cit.
21. C. O. Carter, *Human Heredity*, Penguin, London, 1962.
22. For a discussion, see P. Broadhurst, in H. J. Eysenck (ed.), *Experiments in Personality*, Routledge, London, 1960.
23. For a discussion see H. J. Eysenck (ed.), *Experiments in Personality*, op. cit.
24. H. J. Eysenck, *The Structure of Human Personality*, op. cit. This book discusses in detail the problems of autonomic specificity and personality. See also J. Fahrenberg, and L. Delius, 'Eine Faktorenanalyse psychischer und vegetativer Regulationsdaten', *Nervenarzt*, 1963, *34*, 437–43.
25. I. Spielmann, unpublished Ph.D. Thesis, University of London Library, 1963.
26. Unpublished study by H. Himmelweit, quoted from H. J. Eysenck, *The Structure of Human Personality*, op. cit.
27. H. J. Eysenck, *The Dynamics of Anxiety and Hysteria*, Routledge, London, 1957; Praeger, New York, 1960.
28. A. Petrie, *Personality and the Frontal Lobe*, Routledge, London, 1952. See also R. A. Willett, 'The Effects of Psychosurgical Procedures on Behaviour', in H. J. Eysenck (ed.), *Handbook of Abnormal Psychology*, op. cit.
29. See C. M. Franks, 'Conditioning and Abnormal Behaviour', in H. J. Eysenck (ed.), *Handbook of Abnormal Psychology*, op. cit. Also H. J. Eysenck, 'Conditioning and Personality', *Brit. J. Psychol.*, 1962. *53*, 299–305.
30. See P. Bakan, 'Extraversion-Introversion and Improvement in an Auditory Vigilance Task', Med. Res. Council, S.P.U., 311/57.
31. H. J. Eysenck and D. Prell, 'The Inheritance of Neuroticism: An Experimental Study', *J. ment. Sci.*, 1951, *97*, 441–65.
32. G. J. G. Wilde, *Neurotische Labiliteit gemeten volgens de Vragenlijstmethode*, Uity. F. von Rossen, Amsterdam, 1962.
33. G. Lienert and H. Reisse, 'Ein korrelativer-analytischer Beitrag zur genetischen Determination des Neuroticisms', *Psychol. Beiträge*, 1961, *7*, 121–30.
34. J. Shields, *Monozygotic Twins*, Oxford University Press, New York, 1962. See also, I. I. Gottesman, 'Heritability of Personality', *Psychol. Monogr.*, 1963. No. 572.
35. For a discussion see R. Gooch, in H. J. Eysenck (ed.), *Experiments with Drugs*, Pergamon, New York, 1960.
36. O. H. Mowrer, *Learning Theory and Personality Dynamics*, Ronald Press, New York, 1950.
37. Watson's paper and many other relevant studies can be found in H. J. Eysenck (ed.), *Behaviour Therapy and the Neuroses*, Pergamon, New York, 1960.

38. H. J. Eysenck, *Uses and Abuses of Psychology*, Penguin Books, London, 1951.

39. H. J. Eysenck, 'Emotion as a Determinant of Integrative Learning: An Experimental Study', *Behav. Res. & Therapy*, 1963, *1*, 197–212.

40. Our account follows a letter by R. L. Solomon, describing his work, which is reprinted in O. H. Mowrer, *Learning Theory and the Symbolic Process*, Wiley, New York, 1960. See also refs. 78, 79.

41. See H. J. Eysenck, 'Personality and Conditioning', op. cit. More recent work has been done by J. H. Johns and H. Quay, 'The Effects of Social Reward on Verbal Conditioning in Psychopathic and Neurotic Military Offenders', *J. Consult. Psychol.*, 1962, *26*, 217–20; and by H. Quay and W. A. Hunt, 'Psychopathy, Neuroticism and Verbal Conditioning', *J. Consult. Psychol.*, 1965, *29*, 283.

42. B. J. Fine, Introversion-Extraversion and Motor Vehicle Drive Behaviour, *Percept. Mot. Skills*, 1963, *12*, 95–100.

43. S. Biesheuvel and M. E. White, 'The Human Factor in Flying Accidents', *South African Air Force J.*, 1949, *1*, 25–31.

44. S. B. G. Eysenck, 'Personality and Pain Assessment in Childbirth of Married and Unmarried Mothers', *J. ment. Sci.*, 1961, *107*, 417–30.

45. I. Syed, unpublished study.

46. T. C. N. Gibbens, *Psychiatric Studies of Borstal Lads*, Oxford University Press, New York, 1962.

47. A detailed discussion of the history and present status of work on body-build is given in H. J. Eysenck, *The Structure of Human Personality*, op. cit.

48. S. B. G. Eysenck and H. J. Eysenck, 'On the Dual Nature of Extraversion', *Brit. J. soc. clin. Psychol.*, 1963, 2, 46–55.

49. G. A. Hooton, *Crime and the Man*, Harvard University Press, Cambridge, Mass., 1939.

50. S. Glueck and G. Glueck, *Unravelling Juvenile Delinquency*, Commonwealth Fund, New York, 1950.

51. W. H. Sheldon, E. M. Hartt and G. McDermott, *Varieties of Delinquent Youths*, Harper, New York, 1949.

52. P. Epps and R. W. Parnell, 'Physique and Temperament of Women Delinquents Compared with Women Undergraduates', *Brit. J. med. Psychol.*, 1952, *25*, 249–55.

53. This point has been particularly strongly made by C. M. Franks, 'Recidivism, Psychopathy and Delinquency', *Brit. J. Delinq.*, 1956, *6*, 192–201. See also the excellent book by G. Trasler, *The Explanation of Criminality*, Routledge, London, 1962.

54. D. J. West, *The Habitual Prisoner*, Macmillan, London, 1963.

55. H. J. Eysenck (ed.), *Handbook of Abnormal Psychology*, op. cit.

56. P. L. Broadhurst, 'The Interaction of Task Difficulty and Motivation: The Yerkes-Dodson Law Revived', *Acta Psychol.*, 1959, *16*, 321–38.

57. For reference, see the excellent summary and discussion of this work by A. Yates, *Frustration and Conflict*, Methuen, London, 1962.

58. R. M. Church, 'The Varied Effects of Punishment on Behavior', *Psychol. Rev.*, 1963, *70*, 369–402.

59. N. L. Teuber and E. Powers, 'Evaluating Therapy in a Delinquency Prevention Program', *Proc. Ass. Res. Nerv. Ment. Dis.*, 1953, *31*, 138–47.

60. H. J. Eysenck (ed.), *Experiments in Behaviour Therapy* Pergamon, New York, 1964.

61. J. Wolpe, *Psychotherapy by Reciprocal Inhibition*, Stanford University Press, Standford, Calif., 1958.

62. H. J. Eysenck and J. Rachman, *The Causes and Cures of Neuroses*, Rout-ledge, London, 1964.

63. This study has been reprinted in H. J. Eysenck (ed.), *Behaviour Therapy and the Neuroses*, op. cit.

64. O. H. Mowrer, *Learning Theory and the Symbolic Process*, op. cit.

65. D. Grant, 'The Treatment of Non-conformists in the Navy', *Annals* (322), 1959.

66. See summary and references in H. J. Eysenck and J. Rachmann, op. cit.

67. C. Bradley and M. Bowen, 'Amphetamine Therapy of Children's Be-havior Disorders', *Amer. J. Orthopsychiat.*, 1941, *11*, 92–103.

68. This point is discussed and experimentally documented, in H. J. Eysenck, *Experiments with Drugs*, op. cit.

69. A possible exception to this is L. Eisenberg, *et al.*, 'A psychopharmaco-logic Experiment in a Training School for Delinquent Boys: Methods, Problems, Findings', *Amer. J. Orthopsychiat.*, 1963, *33*, 431–47; the conclusions reached were quite positive.

70. H. Mannheim and L. T. Wilkins, *Prediction Methods in Relation to Borstal Training*, H.M.S.O., London, 1955.

71. Fitch, J. H. 'Two Personality Variables and their Distribution in a Crim-inal Population: an Empirical Study', *Brit. J. Soc. clin. Psychol.*, 1962, *1*, 161–7. Little, A. 'Professor Eysenck's Theory of Crime: an Empirical Test on Adolescent Offenders', *Brit. J. Criminol.* 1963, *4*. 152–163. Peterson, D. R., Omay, H. C. and Tiffany, T. L., 'Personality and Background Factors in Juvenile Delinquency as Inferred from Question-naire Responses', *J. Consult. Psych.*, 1959, *5*, 395–9. Peterson, D. R., Omay, H. C. and Tiffany, T. L., 'Personality Factors Related to Juvenile Delinquency', *Child Develop.*, 1961, *32*, 355–72. Warburton, F. W. 'Observations on a Sample of Psychopathic Prisoners', *Beh. Res. Ther.*, 1965, *3*, 129–35. Price, J. B., 'Some Results on the Maudsley Personality Inventory from a sample of girls in Borstal,' *Brit. J. Crim.*, 1968, *8*, 383–401.

72. S. R. Hathaway and E. P. Monarchesi, 'The Personality of Pre-Delin-quent Boys', *J. Crim. Law & Criminol.*, 1957, *48*, 149–63.

73. C. N. Michael, 'Follow-Up Studies of Introverted Children: Relative Incidence of Criminal Behaviour', *J. Crim. Law, Criminol. & Police Sci.*, 1950, *47*, 414–22.

74. C. Burt, 'Factorial Studies of Personality and Their Bearing on the Work of the Teacher', *Brit. J. Educ. Psychol.*, 1965, *35*, 368–78.

75. G. R. Pierson and R. F. Kelly, 'Anxiety, Extraversion and Personality – Idiosyncrasy in Delinquency', *J. Psychol.*, 1963. *56*, 441–5.

76. B. Marcus, 'A Dimension Study of a Prison Population', *Brit. J. Criminol.*, 1960, *1*, 130–53.

77. J. G. Field, *Report to the Prison Commission on an Investigation into the Personality of Recidivists*, 1960.

78. J. Aronfeld and A. Reber, 'Internalized Behavioural Suppression and the Timing of Social Punishment', *J. Person. Soc. Psychol.*, 1965, *1*, 13–16.

79. R. L. Solomon, L. H. Turner, and M. S. Lessac, 'Some Effects of Delay of Punishment on Resistance to Temptation in Dogs, *J. Person. Soc. Psychol.*, 1968, *8*, 233–8.

Index

Accident-proneness, 34
'Albert', 116, 117, 160, 161
Alcoholism, 68, 173
Amytal, 174
Ascending reticular formation, 103
Athletic body build, 136
Anxiety, 117
Anxiety neurotic, 171
Anxiety state, 53
'Audio-analgesia', 87
Autonomic nervous system, 77, 103, 119

Behaviour disorder, 90
Behaviour therapy, 160, 165
Benzedrine, 175
Biometrics, 74
Blood, 59
Body build, 135, 138
Borstals, 190
Brain-damage, 90
Brain lesions, 66
Brain-washing, 181, 188
Burt, Sir Cyril, 196

Cambridge-Somerville Youth
    Study, 158
Cat phobia, 162
Cattell Personality Scales, 133
Cauchy, R., 187
Cerebrotonia, 137
Character, 23
'Character Education Enquiry',
    23
Cheating, 26
Choleric, 47, 52
Cleckley, C., 54
Conditionability, 94, 145
Conditioned reflex, 80
Conditioned stimulus, 21

Conditioning, 93, 94, 110, 114, 148
'Contraband', 118
Conscience, 113, 120, 126, 129, 144,
    199
Correlation, 24
Cortex, 80
Cortical fatigue, 84
Crime, 62, 171
Criminal, 55, 110
Criminality, 74, 139, 145
Crusoe, Robinson, 75
Cutts, K., 174

Darwin, Charles, 59, 71
Deceit, 23
Delinquency, 55, 171
Delinquents, 134, 135
Depression, 53
Determining tendency, 24
Deterrence, 157
Dexedrine, 174
Distance gradient, 161
Dizygotic twins, 59, 62
'Double testing technique', 26
Dreams, 49
Drive, 84
'Duplicating technique', 26
Dysthymic, 54, 57, 98, 130

Ectoderm, 137
Ectomorph, 136
'Element', 23
Emotion, 95, 152
Emotionality, 47, 52, 77, 79, 100
Endocrine glands, 47
Endoderm, 136
Endomorph, 136
Enuresis, 166, 191
Environment, 74, 97
Excitation, 80, 87, 103

Extraversion, 41, 43, 48, 49, 50, 52, 56, 79, 87, 88, 97, 102, 103, 138 , 142, 145, 172, 178, 179, 195
Extraverts, 93, 94, 97
Eye-blink conditioning, 93, 95, 144

Fantasies, 49
Ferric chloride, 72
Fetishism, 163
Fingerprints, 59
Fixated behaviour, 154
Foelling, C., 72
Ford, Henry, 185
Free will, 71
Freud, Sigmund, 115, 151
'Frustration-instigated behaviour', 155

Galen, 47, 48, 50, 52
Galileo, G., 76
Galton, Sir Francis, 59
Generality, 20, 32
Generalization, 22
Genotype, 97, 99
Grassi, J., 91
GSR, 96, 114
Guilt, 129, 200, 201

Habits, 19
Habitus apoplecticus, 136
Habitus phthisicus, 136
Halo effect, 38
Hamilton, G. V., 154
Harvard Law School, 140
Hedonism, 111
Heredity, 67, 76
Hippocrates, 135
Homo sapiens, 183
Homosexuality, 33, 65, 68, 73, 163
Honesty, 29
Hysteric, 53, 57, 98

'Improbable achievement technique', 26
Impulsiveness, 142
Inhibition, 29, 80, 84, 85, 86, 103, 173, 179
Institute for Criminal Biology, 61
Integration, 29, 47
Integrative learning, 112
Intelligence, 27, 47, 74, 93, 102, 103, 134

Introversion, 41, 43, 48, 49, 50, 52, 56, 79, 87, 88, 97, 102, 103, 172, 178
Introvert, 93, 94, 97
Involuntary rest pause, 85, 86
'Irrational functions', 49

James, William, 22
Janet, Pierre, 53
Jasper, K., 174
Joliet Penitentiary, 133
Juvenile delinquent, 68, 110

Kant, Immanuel, 47, 48, 50, 52
Kranz, N., 68
Kretschmer, E., 136, 137

Law of effect, 111
Learning, 20, 113
Legras, J., 68
Leptosome, 136
Lombroso, C., 58, 139
Lykken, D., 131

McNaughton Rules, 183
Maier, N. R. F., 154, 155
Massed practice, 82
Melancholic, 47, 52
Mendel, G., 73
Mesoderm, 137
Mesomorph, 136
Minnesota Multiphasic Personality Inventory, 133
Mongolism, 139
Monozygotic twins, 59, 62
'Motivation-instigated behaviour', 155
Motoring offences, 34

Napoleon, 113
Negative drive, 84
Neurosis, 52
Neuroticism, 41, 42, 48, 56, 77, 97, 102, 103, 143, 195
Newton, I., 76, 187

Pain, 87, 109, 192
Pain tolerance, 109
Parasympathetic nervous system, 77
Patrick, J. B., 154
Personality, 17, 23, 47, 94, 97, 100, 106, 138, 139, 193, 194
Phenobarbital, 174

Phenotype, 97, 99
Phenylalanine, 72
Phenylketonuria, 72
Phlegmatic, 47
'Pleasure principle', 115
Porteus, S. D., 135
Porteus Mazes Test, 134
Pre-frontal lobotomy, 90
Promiscuity, 132
Psychasthenic, 53
Psychopath, 54, 55, 57, 90, 178
Psychotherapy, 151
Psychoticism, 198
Punishment, 120, 156
Puppies, 127
Pursuit-rotor, 82
Pyknic, 136

Q score, 135

Rampton, 131
Rat 'etiquette', 122
Ratings, 37
'Rational functions', 49
Rats, 122
Raymond, N. J., 164
'Reality principle', 115
Recidivism, 70, 134
Reminiscence, 82
Response, 20
'Response set', 40
Responsibility, 71
Rogers, Carl, 158
Rosanoff, A. J., 68

Sanguine, 47
Self-control, 23, 29
Self-ratings, 39
Sensory deprivation, 107
Service, 23
Sociability, 43
Social immaturity, 169
Social maturity, 169
Somatotonia, 137
Somatotype, 138
Soviet Union, 71

Spaced practice, 82
Specificity, 20, 32, 78
Spontaneous remission, 191
Stimulation, 106
Stimulus, 20
Stumpfl, F., 68
Suggestibility, 38, 44, 46, 100
Sweating, 95
Sympathetic arousal, 77, 162
Symptoms, 52
Syndromes, 52

'Taboo situations', 127
Tapping test, 89, 91
Television, 182
Temper tantrums, 33
Temperament, 48
Temptation, 118, 129
Therapeutic nihilism, 72
Tong, J. E., 131
Traffic violators, 132
Trait, 18, 23, 43 74
Transfer of training, 22
Transvestism, 163
Trouton, D. S., 174
Truancy, 33
Twins, 59, 100, 102, 103
Type, 18, 47
Tyrosine, 72

Unconditioned stimulus, 21
Unconscious, 49
Unconscious bias, 39
Unmarried mothers, 132

Values, 188
Venereal infection, 67
Vengeance, 157
Vigilance, 96
Viscerotonia, 137, 138

White, N. E., 132
Wundt, W., 48, 50, 52, 53

Yerkes-Dodson Law, 152

Bomb Culture
Jeff Nuttall

'Fragment of autobiography? Anarchist manifesto? Slice of
contemporary cultural history? Manual for young guerillas in the
generation war? The Underground's epitaph by one who was in
at its birth? Jeff Nuttall's book is all these and more . . . his book
is a letter from a man who desperately wants to share his terrible
healing vision in the hope that we may profitably pool our
madnesses and our sanities. He is a man I should like as a friend.'

Peter Fryer in NEW SOCIETY

'*Bomb Culture* is an abscess that lances itself. An extreme book,
unreasonable but not irrational. Abrasive, contemptuous,
attitudinising, ignorant and yet brilliant. . . . A book which you
must read, as soon as possible.'

Dennis Potter in THE TIMES

. . . a book which burns off the page, a book which is like a
heap of searing photographs from the battlefronts, both physical
and psychic, a book which sings and dances and won't lie still.'

Michael Kustow in SANITY

The Pursuit of the Millennium
Norman Cohn

A new, revised and enlarged edition

The Pursuit of the Millennium tells how the desire of the medieval poor to improve the material conditions of their lives was sometimes transformed by prophecies of a prodigious final struggle between the hosts of Christ and the hosts of Antichrist, out of which the world would emerge as a new paradise. In the earlier centuries the poor who were inspired by such prophecies would set off on people's crusades or on flagellant processions, and end by massacring the Jews. But gradually their hatred became concentrated on the clergy and the rich. The last chapters of the book show how at the close of the Middle Ages certain groups planned to exterminate the wealthy in preparation for the Second Coming, and then to impose an anarcho-communistic order on the whole world. In the Conclusion the author analyses the significance of these medieval phantasies and strivings from the standpoint of sociology and social psychology, and suggests how they relate to the revolutionary movements of our own times.

'A haunting and significant book.'

TIMES LITERARY SUPPLEMENT

'A piece of great originality and power ... it deserves study and emulation.' ....

Sir Isaiah Berlin

'Full of rich, fascinating, interesting scholarship ... What a field he covers!'

H. R. Trevor-Roper in the NEW STATESMAN

A New History of the United States
William Miller

In this new, revised and up-to-date edition of a work described as 'the most readable history of the United States ever written', William Miller brilliantly spans the events and ideas which have shaped American history from the early Renaissance voyages of exploration and discovery to the latest American and Russian explorations of space.

With its emphasis on placing American history in a world setting, and a virtually new chapter on American foreign relations, *A New History of the United States* is indispensable to the student and the general reader.

'Mr Miller does not merely digest ably and clearly the vast body of modern American historiography, he writes with a point of view. ... A great many complacent beliefs about the past are quietly inspected and revised; a good many historical judgments appealed against ... how much there is to be grateful for! Mr Miller is a master in the difficult art of apt and illuminating quotation, admirable in giving the temper of an age by the revealing illustration, willing to speak his mind and with a mind worth attending to. This is a most able and most welcome book.'

TIMES LITERARY SUPPLEMENT

Russia in Revolution
Lionel Kochan

Russia in Revolution is a panorama of Russian society as first industrialism, then the First World War, destroyed the old order while Lenin preached the new. It is a comprehensive and dramatic analysis of the economic, social and ideological factors which provoked the overthrow of the Tsars and the final triumph of the Bolsheviks.

'Lionel Kochan presents a lucid, down-to-earth and well documented study of the revolution and its roots in Russian history. It is good history and good reading. An excellent study, both for the general reader and for the increasing number of students of Russian history.'

THE DAILY TELEGRAPH

'A vivid panoramic narrative . . . it is the combination of clear outline and interesting detail in this story which is impressive.'

NEW SOCIETY

Love and Death in the American Novel
Leslie Fiedler

Love and Death in the American Novel views in depth both
American literature and American character from the time of the
revolution to the present. From it there emerges Professor
Fiedler's once scandalous – now increasingly accepted –
judgment that American literature is incapable of dealing with
adult sexuality and is pathologically obsessed with death.

'One of the great, essential books on the American imagination.'

Richard Kostelanetz

'Dr Fiedler's witty, exasperating, energetic, penetrating book
will prove indispensable . . . a high level of scholarship and
intelligence.'

SPECTATOR

'Something of a classic . . . witty and arresting . . . He has
contrived to make the American heritage less wholesome, but far
more interesting than once seemed likely.'

ENCOUNTER

The Politics of Ecstasy
Timothy Leary

Dr Leary, 'the high priest of the psychedelic', was dismissed in 1963 from the faculty of Harvard University where he was a lecturer in clinical psychology, when it was learned that he had been experimenting on himself, his associates and hundreds of volunteer subjects with measured doses of psilocybin, the chemical derivative of the sacred mushrooms. Still harassed by what he calls 'the forces of middle-aged, middle-class authority', Dr Leary continues to enforce his bid that 'anyone who wants to have a psychedelic experience and is willing to prepare for it . . . should be allowed to have a crack at it . . .' This startlingly candid collection of essays in defence of ecstasy are the documents of his own spiritual search and the fantastic entrance to the psychedelic world.

On The Track of Unknown Animals
Bernard Heuvelmans

At the beginning of the nineteenth century George Cuvier, the 'Father of Palaeontology', categorically stated that there was little hope that any large animals were still unknown. Since then have been discovered the largest species of bear and gorilla, a white rhinoceros, the pygmy elephant, the okapi, the fabulous Komodo dragon and dozens of other unusual animals. Bernard Heuvelmans, 'The Sherlock Holmes of Zoology', believes, in the face of official zoology, that there are more animals yet to be found. He examines the evidence for the spotted lion of Kenya, the Queensland marsupial tiger, the abominable snowman and other equally 'fantastic' animals.

'Dr Heuvelmans' original research beats any alleged thriller for enthralling excitement; incredible too, this is first-rate authoritative science written without jargon.'

DAILY MAIL

'This is the well reasoned thesis of a scientist who is a good deal more open-minded than many of his fellows ... Even if none of these questionable beasts should be discovered, which is unlikely, the author has documented their legends in a masterly and useful way.'

TIMES LITERARY SUPPLEMENT

Homo Ludens
Johan Huizinga

Introduction by George Steiner

The classic study of culture as play by the author of *The Waning of the Middle Ages*.

'*Homo Ludens* is the most important work in the philosophy of history in our century. A writer with a sharp and powerful intelligence, helped by a gift of expression and exposition which is very rare, Huizinga assembles and interprets one of the most fundamental elements of human culture: the instinct for play. Reading this volume, one suddenly discovers how profoundly the achievements in law, science, poetry, war, philosophy, and in the arts, are nourished by the instinct of play.'

Roger Caillois, editor of DIOGENES

'The unrivalled historian of culture has in his work on Man at Play prepared the ground for the interpretations of history as developed by Toynbee, Sorokin, Alfred Weber, Gabriel Marcel, and even Camus.'

HUMANITAS

'Huizinga's essay on *homo ludens* is one of the few works informed about the problem of man.'

Martin Buber

The War of the Flea
Robert Taber

'The guerrilla fights the war of the flea, and his military enemy
suffers the dog's disadvantages: too much to defend, too small,
ubiquitous, and agile an enemy to come to grips with.'
The War of the Flea is the war of popular resistance that drove
the British out of Cyprus and Israel, the French out of Indo-
China and Algeria, and is now confronting the United States in
South-East Asia. In this fascinating and authoritative book (the
first printing was bought in its entirety by the U.S. armed
services) Taber covers guerrilla theory and practice from Mao
Tse-tung to General Grivas and Che Guevara: how it works,
why it succeeds and the options open to the western countries
engaged in confronting the rising tide of revolution.

The War Business
George Thayer

Since 1945 there have been 55 wars. There are 750 million operable military rifles and pistols in existence (one small arm for every adult male on earth).

Commerce in arms is frequently at odds with accepted foreign policies and national images. Britain has sold arms to both sides in the Nigerian civil war; West Germany trades simultaneously with Israel and Egypt; the USSR sells arms to South Africa, while the US is the biggest seller of arms in the world; and Switzerland and Sweden, despite their long histories of peace, are two of the world's most aggressive exporters of arms.

The War Business demonstrates how the presence or acquisition of weapons influences the outbreak or continuation of hostilities, and draws a detailed and engrossing picture of the workings of the international arms trade.

Paladin

BOMB CULTURE Jeff Nuttall

THE PURSUIT OF THE MILLENNIUM Norman Cohn

LOVE AND DEATH IN THE AMERICAN NOVEL
Leslie Fiedler

THE WAR BUSINESS George Thayer

A NEW HISTORY OF THE UNITED STATES
William Miller

HOMO LUDENS Johan Huizinga

CRIME AND PERSONALITY H. J. Eysenck

THE POLITICS OF ECSTASY Timothy Leary

ON THE TRACK OF UNKNOWN ANIMALS
Bernard Heuvelmans

THE WAR OF THE FLEA Robert Taber

RUSSIA IN REVOLUTION Lionel Kochan

RENAISSANCE AND RENASCENCES IN
WESTERN ART Erwin Panofsky